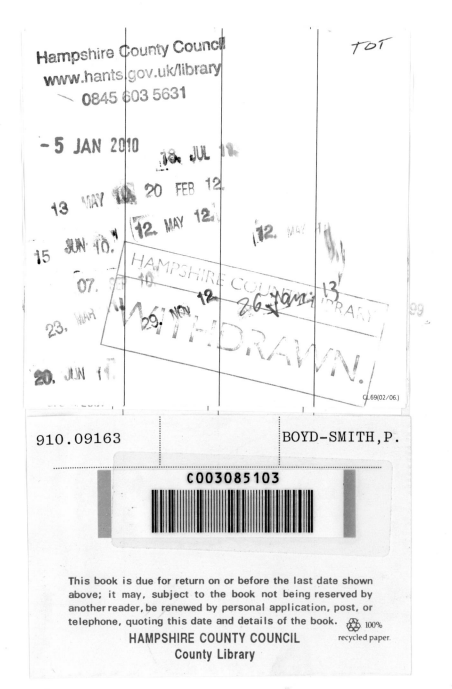

# From Rare Historical Reports

# TITANIC

# From Rare Historical Reports

*Peter Boyd-Smith*

**Steamship Publications**

# From Rare Historical Reports

## Peter Boyd-Smith

Steamship Publications

*For Jan*
*and for my parents*
*who gave me a love of ships*

Peter Boyd-Smith

This book is dedicated to the memory
of the passengers and crew of
R.M.S. TITANIC

Thanks to Jan Boyd-Smith for the cover
photograph and additional
photography. Brian Ticehurst for Titanic
Relief Fund research and crew information.
Harland & Wolff, Southampton Maritime
Museum, The Daily Mirror, The Daily Mail.

Unless otherwise captioned, all items are,
or were, the property of the author.

Many of the items shown in this book
were produced by companies who are no
longer in existence or who I have been
unable to trace. If I have inadvertently
infringed anyone's rights, I hope that they
will excuse me.

Peter Boyd-Smith
Southampton
April 1992

**T**itanic was designed to be one of a trio of the largest liners in the world, and with her sisters *Olympic* and *Britannic* would provide trans-atlantic service to rival Cunard's *Lusitania* and *Mauretania*.

*Olympic* was the first to be built at Harland and Wolff's Belfast shipyard, and was launched on October 20th 1910, whilst work proceeded on Titanic in the adjoining slip.

*Titanic* was launched on May 31st 1911 and at that time she was the largest movable object ever made by man. On the same day, *Olympic* sailed on her maiden voyage to the United States.

*Titanic* spent ten months fitting out with only the best quality furniture, carpeting, artwork and workmanship being accepted. She sailed from Belfast on April 2nd 1912, arriving at Southampton on April 3rd where she was to be provisioned and the majority of the crew embarked. She was so large that the passengers would be given maps to find their way around her. On Good Friday she hosted a banquet for the Mayor of Southampton, and this was the only occasion that she was dressed overall.

*Titanic* left Southampton on her maiden voyage at noon on April 10th with 1308 passengers and 898 crew on board. As she left the White Star dock and proceeded down river, she passed the *New York* moored outboard of the *Oceanic* at 38 berth (which is where *QE2* now docks). The suction from the *Titanic* broke the mooring ropes holding the *New York* to the *Oceanic* which caused the *New York* to swing out towards the *Titanic*, and only the superb seamanship of the crews of the tugs and the *Titanic* averted a collision. One wonders, with the benefit of hindsight, if they had collided, would *Titanic* have been damaged enough to have cancelled her maiden voyage?

She sailed down Southampton Water and turning into the Solent, set course to Cherbourg in France where she collected more passengers and then sailed to Queenstown (now Cobh) in Ireland to collect her remaining passengers who were mainly emigrants hoping for a better life in the New World. At 1.30 on April 11th, she left Ireland and headed south and then west into the Atlantic and into the history books...

*Workers leaving Harland & Wolff in Belfast. Titanic is on the slip and white Star's tender, Nomadic, is berthed on the left. She is still afloat today as a nightclub on the River Seine at Paris. (Harland & Wolff)*

*Titanic on the slip prior to launching (Harland & Wolff)*

SOME OF THE MEN WHO BUILT THE "OLYMPIC" AND "TITANIC." No. 10
19,000 MEN WERE EMPLOYED AT ONE TIME BY MESSRS. HARLAND & WOLFF DURING THE BUILDING OF
THESE LEVIATHANS.   THE ILL-FATED "TITANIC" IN THE BACKGROUND.

The passengers enjoyed unsurpassed luxury on this beautiful ship with a gymnasium and electric and turkish baths for which you paid four shillings (20p) or $1, luxurious public rooms and superb restaurants. Even the third class or steerage passengers had far better amenities than did second class on some other ships.

Apart from a fire that had been burning in the coal since leaving Southampton, the ship performed as expected. On the 14th of April she received wireless warnings of icefloes in her path, but her speed of 21 knots was not reduced. At 10.30 pm. she received further warnings of icefloes and bergs but she still did

not reduce speed. Although today a large liner travelling at speed in an area where icebergs or floes were would constitute a criminal act, in 1912 it was common policy for most of the large shipping companies to order their captains to make the fastest possible crossings — so the *Titanic* was only doing what every other transatlantic liner did!

At 11.40 p.m. the lookout, Frederick Fleet, saw an object dead ahead and rang the bridge telephone which was answered by junior officer Moody. Murdoch, the Chief Officer, immediately ordered the wheel to 'hard a starboard', ordered the engines stopped and reversed, then activated the watertight

No. **193**

↑

**"TITANIC"**

**Launch.**

↑

To be retained for
admittance to Stand.

No **193**

**Launch**

OF

White Star Royal Mail Triple-Screw Steamer

**"TITANIC"**

At BELFAST.

Wednesday, 31st May, 1911, at 12-15 p.m

TO BE PRESENTED AT GATE.

*A Ticket to view Titanic's launch. This must have belonged to a V.I.P., as most of the viewers would have stood in the yard, and stand ticket holders would have been invited guests.*

doors. She started swinging to port, but a ledge of ice protruding from under the berg ripped a 300ft gash in her starboard side as easily as opening a can with a can opener.

From that moment she was doomed...

The *Titanic* was designed with safety in mind, and although there were not enough lifeboats for everyone on board, she was carrying the requisite number as required by the Board of Trade. However, there had been no boat drill, and many of the crew did not know their assigned boat positions.

A recent television documentary seemed to have proof that her original design had enough boats for all, but cost-cutting and disagreement about the ship's appearance seemed to win the day. Too many boats might imply that the ship was unsafe!

Her watertight doors were the best and latest available, and were designed so that she could float with up to four of her watertight compartments flooded, but the gash extended into the fifth compartment and her fate was inevitable. The sea flowed from one compartment over the top into the next and so on until she sank. The boats were ordered to be lowered at 12.15 a.m. and although most were filled to capacity with women and children, some had only a few first class passengers and crew in them.

*Titanic; launched without the traditional champagne bottle broken across her bow.*

*Titanic and Olympic together in Belfast. Olympic had been involved in a collision with HMS Hawke in the Solent, and been returned to Harland & Wolff for repairs. She is shown entering the graving dock with Titanic almost completed in the foreground. This was the only time that the two sister-ships were together. (Harland & Wolff)*

THE ILL-FATED "TITANIC" NEARING COMPLETION. DOCKED IN THE LARGEST GRAVING DOCK IN THE   No. 3
WORLD, BELFAST, FEBRUARY, 1912. LOST WITH 1,500 SOULS, APRIL 15th, 1912.

By 2.00 a.m. the last boat had gone, leaving over 1500 people still on board, and at 2.20 a.m. her stern rose out of the sea and she plunged to the seabed nearly two miles down. Luckily, she did not have her full complement of 3350 aboard, but to this day, she is the world's worst peacetime shipping disaster.

When it became apparent that the *Titanic* was sinking, the radio operator broadcast the world's first SOS which superseded the old distress call CQD, and amongst the ships that heard it was the Cunarder *Carpathia*, which

arrived on the scene in the morning. She picked up 705 survivors and sailed to New York where the passengers disembarked. The crew were kept together and transferred to the *Lapland* of Red Star Line for their return to England. Their pay stopped the moment that the *Titanic* sank.

It is perhaps difficult to imagine what a 46.000 ton ship looks like, so I compare the *Titanic* with the *Canberra*. Both were built at Har-

5150   P. & O. — ORIENT LINER "CANBERRA". 45.270 TONS

land and Wolff in Belfast and both had a crew complement of 900:

*Titanic*: 46,329 tons. 883 ft long, 93 ft wide. 900 crew, 2603 passengers.

*Canberra:* 45,270 tons. 820 ft long, 102ft wide. 900 crew, 2198 passengers.

In 1912, the area of Southampton known as Northam, Chapel and St. Mary's were the poorest areas of the town, and as many crew members lived here were also the hardest hit. In Millbank Street alone, eight homes within 100 yards of each other lost thirteen relatives between them. During the Second World War, a lot of this area was destroyed, but even today, (April 1992) I meet a large number of people who come into

*Titanic dressed overall for the Mayor's reception on board in Southampton on Good Friday, 1912. She is riding high out of the water, indicating that coal and cargo had not yet been loaded. The bollards that held her ropes are still in the same position today.*

our business premises, which are in the heart of Northam, whose relatives were on the *Titanic* and treat it as an important piece of local history. Some of their stories are fascinating, such

as the lady who arrived one day and said that she had a china tea service from the *Titanic*! I must have appeared rather surprised, so she told me how it was obtained. Her parents owned a

*Titanic viewed from astern in the White Star Dock. This rare photo shows her graceful counter-stern and huge rudder.*

F.G.O. Stuart, 2033

White Star Dock. Southampton.

Oceanic.    New York.    Titanic    leaving
Southampton on her maiden voyage
Wednesday April 10th — Lost, Monday April 15th 2.20 a.

*Previous page: This previously unpublished photograph shows the New York being held by the tug Vulcan whilst Titanic steams down river, just a few minutes after their near collision.*

*Departure. At noon on April 10th 1912, Titanic sailed on her maiden voyage. The gentleman in the foreground was the White Star Line superintendant.*

*Left: Captain Smith, her master, photographed on Titanic prior to sailing. He lived with his wife and daughter at Woodhead in Winn Road, Southampton, and until quite recently, the house was still standing. A block of flats now stands in its place.*
*(Southampton Museums)*

small guest house and one of their clients was one of the second stewards who invited them to look around the ship. Her mother commented about how lovely the chinaware was, and just before sailing they received a parcel from the second steward containing the tea service. After the sinking, it was boxed up and never used and even now is still in it's box somewhere in Southampton.

*The White Star wharf at Queenstown in Ireland. From here, many emigrants hoped to escape the grinding poverty and make a new life in the wealthy United States. As Titanic was too large to come close inshore, passengers and baggage were tendered out to her.*

*No.*

**WHITE STAR LINE.**

**R.M.S. "TITANIC."**

This ticket entitles bearer to use of Turkish or Electric Bath on one occasion.

**Paid 4/- or 1 Dollar.**

*No.*

WHITE STAR LINE.

**R.M.S. "TITANIC."**

This ticket entitles bearer to use of Turkish or Electric Bath on one occasion.

**Paid 4/- or 1 Dollar.**

WHITE STAR TRIPLE-SCREW STEAMER "TITANIC" (45,000 TONS).
THE LARGEST VESSEL IN THE WORLD
FIRST VOYAGE FROM SOUTHAMPTON TO NEW YORK, WEDNESDAY, APRIL 10th, 1912.

THIS VESSEL IS LUBRICATED WITH "VACUUM" TURBINE OIL.    VACUUM OIL CO. LTD.
LONDON.

*Above: An artist's impression of the Titanic at speed, promoting turbine oil.*
*A representative of Vacuum Oil was on the ship and listed as missing.*

R.M.S "TITANIC" ON HER MAIDEN VOYAGE. 10 APRIL 1912. SILK.2.
STERN VIEW, SHOWING THE VESSEL'S GREAT LENGTH.

*Previous page: Suite B57. These special staterooms located on B and C decks consisted of three combined bed and sitting rooms with connecting doors and lavatory. At the other end of the scale, some third class passengers shared up to ten in a cabin, and up to 160 in dormitories way down on G deck. (Harland & Wolff)*

R M S TITANIC

APRIL 14. 1912

### LUNCHEON.

CONSOMME FERMIER      COCKIE LEEKIE

FILLETS OF BRILL

EGG A L'ARGENTEUIL

CHICKEN A LA MARYLAND

CORNED BEEF, VEGETABLES, DUMPLINGS

### FROM THE GRILL.

GRILLED MUTTON CHOPS

MASHED, FRIED & BAKED JACKET POTATOES

CUSTARD PUDDING

APPLE MERINGUE      PASTRY

### BUFFET.

SALMON MAYONNAISE      POTTED SHRIMPS

NORWEGIAN ANCHOVIES      SOUSED HERRINGS

PLAIN & SMOKED SARDINES

ROAST BEEF

ROUND OF SPICED BEEF

VEAL & HAM PIE

VIRGINIA & CUMBERLAND HAM

BOLOGNA SAUSAGE      BRAWN

GALANTINE OF CHICKEN

CORNED OX TONGUE

LETTUCE      BEETROOT      TOMATOES

### CHEESE.

CHESHIRE, STILTON, GORGONZOLA, EDAM,

CAMEMBERT, ROQUEFORT, ST IVEL

CHEDDAR

*Iced draught Munich Lager Beer 3d. & 6d a Tankard*

*Left: Lunch menu for April 14th. The last lunch that was ever served on her.*

*Below: The Cunard liner Carpathia raced to the rescue and arrived on the scene at daybreak, only to find wreckage and a few lifeboats.*

CUNARD R.M.S "CARPATHIA"

| No. | *No. of ship, and official number, Port of registry, and tonnage.† | *Date and place of engagement. | *Rating : and R.N.R. No. (if any). | Date and place of discharge. | Description of voyage. | Signature of Master. |
|---|---|---|---|---|---|---|
| 13 | *Olympic* 131346 *Liverpool* | 29 Nov 1911 South'ton | Stwd | 16 Dec 1911 South'ton | New York. | |
| 14 | Do | 20 Dec 1911 South'ton | Stwd | 6 Jan 1912 South'ton | Do | |
| 15 | Do | 10 Jan 1912 South'ton | Stwd | 31 Jan 1912 South'ton | Do | |
| 16 | Do | 7 Feb 1912 South'ton | Stwd | 28 Feb 1912 South'ton | Do | |
| 17 | *Titanic* 131428 *Liverpool* 0831 OLYMPIC | 10 April 1912 South'ton | Stwd | 15 April 1912 at Sea | Intended New York. | |
| 18 | OLYMPIC 131346 LIVERPOOL ... | 20 Aug ... SOUTHAMPTON STEWARD | | 14 SEP 1912 SOUTHAMPTON | | |

*Extracted from Agreement* *Registrar General* *16th June 1912*

* These columns are to be filled in at time of engagement.
† In Engineers' Books insert Horse Power.

680582

*Seaman's discharge book for E. Brown of Liverpool, steward on the Titanic who joined on the 10th April. He was an important witness at the inquiry, and later served on Olympic and Baltic until 1914.*

The crew were badly treated by the authorities on both sides of the Atlantic and by White Star who stopped their pay the moment that the *Titanic* sank. It appears that no *Titanic* officer or crewman ever attained promotion on any other White Star ship that they were employed on. It was almost as if they were all blamed for the sinking.

The newspapers that reported the sinking asked for donations to be sent for the widows and orphans and within a few days of the disaster The Daily Mail alone had raised the sum of £39,000

In March 1913 The *Titanic* Relief Fund was raised by public subscription upon the invitation of the Lord Mayor of the City of London for the aid and relief of the widows, orphans and dependent relatives of the people (whether crew or passengers) who lost their lives on the *Titanic*. The total sum raised was £413,212.

The allowance to a widow ceased if she remarried, to a male child it ceased at age 16, and a female at 18. Today there are still two people receiving the *Titanic* Relief Fund.

The following payments were the monthly amounts that the dependents received on January 29th 1917

2.00. to Mrs. Parsons
Ashbrittle, Somerset.

10s. to Mrs. Smith
Sir Georges Rd. Southampton.

4.2.0d to Mrs. Ranson
Knowle, Bristol.

1.2,0d to Mrs. Pook
Alexandra Rd. Southampton.

3.00d to Mrs. Bristow
Westridge Rd. Southampton.

14s. to Mrs.Thomas
Newman St. Southampton.

1.2.0d to Mrs. Banfield
Oreston Plymouth.

1.0.0d to Mrs.Carbines
St. Ives. Cornwall.

3.10.0d. to Mrs.Gill
Suffolk Ave. Southampton.

1.2.0d to Mrs. Coleman
Oaktree Rd. Southampton.

Memorial services were held for the victims in Britain, America, France and many other countries and ranged from simple services in village churches to large national services in cathedrals attended by the most important dignitaries of the day. Many churches especially in the Southampton area had memorial plaques made to commemorate members of their congregation who perished, but sadly due to wartime bombing and the current trend of demolishing or closing churches, not many memorials survive.

*Below: A Mrs Hocking's relief fund cheque for January 1917. Her son was a second class passenger travelling to Akron, Ohio with his wife and daughter. They were both saved but Mr Hocking perished.*

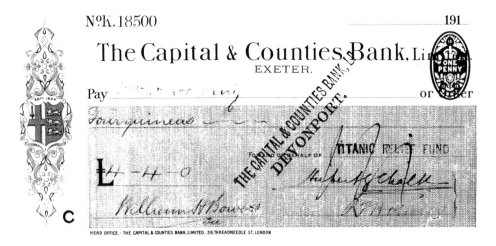

Today there is a growing interest in our nautical past and since the *Titanic* was found by Dr. Ballard in 1985 and the television pictures were flashed around the world, many more people have become interested in her. She has been the most discussed and written about ship ever, and will probably continue to be so.

She has had films made about her from the 1930's to the present day including the memorable *Night To Remember* in 1958, based on the excellent book by Walter Lord. I have found that more people have become interested in the *Titanic* through his book or the film than any other source.

In 1987 a French team with an American film crew dived to the *Titanic* and started raising items from her which included her foremast bell, rudder indicator, silverplate, chinaware, a safe, and numerous other artifacts. Subsequent dives brought up the bronze statue from the Grand staircase and many items of passenger's effects including jewellery. The *Titanic* lies in International waters, and is fair game for anyone with the resources to dive on her, although the Americans have passed a bill

### All Saints' Parish Church,

**SOUTHAMPTON.**

### SUNDAY, April 21st,

#### 1912.

✠ ✠

### The Loss of the White Star Liner " Titanic."

WARREN & SON, STEAM PRINTERS, SOUTHAMPTON.

*Programme of prayers for a memorial service at All Saints Church in Southampton. The church was full with standing room only. It was destroyed in the blitz on December 2nd 1940.*

prohibiting the sale of items from the wreck on U.S. soil. Canada has also refused to permit wreck items to be sold, and although Britain was asked to join the Americans and Canadians she refused, so presumably this once beautiful ship which is a grave to 1500 men, women and children will be steadily vandalised until there is nothing left.

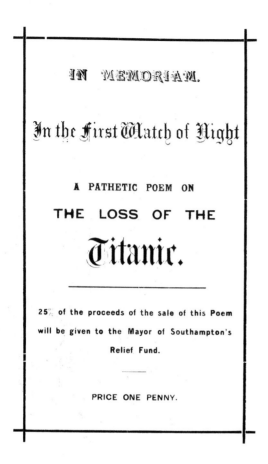

**IN MEMORIAM.**

**In the First Watch of Night**

A PATHETIC POEM ON

**THE LOSS OF THE**

**Titanic.**

25% of the proceeds of the sale of this Poem will be given to the Mayor of Southampton's Relief Fund.

PRICE ONE PENNY.

*One of the many poems written about the Titanic. Part of the proceeds of this one are given to the relief fund.*

*Southampton Times and Hampshire Advertiser. April 5th 1912.*

## A Wonderful Ship.

In a port where the magnificence of the appointments of the *Olympic* are so well known, it seems scarcely necessary to say much about the *Titanic*. The priviliged few who have had the pleasure of visiting the ship since her arrival at Southampton on Thursday morning have been at a loss to express their admiration. One person said that the *Olympic* was all that could be desired, and the *Titanic* was something even beyond that! And if his hearers smiled at his method of putting it, they were to agree that the White Star Line had taken every possible opportunity of effecting improvements, their experience with the *Olympic* having been brought to bear. The *Titanic* had a delightful trip from Belfast to Southampton, and among those on board were Mr. Morgan (Morgan, Grenfall and Co.), and representatives of the London and Southampton offices of Cafe Parisienne.

These gentlemen were quick to notice that several changes had been made in the *Titanic*, and particularly was it noticed that increased state room accommodation had been provided. The

*Almost immediately, the Newspapers launched appeals for the widows and orphans using any means; including decorated dogs.*

two private promenade decks were inspected with interest, and they have been instituted in connection with the parlour suite rooms. Then a delightful addition is the Cafe Parisienne which has been arranged in connection with the restaurant. The deck space outside the restaurant has been utilised for it and it represents an entirely new feature on steamers.

The Cafe Parisienne has the appearance of a charming sun lit verandah tastefully arranged with trellis work, and chairs in small groups surrounding convenient tables. It will also form a further addition to the restaurant, as lunches and dinners can be served with the same excellent service and all the advantages of the restaurant itself.

## I Plead for the "TITANIC" Sufferers.

JOHN DREW, PRINTER, SWINDON.

In the first class dining room over 550 passengers can dine at the same time, and a feature of the room is the arrangement of recessed bays where family and

## ◇ **In Memoriam** ◇

## "TITANIC"

**SUNK ON HER MAIDEN VOYAGE OFF CAPE RACE, APRIL 15th, 1912.**

*The most appalling disaster in Maritime History, with a loss of over 1,500 lives.*

*Within hours of the disaster, entrepreneurs on both sides of the Atlantic started manu-facturing souvenirs commemorating the tragedy. Most used pictures of the Olympic, and some even substituted Cunard's Lusitania. Over 170 postcards were printed. This one shows Olympic named as Titanic.*

other parties can dine together in semi privacy. The second class passengers have been very generously provided for. The dining saloon extends the full breadth of the vessel, and will seat 400. The state rooms are of very superior character, and the promenades are unusually spacious, a unique feature being the enclosed promenade. The accommodation for third class is also very good, and the vessel will accommodate in all about 3,500 passengers and crew.

## ARRIVALS AND DEPARTURES.

**The "Combine" Sailings.**

TITANIC, for New York, leaves Southampton Wednesday next.
OLYMPIC, for New York, left Southampton Wednesday.

BOURNEMOUTH BEACH.

*A very rare postcard of a sand sculpture on Bournemouth beach to raise money for the relief fund.*

*Southampton Times And Hampshire Express 13th April 1912*

## MAIDEN VOYAGE OF THE TITANIC

The departure of the *Titanic* on her maiden voyage on Wednesday was marred by an untoward incident which caused considerable consternation among the hundreds of people on the quayside. By some means or other the passing of the *Titanic* caused the *New York* to break away from her position alongside the *Oceanic* with the result that the *New York* and the *Titanic* narrowly missed colliding with each other. Fortu-nately the captain of the tug *Vulcan* was able to hold the *New York* whilst the *Titanic* got clear.

It was a narrow squeak. From the quayside it seemed that there were not more than three or four feet between the two vessels. It was stated that the vessels actually touched, but this was not so. When the *Titanic* finally passed down channel the bow of the *New York* was pointing towards the Floating Bridge. Apparantly the tugs just held her and when the danger was past she was bought back to her berth alongside the *Oceanic*.

*The Cafe Parisienne on board*

NOW LYING TWO MILES DEEP IN THE ATLANTIC—THE "TITANIC" (TONNAGE 60,000)

Some idea of the tremendous size of the "Titanic" may be conveyed by the following figures:—

Length, over all - - - - 882 ft. 9 in.
Breadth, extreme - - - - 92 ft. 6 in.
Total height, from keel to navigating bridge - 104 ft.
Gross tonnage - - - - 46,382
Displacement (tons) - - - - 66,000

Horse-power of reciprocating engines - 30,000
Shaft horse-power of turbine engines - 16,000
Speed (knots) - - - - 22
Value of the ship - - - £1,250,000
Value of the cargo - - - £1,000,000

She had accommodation for 750 first-class passengers, 650 second-class, and 1,200 third-class, and her crew was reckoned at 860, of whom 65 were attached to the navigating department, 320 to the engineers' department, and 475 to the stewards.

The rudder of the vessel weighed 100½ tons, with a length of 78 ft. 8 in. A 15-ton anchor held her at her moorings.

Total height, over 100 ft.

# The Daily Mirror

THE MORNING JOURNAL WITH THE SECOND LARGEST NET SALE.

No. 2,645.    Registered at the G.P.O. as a Newspaper.    TUESDAY, APRIL 16, 1912    One Halfpenny.

## DISASTER TO THE TITANIC: WORLD'S LARGEST SHIP COLLIDES WITH AN ICEBERG IN THE ATLANTIC DURING HER MAIDEN VOYAGE.

Disaster, it was reported yesterday, has overtaken the great steamer Titanic, the largest and most luxuriously appointed vessel afloat. The liner, which is the latest addition to the White Star fleet, left Southampton last Wednesday on her maiden voyage to New York, and was in the vicinity of the Newfoundland banks, to the south of Cape Race, when she struck an iceberg, an ever-present peril in those latitudes at this time of the year. "Wireless" has again demonstrated its immense value, assistance being summoned by this means. The photograph shows the mighty vessel leaving Southampton on Wednesday.—(*Daily Mirror* photograph.)

# Section of the White Star Liner, TITANIC

## Shown in the New Dock at Southampton which She will Use when Completed.

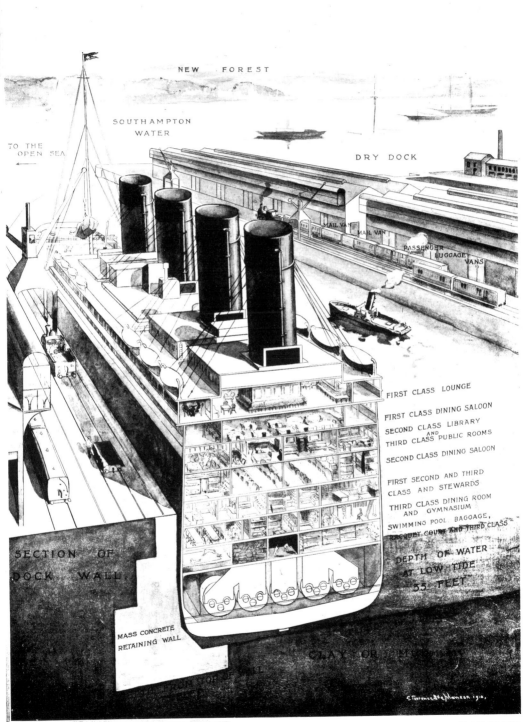

NEW FOREST

SOUTHAMPTON WATER

TO THE OPEN SEA

DRY DOCK

MAIL VAN · MAIL VAN

PASSENGER · LUGGAGE VANS

FIRST CLASS LOUNGE

FIRST CLASS DINING SALOON

SECOND CLASS LIBRARY
AND
THIRD CLASS PUBLIC ROOMS

SECOND CLASS DINING SALOON

FIRST SECOND AND THIRD CLASS AND STEWARDS

THIRD CLASS DINING ROOM AND GYMNASIUM

SWIMMING POOL BAGGAGE, RACQUET COURT AND THIRD CLASS

DEPTH OF WATER AT LOW TIDE 35 FEET

SECTION OF DOCK WALL.

MASS CONCRETE RETAINING WALL

CLAY OR MUD

C. Terence Stephenson 1912.

*Special Sphere picture*

## THE VARIED USES OF THE DECKS OF THE GREAT LINER, 'TITANIC,' TO BE LAUNCHED NEXT WEEK

This view has been specially drawn by a SPHERE artist from plans and drawings prepared by the engineers of the ship and dock. For this assistance THE SPHERE has to thank the authorities of the London and South-Western Railway Company at Southampton and of the White Star Line and the builders at Belfast. When the giant vessel arrives at Southampton there will be a depth of 35 ft. at low water, in order to facilitate the entry of the huge bulk of the *Olympic*

**VULCAN TO THE RESCUE.**
**The Captain's Story.**

Captain C. Gale the captain of the tug *Vulcan*, stated to our reporter that he assisted the *Titanic* out of the new dock and had hold of her aft. "We let go by the starboard quarter and dropped astern in order to go alongside and pick up a number of workmen who were about to leave the *Titanic*. The *Titanic* was drawing about 35 ft. of water and she was near the sea bed. As soon as she drew abreast of the *New York* her ropes snapped caused either by the backwash or suction and I turned the *Vulcan* round and got a wire rope on the port quarter of the *New York*, and got her clear of the *Titanic*."

"The *Titanic* arrived at Queenstown on Thursday. She had a good passage from Southampton and Cherbourg, and arrived at the Irish port shortly before noon. On her departure at 1.30. she had on board 350 saloon, 300 second, and 740 third class passengers. 903 crew and 3,814 sacks of mail"

The first reports of the disaster were wired to New York and then England and appeared in the newspapers of the 16th of April,

and some of the earlier editions reported that all the passengers were safe and that the Titanic was being towed to Halifax by the Allan liner *Virginian*. By the evening of the 16th the real story was unfolding and the following morning all the papers were reporting the true story.

*NEW YORK TRIBUNE April 16th 1912.*

# LONDON HEARS LATE OF LOSS OF TITANIC.

**Newspapers Went to Press Supposing All on Board the Ship Were Safe.**

**CROWD COMPANY'S OFFICES.**
*London, April 16th (Tuesday)*
Some of the London newspapers went to press this morn-

ing under the belief that all aboard the *Titanic* were safe, and that the vessel was proceeding for Halifax. These in editorials congratulate all concerned that man's inventive genius has reduced the perils of a sea voyage to a minimum.

Later dispatches recording the sinking of the *Titanic,* with loss of life, appear only in the very latest editions, and the terrible extent of the disaster will not become known to the British public until much later in the day.

All news on the subject still comes exclusively from New York. No wireless communication appears to have been established with this side.

A dispatch just received from Liverpool says that the White Star officials have received information from the *Olympic* of the sinking of the *Titanic* and of the saving of many of the passengers and crew, and adds that the offices are besieged by friends of the passengers making inquiries.

Writing under the impression that the *Titanic* was saved, the newspapers call attention to the absence of any drydock on the American seaboard large enough to accommodate such a vessel, and also to the coincidence of accidents happening to the sisterships *Olympic* and *Titanic*.

Exciting scenes were witnessed at Lloyds underwriting rooms yesterday. Insurance losses in the last six months have been unparalleled in the history of Lloyd's in liners of the biggest class.

It is understood that there was no specie on board the liner, but large insurances had been written on diamonds and other valuables in her cargo.

*DAILY MIRROR APRIL 16th 1912.*

# Every one on board World's greatest liner safe after collision with iceberg in Atlantic Ocean.

**TITANIC'S WIRELESS SIGNAL BRINGS VESSELS TO SCENE.**

**ALL ON BOARD SAFE.
PASSENGERS TAKEN OFF.**

**Helpless Giant Being Towed to Port by Allan Liner.**

The White Star liner *Titanic*, the greatest ship the world has ever known, has met with disaster on her maiden voyage.

She left Southampton on Wednesday last and carried about 2,300 passengers and crew on board, with 3,400 sacks of mail.

On Sunday she came into collision with an iceberg, and immediately flashed out wireless messages for help.

Many steamers rushed to her aid, but her fate and that of the thousands on board remained in doubt on both sides of the Atlantic for many hours.

It was at length known that every soul was safe, and that the vessel itself was proceeding to Halifax either under her own steam or towed by the Allan liner *Virginian.*

All her passengers had by that time been taken aboard two of the liners that hurried to the scene in reply to the wireless message. They are due at Halifax (Nova Scotia) today and will be taken thence by train to New York.

Last night direct news from the *Titanic* was received by the parents of the wireless operator on board, who announced cheerfully that the boat was practically unsinkable and that she was making slowly for Halifax.

*DAILY MIRROR. April 16th.*

# LINER THAT COST £1,500,000.

**Titanic's Two Miles Of Walks and Beds Of Roses on Board.**

**MAPS FOR PASSENGERS.**

To be a passenger on the *Titanic* is to be a resident in a luxurious town of over 3,000 inhabitants.

Life on board is life timed and arranged always with a view to comfort. Indeed, the passenger is almost safer when crossing the Atlantic than in crossing a busy London street.

There are ten decks, and so complicated are the numerous passages, saloons and stairways that passengers are provided with special guide maps in their staterooms to show them the way about.

Glass enclosed "sun parlours" are one of the most delightful innovations on the *Titanic*. Those who wish to take their meals on deck may visit the verandah cafe, made to represent those on the Riviera.

The lighting of one of the first class dining saloons is so arranged that the room appears to be bathed in sunshine, a warm sunset light shining through the windows.

The most expensive suite costs £870 and the lowest first class passage is £23 without meals.The cheapest passage on the *Titanic* is £7.15s, third class which includes meals.

*(Daily Mail, April 16)*

## 'TITANIC SUNK'.

**FEARED LOSS OF 1,800 LIVES.**

**MESSAGE FROM 'OLYMPIC'.**

**675 RESCUED.**

**CHILDREN AND WOMEN.**

**COLLISION WITH ICEBERG.**

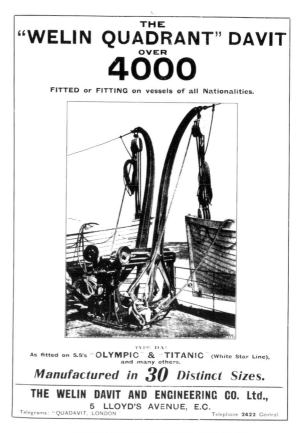

THE
## "WELIN QUADRANT" DAVIT
OVER
# 4000
FITTED or FITTING on vessels of all Nationalities.

TYPE DAY
As fitted on S.S's OLYMPIC & TITANIC (White Star Line), and many others.

*Manufactured in* **30** *Distinct Sizes.*

**THE WELIN DAVIT AND ENGINEERING CO. Ltd.,**
5 LLOYD'S AVENUE, E.C.
Telegrams: "QUADAVIT, LONDON. Telephone 2422 Central.

**ONLY FOUR HOURS AFLOAT.**

The White Star liner *Titanic*, the greatest ship in the world, has sunk on her maiden voyage.

It is feared there has been loss of 1,800 lives.

She collided with an iceberg 300 miles south-east of Cape Race at 10.25 p.m. on Sunday (about two o'clock yesterday morning by our time).

She sank at 2.20 yesterday morning, that is about six o'clock English time.

*(Daily Mail, April 16)*

# GREAT LOSS OF LIFE.

**CAPTAIN'S MESSAGE.**

*FROM OUR OWN CORRESPONDENT.*
*NEW YORK, Monday (midnight).*

It is now known that 1,800 lives have been lost in the wreck of the *Titanic*.

A special despatch to the New York Times from Cape Race says: —

"It can be positively stated that up to eleven o'clock tonight nothing whatever had been received at, or heard by, the Marconi station to the effect that the *Parisian, Virginian,* or other ships than the *Carpathia* picked up survivors."

*FROM OUR OWN CORRESPONDENT.*
*NEW YORK, Monday Night.*

A message from Cape Race states:

"The *Olympic* reports that the *Carpathia* reached the *Titanic's* position at daybreak."

"She found boats and wreckage only. The *Titanic* had foundered about 2.20 a.m. in 41.deg. 16min. North, 50deg. 14min. West. All her boats are accounted for."

"About 675 souls are saved of the crew and passengers, the latter nearly all women and children. The Leyland liner *California* is remaining searching the position of the disaster. The *Carpathia* is returning to New York with the survivors."

The foregoing message has shocked New York most profoundly. If its truth is sustained, as seems only too probable, the loss of life is approximately 1,800 passengers and crew.

The public is stunned by the news, and is assembling in huge crowds outside the newspaper offices. The grief is more intense as the messages published throughout the day had established the conviction that all the passengers were saved.

The reaction from the buoyant spirits that prevailed as the result of these optimistic reports is most tragic.

The White Star authorities have not given out the full text of the message from Captain Haddock, of the *Olympic*. The message, they say, is very brief, and intimates that there has been loss of life.

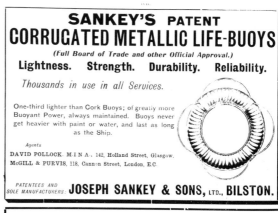
It is understood that the *Carpathia* has six or seven hundred passengers aboard, including all the first-class passengers. They were taken aboard the *Virginian* first and then retransferred to the *Carpathia*, as the former ship was carrying mails east, while the *Carpathia* was bound for New York. She is expected to reach this port on Friday morning.

Early this afternoon rumours were circulated that the *Titanic* had sunk. They were denied in the most emphatic terms by the White Star authorities, who confirmed the message stating that the *Titanic* was proceeding under her own steam to Halifax.

The first intimation that mystery still surrounded the fate of the ill-starred vessel was given at six o'clock, when the Marconi operator at Cape Race reported that all connection with the *Olympic* and surrounding steamers had been lost.

*8.15 p.m.*

The White Star Line admits that many lives are lost. In its official statement the White Star declares that no definite estimate of the loss of life can be made until it is known whether any passengers were picked up by the *Virginian*.

Mr. Alfred Vanderbilt, who was supposed to be on board, has cabled his mother that he is safe in London.

*8.30 p.m.*

The text of Captain Haddock's message is now given out. It runs:

At 2.20 a.m. the *Titanic* foundered. The *Carpathia* is proceeding to New York with passengers.

There is reason to believe that the message was considerably longer than this, but that the White Star are suppressing other passages until the reports of great loss of life are confirmed.

It is still unknown if the *Parisian* has any of the *Titanic's* passengers on board.

*9.30 p.m.*

The White Star Line now admit that probably only 675 persons of the 2,358 on board the *Titanic* have been saved.

*9.35 p.m.*

Mr. Franklin, vice-president of the White Star Company, now admits that there has been "horrible loss of life."

Official figures of those known to be saved are 675. Mr. Franklin adds that the monetary loss cannot be estimated tonight, but the amount is in the millions. "We can replace the money," he said, "but not the lives."

*9.45 p.m.*

The official admission that there has been "horrible loss of life" was made after representations from the New York Times to the effect that despatches to that newspaper gave no indication whatever of any lives being saved beyond the 675 persons picked up by the *Carpathia*.

**A GLEAM OF HOPE.**

*10 p.m.*

It is estimated that the twenty boats picked up were manned by at least eighty of the crew. Of the 800 third-class passengers one-

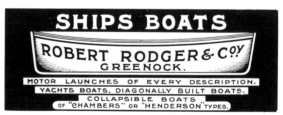

third probably were women, and thus 313 of the 675 persons rescued would be accounted for.

It seems therefore only too probable that many of the men among the first-class passengers must have perished.

In a statement issued tonight, Mr. Franklin declared that the *Titanic* had enough boats to accommodate all the passengers and crew. He still had hopes, he said, that the *Virginian* and *Parisian* had picked up some of the boats. He admitted, however, that he had no information on which to base these hopes, and concluded, "The situation is very alarming."

*(Daily Mail, April 16)*

## THE WRECK.

**SINKING BY DEGREES.**

Practically all that is known of the circumstances of the collision is summarised in the following telegram from Lloyd's agent: —

*CAPE RACE, Monday.*
10.25 p.m. yesterday *Titanic* reports by wireless struck iceberg and calls for immediate assistance. At 11 p.m. she reported sinking by head. Women being put off in boats. Gave position as 41.46 N., 50.14 W. Steamers *Baltic, Olympic,* and *Virginian* all making towards scene of disaster. Latter was last to hear *Titanic* signals at 12.27 a.m. today. Reported them then blurred and ending abruptly. Believed *Virginian* will be first ship to reach.

Lloyd's agent at New York cabled:
Allan Line steamer *Parisian,* from Glasgow for Halifax, reports by wireless that steamer *Carpathia*, from New York April 11 for Naples, is in attendance on the *Titanic,* and that the *Carpathia* has picked up twenty boats of passengers.

The blow fell when the passengers were preparing to retire for the night after the peaceful monotony of a Sunday at sea. The shock that damaged the vast ship startled and alarmed them, but order was kept, and in half an hour the women were being placed in the lifeboats.

Meanwhile the *Titanic's* call had been picked up and passed on until it rang all over the Atlantic. Fifty ships received it. Those nearest the *Titanic*, the *Parisian*, *Virginian*, *Carpathia* and *Olympic*, hastened with all speed to her help.

# THE MAGNIFICENCE OF THE TITANIC AND SOME OF THE

A photograph which gives an idea of the immense size of the Titanic. Her length over all is 882ft. 6in., and her breadth 92ft. 6in.

The cooling room of the Turkish bath, one of the features of this sumptuous and luxurious vessel.

Colonel J. J. and Mrs. Astor.

Mr. Bruce Ismay.      Captain Smith, the

Photograph showing an iceberg as see

Mr. Isidor Straus.

Mrs. Cavendish.

Mr. Clarence Moore.

Major A. W. Butt.      Mr. Charles M. Hays.

In the furnishing and equipment of the Titanic the last note in ocean luxury had been struck, and the passengers—some of whose photographs are reproduced above—who travelled on th
luxurious vastness.—(Daily Mirror, Downey, Langfier,

# L-KNOWN PASSENGERS ON BOARD THE ILL-FATED VESSEL.

An evil omen. The Titanic and the New York nearly collide at Southampton at the start of the Titanic's first voyage last Wednesday.

The Countess of Rothes.

Lord Ashburton.

of the Titanic.

A bed in one of the staterooms, showing the modern magnificence of some of the Titanic's apartments.

eck of a mail steamer in mid-ocean.

Mr. Benj. Guggenheim.

Miss Gladys Cherry.

Major A. Peuchen.

Miss Esther Bowen.

Mr. W. T. Stead.

ing her maiden trip enjoyed while they were journeying across the ocean all the comforts of the Carlton Hotel. The photographs reproduced above give some idea of the vessel's
d Walery.)

The list of passengers and crew issued by the company was as follows: —
First-class passengers 350
Second-class passengers 305
Steerage passengers 800
Officers and crew 903
Total: 2,358

*(Daily Chronicle, April 17)*

# THE 'TITANIC' CATASTROPHE.

**THE KING'S MESSAGE.**

It is now certain that the huge White Star liner *Titanic,* the biggest and most luxurious ship in the world, lies sunk in two miles of water, some 400 miles from Newfoundland, and that of the 2,100 souls on board only 868 have been saved.

She sank three or four hours after striking the iceberg on Sunday night, and none of the liners that, in response to her wireless cry for help, raced to her aid, arrived in time to do more than pick up the boats that contained the 868 survivors.

Among the total rescued are only 79 men—all of whom were probably necessary to man the boats.

All honour to the brave crew and passengers who died doing their duty!

The King and Queen last night sent the following message to the White Star Company: —

The Queen and I are horrified at the appalling disaster which has happened to the *Titanic*, and at the terrible loss of life. We deeply sympathize with the bereaved relations, and feel for them in their great sorrow with all our hearts.
*George R. and I.*

To this the following reply was sent: —

"We are deeply grateful to your Majesty and the Queen for the gracious message of sympathy. The calamity is indeed overwhelming in its magnitude, and in the sorrow it must bring to so many hearts. We are taking necessary steps to ensure that the knowledge of your Majesties' sympathy shall reach all for whom it is intended."

Queen Alexandra telegraphed: —
"It is with feelings of the deepest sorrow that I hear of the terrible

# DISASTER TO THE TITANIC

How the "Titanic" struck the iceberg. The blow was received forward on the starboard side, and tore open the ship's side and bottom from the bows to the engine-room.

## FIRST TO RACE TO ASSISTANCE OF THE TITANIC.

The Allan liner Virginian, the first vessel to go to the assistance of the Titanic.

### Greatest Ship Ever Built Lies in Two Miles of Ocean.

### TITANIC'S LAST "GOOD-BYE."

The last known message from the Titanic before the disaster was received by the Tunisian, which yesterday reported on arrival at Liverpool, speaking the Titanic by wireless on Saturday midnight, and sending a message, "Good luck." To this the Titanic replied: "Many thanks. Good-bye."

### FOUNDERED ALONE.

#### No Ship Near When The Liner Went Down.

NEW YORK, Monday night.

Mr. Franklyn, in a statement issued at 10.45 to-night, states that no ship was by the Titanic sank.

## "TITANIC"

**Authentic Copyright Photographs of this ship, TAKEN AT SEA on her MAIDEN VOYAGE, April 10th.**

Size 11 in. by 9 in., unmounted, P.O.P., 2/1; Permanent Platinotype, 3/1 post free.
Size 14 in. by 10 in., unmounted, P.O.P., 3/7; Permanent Platinotype, 4/7 post free.  Mounting 9d. and 1/- extra.
Safely Packed and despatched to any address.

**PRATT, PHOTOGRAPHER, SOUTHAMPTON.**
Telephone 1229.

disaster to the *Titanic* and of the awful loss of life. My heart is full of grief and sympathy for the bereaved families of those who have perished."

*(Daily Chronicle, April 17)*

## 1,000 BEREAVED AT SOUTHAMPTON.

In Southampton people held out hope till the last moment that better news would be received with regard to the *Titanic* disaster; but yesterday afternoon the whole town was in the depth of gloom. All flags were flown at half-mast on the public buildings and in the docks.

*The same building in 1992.*

*The White Star offices in London & Southampton were beseiged with anxious relatives. This scene is from the Canute Road offices in Southampton (Southampton Museums)*

**Greatest Disaster Town Has Ever Known.**

A meeting of the Harbour Board, which was held in the afternoon, was adjourned as a mark of sympathy with the sufferers, and a letter was read from Colonel Philipps, M.P. for the borough, expressing his deepest sympathy with the inhabitants. The mayor made a feeling reference to the disaster, and said that the sympathy of Southampton and of the whole civilized world went out to the sufferers through this frightful calamity. Colonel Bance seconded the mayor's resolution of sympathy and condolence, which was carried. One member of the Harbour Board had a son on board the *Titanic,* and another ex-member was a passenger.

The scenes in some parts of the town were heartrending. Nearly a thousand families are directly concerned in the fate of the crew alone, and in most cases the only breadwinner of the family is lost. It was impossible to walk through the principal streets without meeting people who had friends on board, and the majority of the officers and crew are well known in the port. The offices of the White Star line were besieged all day by distressed women; for since the report was received that a considerable number of the crew had been saved the anxiety for further particulars was naturally all the keener.

In some of the poorer streets, where firemen and seafarers live in large numbers, very sad sights have been witnessed. In some streets nearly every house is represented on board the *Titanic,* and the manner in which bereaved women fasten on to the faintest glimmer of fresh intelligence is painfully pathetic. This is the greatest disaster Southampton has ever known. Steps will be taken by the Mayor immediately to open a local relief fund.

As usual, stories of premonitions of disaster are current. It is said that one fireman, who felt that something was sure to happen, deserted at Queenstown. Six firemen who had been signed on arrived on the quayside at Southampton last Wednesday in time to see the last gangway removed, and they are now congratulating themselves on having missed the boat.

Fully 90 per cent of the crew of the *Titanic* (stewards excluded) were members of the newly-formed British Seafarers' Union, and the widows or dependents of those drowned are entitled to a death benefit of five pounds.

*(Daily Mail, 17 April)*

## VAIN SEARCH FOR SURVIVORS.

### FRANTIC GRIEF IN NEW YORK.
*NEW YORK, Tuesday.*

The *Titanic* lies two miles deep at the bottom of the sea, probably some 420 miles east south-east of Sable Island.

# TITANIC

## 1,300 LIVES LOST IN THE GREAT DISASTER.

### THE SUNKEN LINER

A photograph which gives an idea of the immense size of the Titanic. Her length over all is 882ft. 6in., and her breadth 92ft. 6in.

## A FLOATING TOWN.

### Boilers Big Enough to Pass a Double-Decker Tram.

The Titanic, which was launched from Messrs. Harland and Wolff's shipbuilding yard at Belfast, and later set out on her disastrous maiden voyage from Southampton last Wednesday, is the largest vessel afloat, and the most luxuriously equipped. She had a registered tonnage of 46,328 tons —over 1,000 tons more than the next largest ship in the world, her sister vessel, the Olympic—is 1,000 feet long, with a beam of 112 feet, with accommodation for 2,500 passengers and a crew of 860, and cost £1,500,000 to build.

The Allan liner Virginian, which arrived yesterday to render assistance to the Titanic. She received a "wireless" message asking for assistance, and immediately sailed from Halifax, Nova Scotia.

## FAMILY OF 11 LOST.

Mr. and Mrs. John Sage and their ni... children, who are given as passengers the White Star list, are believed to ha... perished in the wreck.

They had left Peterborough, where t... father was in business as a grocer, to set... in Florida. The whole family seems to ha... been drowned. Mr. Sage was a London ma... and before going to Peterborough wa... business at King's Lynn.

## AWFUL DEATH ROLL.

Photograph showing an iceberg as seen from the deck of a mail steamer in mid-ocean.

# How the Titanic Struck

**HOW THE TITANIC WAS RIPPED FROM STEM TO STERN BY THE ICEBERG.**

The whole bilge was ripped out where the iceberg struck her. She struck the berg a blow on the starboard side."—(Extract from Mr. Bruce Ismay's statement.) (Drawn by Charles Dixon, R.I., from telegraphic description.)

## FOUNDERS IN MID-OCEAN

[By courtesy of "The Sphere."

Special drawing to show the relative position of the "Titanic" and other liners on the icefield. The "Carpathia," which picked up the survivors, raced to the rescue from the westward.

The *Carpathia*, with the 800-odd survivors, is now steaming towards New York through a perilous field of ice. "Lat. 41deg. 45min. north, long. 50deg. 20min. west. Am proceeding to New York unless otherwise ordered with about 800", runs the message received this morning from Captain Rostron, of the *Carpathia*, who adds, "After consulting with Mr. Ismay and considering the circumstances with so much ice about, we consider New York the best. There is a large number of icebergs and twenty miles of field ice with bergs among it."

The fact that the *Titanic* apparently drifted some thirty miles from the time she struck until she sank gave rise to the hope that some lifeboats might have drifted too, but this hope was dissipated by the repetition of the intelligence that all the lifeboats that were not damaged by the collision were picked up, and by definite reports from the liners *Virginian* and *Parisian* that they found no survivors.

In contradiction of various statements published yesterday, the *Virginian* today informed the Allan agents that she arrived on the scene of the disaster too late to be of any assistance, and could not say if any bodies or survivors were amid the mass of wreckage. It covered a large area of the sea. In the improbable event of any of the ill-fated passengers and crew being adrift on rafts, the piercing cold and heavy weather in all probability long ago ended their sufferings, for according to the weather reports, heavy fogs lay off Nova Scotia and a violent thunderstorm broke in that neighbourhood last night.

The Leyland liner *Californian*, however, is still cruising in the forlorn hope of making further rescues in the neighbourhood of the catastrophe. The *Virginian* has resumed her voyage eastwards.

The City of New York is hushed today by the depression caused by the greatest of all sea tragedies, and telegrams from Boston, Philadelphia, and other towns bear witness to the national grief. Men and women who a few days ago were proudly discussing the qualities of "the biggest and finest ship afloat" today can only speak of the most awful loss of life in the history of ocean travel.

# A FLOATING PALACE THAT NEVER REACHED PORT.

## HOW THE OLYMPIC AVOIDED THE ICE.

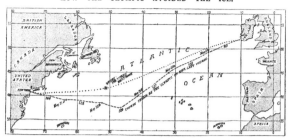

Chart showing the Olympic's course from Ireland to New York. No vessel of any importance has ever gone so far south (nearly down to the tropics) to avoid the ice. On her next trip she is coming down nearly a degree further south. The chart was supplied by Mr. A. S. Manders, manager of the Third International Rubber and Allied Trades Exposition, which opens in New York next September.

## The Largest British Steamer.

SECOND CLASS PROMENADE DECK. A GRAND EXPANSE FOR A BRISK WALK.

# MARVELS OF THE TITANIC

The Parisian cafe on board the Titanic—an innovation in ocean travelling.

## "BE BRITISH!"

Captain Smith, the commander of the Titanic.

MR. BRUCE ISMAY

## FRANTIC GRIEF.

Their mental picture of eleven sumptuous decks, with the lifts, gymnasiums, swimming baths, luxurious apartments, saloons and restaurants, has been rudely dispelled by the vision of twenty small boats crowded with women and children waiting in Arctic cold until the great ship with husbands, brothers, and fathers on board took the final plunge into the depths of the ocean.

Scenes of frantic grief are witnessed at the White Star offices, outside which a special force of police gently kept order among the multitudes of the bereaved.

With swollen eyelids they thronged the corridors, ever coming and going, listening, where they dared not ask, for a word of the safety of kin or friends and now and then breaking into hysterical inquiries. At an early hour an official of the White Star Line was called up on the telephone by Mr. William Vincent Astor, the son of the great millionaire. The official informed him that Mrs. John Jacob Astor and her maid had been saved. "But what of my father?" cried the boy, and made no effort to choke back his sobs when the faltering reply came, "No word has been received of the fate of Colonel Astor."

Grief such as his has visited hundreds of families, and wealthy women and poor awaited news side by side. With a tall woman in blue velvet Mr. Cornell, a popular magistrate, elbowed his way into the offices to get some word of his wife and two sisters. Mrs. E.D. Appleton and Mrs. Murray Brown, of Boston. No sooner had he gained the counter than the tall woman fainted. She was revived and said that she was Mrs. Weir, and that her husband was in the *Titanic*. When told that there was no news of him she fainted again, and was carried to her motor car by policemen.

Mr. Cornell's face went ghastly white when he was told that his sisters were safe but that there was no word of his wife. "I can't understand it," he cried, "they were all in the same cabin. They had been abroad for only a week just to attend the funeral of their sister." Later, to his intense relief, the name of Mrs. Cornell was included in the list of survivors.

A still more painful scene was enacted when Mrs. Benjamin Guggenheim entered with her brother-in-law, Mr. Daniel Guggenheim, and hysterically asked for news of her husband, one of the famous smelter millionaires. The clerk shook his head, and the bereaved lady burst into uncontrollable weeping, crying, "It's a shame, it's a crime. The *Virginian* should have done something. Where is the *Olympic*? Why weren't there lifeboats enough?"

## ONE MAN'S GOOD NEWS.

One man, on learning that his relatives were safe, burst through the mourning throngs with a loud whoop, sprang into a motor car, and rushed away.

Among the most eager inquirers by telephone was President Taft, who mourns Major Butt, one of his closest friends and his aide-de-camp. The major was returning from a special mission to Rome, where he went to ascertain certain points of etiquette governing the precedence of new American cardinals. Mr. Taft finally directed the Secretary of the Navy to despatch the speedy cutter *Salem* to meet the *Carpathia*.

The *Salem* is equipped with the best wireless apparatus in the Navy, and is capable of sending 1,000 miles. Her commander will obtain complete lists of the survivors and send them to the Government.

Frequently the White Star officials were required to answer angry questions as to why they kept the news of the dreadful extent of the disaster a secret for so many hours. They reiterated that the wireless message with the information that the *Titanic* had sunk had been issued as soon as it was received, and explained that the absence of any authentic details of how the collision occurred is due to the congested state of the wireless stations, which were busily occupied with the transmission of names and inquiries regarding survivors.

Elucidation of the disaster is therefore left entirely to the experts, who, on the basis of the meagre details to hand, unanimously incline to the view that the *Titanic* struck with tremendous force either a "growler" or mostly submerged berg, or a huge, towering berg with a submerged pointed shelf or beach extending a long distance under the water.

"Such a beach," said one engineer, "would tear the bottom off any ship coming at even less than half-speed. All the *Titanic's* bulk heads would not help her in such an emergency, for it would be like striking against solid rock. I believe the ship's vitals, her engines and boiler compartments, were penetrated by the first blow. That the wireless was so quickly put out of commission proves there was trouble down there."

Mr. Lewis Nixon is another of those who are convinced that the *Titanic* struck a sharp submerged berg-reef, which either tore her side out or ripped the keel and buckled the vessel in such a manner as to render the watertight compartments useless. He sees no reason to criticise the White Star Company because the *Titanic* was equipped with only twenty boats. The number of lifeboats, he observed, undoubtedly complied with the law. What ought to be done, in his opinion, is to furnish all big liners with huge detachable rafts. "Possibly," he said, "a certain portion of the stern superstructure might be made detachable so that if the liner begins to sink it will float free with the passengers left aboard. I have not worked out the idea scientifically, but I am convinced that a stern platform twelve feet deep and as wide as the ship might be made so that it could be detached in the presence of imminent danger."

**STILL BIGGER SHIPS.**

Steamship owners said today that the sinking of the *Titanic* would have no effect on their plans for the future construction of Transatlantic vessels. Representatives of the Cunard, North German Lloyd, and Hamburg-American lines declared that, notwithstanding the danger of losing ships valued at £1,400,000 or more, the companies would go on building larger vessels whenever the need for them developed.

Accidents, they said, would only make them exert greater efforts towards ensuring the safety of passengers. Mr. Emil L. Boas, general manager of the Hamburg-American Line, declared that all of the large transatlantic liners to be built in future would be of the type of the *Titanic*, Imperator and *Aquitania*. "The appliances now known to man have made the vessels of the present day so secure that it has been considered there was no danger of any of our big ships going down. If any lesson is to be learned from this accident it is to build still bigger ships."

*(Daily Mail, 17 April)*

## SEARCH ABANDONED.

*From Our Own Correspondent.*
*ST. JOHN's, Newfoundland, Tuesday.*

Everything indicates that the loss of life is about 1,500. The *Carpathia*, the first liner to arrive, rescued all the survivors in boats. Most of them are women and children.

Other liners have found no survivors in their searches on the scene of the wreck and are now continuing their voyages.

*(Daily Mail, 17 April)*

## MASSES OF WRECKAGE.

*NEW YORK, Tuesday.*
The Leyland Company have instructed the captain of the *Californian* by wireless to remain near the scene of the wreck and to render whatever aid is possible until he is relieved or until his coal supply runs low.

A telegram from Montreal states that notwithstanding the reports

to the contrary, the officials of the Allan Line still cling to the hope that the *Parisian* may have on board some survivors from the *Titanic*. This assumption is apparently based upon the fact that the *Parisian* is heading for Halifax, although her original destination was Philadelphia. — *Reuter.*

*HALIFAX (Nova Scotia), Tuesday.*
The *Parisian* steamed through much ice looking for survivors. No life rafts or bodies were sighted among the floating wreckage, which covered a large area. The weather was cold, and even if persons had been on the wreckage they would in all probability have perished from exposure before they could have been picked up. The *Parisian* is expected to reach here tomorrow. — *Reuter.*

*(Daily Mail, 17 April)*

## ANOTHER HOPE GONE.

*HALIFAX (N.S.), Tuesday.*
The Sable Island cableship *Minia* reported this afternoon by wireless that she had sighted a great mass of wreckage, but no boats or rafts from the *Titanic*.

This disposes of the hope that the *Minia*, which was anchored off Cape Race when the *Titanic* first cabled for help, might have picked up some of the *Titanic's* passengers. — *Reuter*.

(*Daily Mail, 17 April*)

# RELIEF FUND.

**MAYOR OF SOUTHAMPTON'S PLAN.**

The Major of Southampton is taking steps to open a fund for the relief of those who suffer by the loss of the *Titanic*, and will come to London today to confer with the Lord Mayor on the subject.

The Mayor of Southampton has sent the following message to the Lord Mayor of London: — "I propose opening a relief fund for distressed dependents of the crew of the *Titanic*, the majority of whom reside in Southampton. May I appeal for your cordial cooperation?"
"HENRY BOWYER."

(*Daily Mail, 17 April*)

# HONEYMOON COUPLE.

**BRIDE SAVED AND HUSBAND MISSING.**

There were no happier persons in the *Titanic* before disaster befell her than Mr. and Mrs. D.W. Marvin, a newly married American couple, aged nineteen and eighteen, who were returning to New York from a three week honeymoon in England. Mrs. Marvin's name appears in the list of survivors, but her husband apparently has not yet been accounted for.

Mr. Marvin was the son of the head of one of the largest cinematograph organisations in America, and was being trained as an engineer. Mr. A. Hamburger, a director of the Dover Street Studios, London, who knew Mr. H.M. Marvin intimately, said yesterday: "He was a splendid specimen of American youth; strong, athletic, and well set up. Mrs. Marvin is an extremely pretty and vivacious girl. They were both of them full of the joy of life and affection for each other, and when in England behaved just like two happy school children on a holiday. They spent most of their time sight-seeing and going to parties, dances, and the like. Everyone made much of them. The girl's parents are wealthy, and she had received $2,000

# TRAGIC SEQUEL TO THE FIRST WEDDING TO BE CINEMATOGRAPHED:
## AMERICAN BRIDE WIDOWED BY THE TITANIC DISASTER.

he latest craze in America is to have your wedding cinematographed. It was the ea of Miss Mary Farquharson, a pretty American girl, to have moving pictures f her wedding, and when she was married to Daniel Marvin, whose father is the ead of a large cinematograph firm, the ceremony was performed twice, the econd occasion in the presence of an operator, whose duty it was to record every cident on his instrument. Little did the happy couple dream that their married life would be cut short before the end of the honeymoon. They made a tour of Europe, and were returning home on the ill-starred Titanic, Mr. Marvin being drowned. One of the photographs shows Mrs. Marvin, who is one of the eleven brides widowed by the terrible tragedy, wearing her wedding dress. The other two are from the film illustrating the wedding ceremony. The portrait is of Mr. Marvin.—(Dover-street Studios.)

from her mother as a wedding present."

Among the survivors are Mr. Edward Beane and Mrs. Ethel Beane, second class passengers, who were married at Norwich several days ago. Both are of Norwich parentage, and Mr. Beane, who has been engaged in the building trade in America, returned to England about three weeks ago to get married. Only a few days of the honeymoon had been spent at Norwich before they started for America.

A Mr. Sedgwick, formerly an engineer at St. Helens Electricity Works, Lancashire, who was going to Mexico to take up an appointment, was one of the passengers. He was married only a week before his departure, and left his wife in England.

A young Russian watchmaker named Harmer, who was married to a Russian girl, aged twenty, in Manchester recently, was a steerage passenger. He had started in business at Strangeways, Manchester, but decided to emigrate and send for his wife later.

*(Daily Mail, 17 April)*

## NOT ENOUGH BOATS.

**SHARP CRITICISM IN THE AMERICAN PRESS.**

*From Our Own Correspondent.*
*NEW YORK, Tuesday.*
A number of newspapers direct sharp attacks against the British regulations for ensuring the safety of passengers at sea.

The *Globe* appears with an article entitled "Safety at sea ignored under British laws," and argues that the regulations for lifeboats, rafts, etc., are twenty years old and take no account of the huge modern liners.

"The rules of the British Board of Trade and Lloyd's," the Supervising Inspector-General of the United States steamboat service, Mr. George Uhler, is quoted as declaring, "are held up to the world as the proper example. The consequence is that great liners make no pretence of carrying enough lifeboats to save the lives of the passengers if the ship goes down."

Mr. Uhler admitted that many American vessels are also lacking in this respect explaining that

## PASSENGERS BOARDING THE TITANIC AT QUEENSTOWN

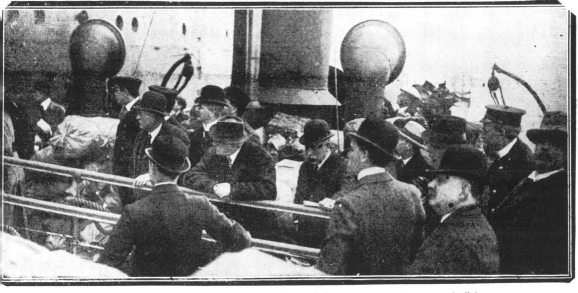

Embarking on the Titanic at Queenstown la st Thursday. This was the last port at which the ill-starred vessel called.

## THE TITANIC

### A LAST GLIMPSE OF THE ILL-FATED TITANTIC.

The last time the Titanic was seen from the shores of the United Kingdom. The photograph shows the mighty vessel steaming away from Queenstown on Thursday last.

## THE WHITE STAR LINE,

J. BRUCE ISMAY, Esq.
White Star Line.

Mrs. Marvin.—(Dover-street Studios.)

Mr. D. W. Marvin, of New York, who was drowned. His wife, who was saved, said: "As our boat shoved off he threw me a kiss, and that's the last I saw of him." The couple were returning home after a three-months' honeymoon trip in England.—(Dover-street Studios.)

it had been found impracticable in the bigger steamships to provide lifeboats for all the passengers.

The *Evening Post*, commenting on this statement, declares that "those 1,400 lives were flung away because the White Star Line, like other steamship companies, persistently refused, with the connivance of the steamboat authorities of this country, to carry sufficient lifeboats and rafts to accommodate those whose passage money they took, to say nothing of the crews whom they employed.

The sole reason every life was not saved was simply because the owners of the *Titanic* were permitted to send her to sea with only a few more lifeboats than were carried by the ocean steamers of 25 and 30 years ago."

The *Post* believes intense feeling will be aroused in America on this subject.

*(Daily Mail, 17 April)*

## LAST SIGNALS.

**WIRELESS RECORD OF THE DISASTER.**

**MIDNIGHT SCENES.**

**Titanic Struck – 10.25 p.m. Sunday**

**Wireless Failed – 12.27 a.m. Monday**

**Titanic Sank – 2.20 a.m. Monday**

The bewildering reports published in New York of wireless messages received concerning the collision have befogged even the scanty details obtainable. The wireless messages printed below are those of the authenticity of which there can be no possible doubt.

They show that the *Titanic* struck on Sunday night at 10.25 p.m. at a point roughly 360 miles from Cape Race, Newfoundland, the nearest land, 1,070 miles from New York and 2,020 miles from Southampton. The sea at the place is 12,000 feet deep.

The women were placed in the lifeboats at once, and wireless appeals for help were sent out. At 12.27 a.m., two hours and two minutes after the collision, the last wireless signal from the *Titanic* was received, showing that the dynamos were then flooded.

# THE MAGNIFICENCE OF THE TITANIC

## THE TITANIC'S FIRST AND ONLY CALL AT QUEENSTOWN LAST THURSDAY.

A tender with mail bags aboard alongside the Titanic. The little vessel is completely dwarfed by the mammoth liner.

# THE SINKING OF THE TITANIC.

"GREATER LOVE HATH NO MAN."

Mr. Phillips, senior "wireless" operator. He sent calls for help, while his assistant, Mr. Bride, strapped a lifebelt upon him. "Phillips was a brave man," said Mr. Bride, "and I shall never forget his work during the last 15 minutes."—(Miss J. Stedman.)

Mr. Bride, of Shortlands, Kent, the junior "wireless" operator, who has been saved. Though suffering great pain as the result of injuries to his feet, he went on crutches to the relief of the overworked "wireless" operator of the Carpathia.

# TRAGEDY OF THE TITANIC.

WORLD'S GREATEST LINER AT THE BOTTOM OF THE ATLANTIC AFTER COLLIDING WITH AN ICEBERG.

# SCENES IN LONDON.

Anxious enquirers outside the White Star offices in London to-day.

High above the traffic in Cockspur Street the flags on all the shipping offices were at half-mast. It was a day of mourning for the whole of the merchant navy.

## THE TITANIC DISASTER IN FIGURES.

| | |
|---|---|
| Number of souls on board (passengers 1,200, crew 900) | 2,100 |
| Number saved | 800 |
| Number drowned | 1,300 |
| Value of the ship | £1,250,000 |
| Value of the cargo | £1,000,000 |

### MR. ASTOR'S WILL.

MR. V. ASTOR.

MRS. ASTOR.

Colonel J. J. Astor, who was drowned in the Titanic disaster, left the bulk of his estate, variously estimated at between fifteen and thirty million sterling, to his son, Mr. Vincent Astor, a young Harvard student. His widow, who is not yet twenty-one, inherits the income from a trust fund of £1,000,000, provided she does not remarry.

## CAPTAIN'S MISFORTUNE.

### Titanic's Commander in Command of Olympic at Time of Collision.

In command of the Titanic on her disastrous maiden voyage is Captain Edward John Smith, who has been a commander on the White Star Line for five-and-twenty years.

It is an unhappy coincidence that Captain Smith was in command of the Olympic last September on the occasion of her collision in the Solent with the cruiser Hawke.

In his evidence before the Admiralty Court he stated that he took charge of the Olympic on her first voyage last June, having formerly commanded the same company's liner the Adriatic.

At the time of the collision the Olympic was in charge of a duly-licensed Trinity House pilot, and the judgment of the Court was that the collision was due to the Olympic's pilot.

Captain Smith, a Staffordshire man, born sixty years ago, is one of the best known and most popular shipmasters on the North Atlantic route. The White Star Line authorities hold him in high esteem for his skill and competence.

Salvation Army band playing a hymn outside the White Star's London offices yesterday.

After that there was an interval of one hour and fifty-three minutes waiting in the dark before the *Titanic* sank. She went down by the bows, and the 1,400 people lost were probably gathered together in the stern, which sank last, while the lifeboats pulled away to avoid the whirlpool caused by the sinking ship. The sea was quiet and the weather clear. The *Carpathia* arrived at daybreak.

The first authentic message was that from the wireless station at Cape Race. It ran:

CAPE RACE, Monday.
10.25 p.m. yesterday *Titanic* reports by wireless struck iceberg and calls for immediate assistance. At 11 p.m. she reported sinking by head. Women being put off in boats. Gave position as 41.46 N., 50.14 W. Steamers *Baltic, Olympic*, and *Virginian* all making towards scene of disaster. Latter was last to hear *Titanic* signals at 12.27 a.m. today. Reported them then blurred and ending abruptly.

The next authentic message, published exclusively in yesterday's *Daily Mail*, was only received when the *Olympic*, with her powerful wireless installation, was able to take the *Carpathia's* messages and forward them to the land.

*(Daily Mail, 17 April)*

# BOAT LOADS OF WOMEN.

**LAST OF THE TITANIC.**

**FEW MEN AMONG SURVIVORS.**

**868 SAVED. 1,490 MISSING.**

**FIRST LISTS OF NAMES.**

The number of the survivors of the *Titanic* is officially stated by the White Star Line in New York to be 868, the great majority of them women and children.

The number of the missing is 1,490. The survivors are on board the Cunard liner *Carpathia,* which is proceeding slowly through the ice, and is expected at New York tomorrow evening or Friday morning.

There are no survivors in the *Parisian* and *Virginian* or other ships, but the Parisian has changed her destination from Philadelphia to Halifax, where she arrives today.

64

# SINKING OF THE TITANIC

## ROUTE TAKEN BY THE TITANIC DURING HER FIRST AND LAST VOYAGE.

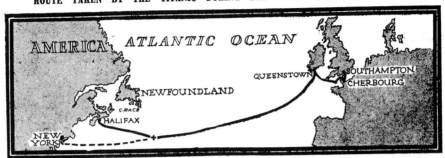

Map showing the course from Southampton to New York, via Cherbourg and Queenstown, the route taken by the Titanic. The point where the collision occurred is shown by a cross. The deep black line is continued to Halifax, to which port the Titanic was steaming when she sunk.

Inside the Parisian café, one of the Titanic's new features. Among the other luxuries are a squash racquets court, swimming bath, gymnasium, ballroom and skating rink.—(*Daily Mirror* photograph.)

The s.s. Birma, which is better known by her old name the Arundel Castle. She left New York —bound for Rotterdam and Libau—three hours after the Carpathia. The photographs reproduced here and on page 1 were sent ashore off Dover when the vessel stopped specially for the purpose.

Mr. J. Maxwell, the ship's carpenter, who was the first man Captain Smith sent for when the accident occurred.

The King and Queen have sent to the White Star Line a telegram expressing their deepest sympathy with the bereaved. The Kaiser has also telegraphed expressions of sympathy.

President Taft has despatched a special ship with very powerful wireless apparatus to meet the *Carpathia* and send direct to New York the full names of all the saved and all the missing.

The magnitude of the disaster, which is the greatest in maritime history, will be realised from the fact that the names and addresses of the crew alone occupy half a page of *The Daily Mail*. Yesterday we published the names of the first and second class passengers, which occupied two columns, and today the lists of the saved and the missing fill three columns more.

Search for survivors on the scene of the disaster has been abandoned. Piercing cold, dense fog, and a thunderstorm have prevailed on the spot beneath which the *Titanic* lies 12,000 feet down.

Among those not accounted for are Mr. W.T. Stead, the famous journalist; Colonel J.J. Astor, the millionaire, whose young bride is saved; Captain E.J. Smith, R.N.R., the commander; Major A.W. Butt, President Taft's aide-de-camp; Mr. Washington Dodge, a Philadelphia millionaire, and his son; Mr. Benjamin Guggenheim, a New York ironmaster and financier; Mr. F.D. Millet, the American artist; Mr. M. Rothschild, Mr. Isidor Straus, a wealthy American, and his wife; and Mr. George D. Widener, a United States railway magnate, and Mr. Harry Widener.

Mr. D.W. Marvin, aged nineteen, is among the missing, while his wife, aged eighteen, whom he married a few weeks ago, is saved.

The ship was not fully insured, but insurances on the hull, cargo and passengers, together with their property and jewels, amount to not less than £2,500,000. In Southampton was a steward who was waiting for news of his father and brother, who had long been in the service of the White Star Line as stewards, and were transferred to the *Titanic* last week. "I only missed the boat myself by a fluke," he said. "I had come back from a trip on the *Oceanic*, and, although my father asked me to sign on with him for the *Titanic*'s maiden voyage, I told him I wanted a holiday."

Mr. E.W. Bill, of New York, and his wife, who were staying at the Hotel Cecil, were very keen on sailing on the *Titanic* on her maiden voyage. A day or two before the *Titanic* sailed, Mrs Bill saw the vessel wrecked in a dream. So impressed was Mr Bill by his wife's story that they cancelled the passage – and sailed on the *Celtic* instead.

Of the eleven passengers on the *Titanic* who landed at Queenstown, two were almost forgotten and narrowly escaped being carried across the Atlantic on the ill-fated voyage.

*(Mirror, 18 April 1912)*

# NOT ENOUGH LIFEBOATS.

*Titanic's* Builder Blames Government for Inadequate Regulations.

One of the most important questions which has been raised in consequence of the disaster is whether there were a sufficient number of lifeboats on the *Titanic*.

The Right Hon. A.M. Carlisle, who, formerly general manager to Messrs. Harland and Wolff, built the *Titanic* and partly designed her, said, when interviewed yesterday by *The Daily Mail*, that he did not consider the lifeboat accommodation required by the Board of Trade regulations was sufficient.

I do not think it is sufficient for big ships," he said, "and I never did. As ships grew bigger I was always in favour of increasing the lifeboat accommodation. Yet it remains the same for a ship of 50,000 tons as for one of 10,000.

When working out the designs of the *Olympic* and the *Titanic* I put my ideas before the davit constructors, and got them to design me davits which would allow me to place, if necessary, four lifeboats on each pair of davits, which would have meant a total of over forty boats.

Those davits were fitted in both ships. But, though the Board of Trade did not require anything more than the sixteen lifeboats, twenty boats were supplied.

The White Star Company did, of course, supply boats of very

# SAVED FROM THE TITANIC:

Titanic survivors on board the Cunard liner Carpathia, the only vessel to rescue anyone from the wreck.

## WORLD'S GREATEST LINER AT THE BOTTOM OF THE ATLANTIC

Rescued passengers on board the Carpathia. They are loud in their praises of the kindness they received from the captain and crew.

much greater capacity than those required by the Board of Trade. I think I am correct in saying that the provision, in cubic capacity, was practically double that which was required.

At the same time, it was nothing like sufficient in case of accident, to take off the majority of the passengers and crew.

I have no doubt that the Government of this country, and the Government of other countries, will now look more seriously into the matter.

*(Mirror, 18 April 1912)*

## CALL FOR BETTER REGULATIONS.

In the House of Commons on Monday Mr. Douglas Hall will ask the Prime Minister whether the Government are prepared, in view of the grave loss of life attending the wreck of the *Titanic*, to appoint a committee to inquire into the whole question of the supply of boats on ships of the mercantile marine, and other means of saving life at sea.

Also to consider the efficacy of the existing Board of Trade regulations, with a view to the adoption of more effective means in the near future.

*(Mirror, 18 April 1912)*

## SAFETY WANTED, NOT LUXURY.

Mr Walter Winans, the millionaire sportsman, expresses himself sensibly on the disaster. "Does it not seem strange, charging a passenger 870 for the best stateroom on the *Titanic*," he writes to *The Daily Mirror*, "and not giving him a private lifeboat? I am sure it would pay better than giving him a lot of useless decoration. By the way, the Titans defied the gods and were thrown into the sea; so it was a bad-omened name to give a ship."

*(Mirror, 18 April 1912)*

## FOUR OFFICERS SAVED.

At a quarter to eleven yesterday morning the White Star Line received the following telegram from their head offices in Liverpool: "Have received following from Captain Haddock, of the *Olympic*, via *Celtic*": —
Please allay rumours that *Virginian* has any *Titanic* passengers. Neither has the *Tunisian*. Believe

only survivors on *Carpathia*. Second, third, fourth, fifth officers and second Marconi operator only officers reported saved.

The names of the officers reported saved are respectively Messrs. E.H. Lightoller, H.J. Pitman, J.G. Boxhall and H.G. Lowe. The Marconi operator is Harold Bride.

*(Mirror, 18 April 1912)*

*Some of the children from one street in Southampton who lost relatives on the ship (Southampton Museums)*

## AMATEURS OF WIRELESS.

The enactment of a law regulating the promiscuous use of wireless telegraphy and the exclusion of amateur and irresponsible operators from the freedom of the air, is likely to be one sequel of the *Titanic* catastrophe, says a Reuter special message from New York.

Measures of this sort have been pending for some time, but the present situation will undoubtedly force immediate action. Of course, no concrete programme for Congress has yet been determined upon, but it is probable that the officials of the White Star Line will be summoned to state the precautions for safety taken on board their liners. Mr. Taft is taking a keen personal interest in all the features of the proposed regulation of passenger vessels.

*(Mirror, 18 April 1912)*

## WIRELESS TO THE DEAD.

**Shoals of Messages to Passengers Destined Never To Be Delivered.**

One of the most pathetic features of the *Titanic* disaster are the shoals of wireless messages sent by relatives and friends to people on the *Titanic* — messages which were destined never to be delivered. On Monday last large numbers of wireless messages were sent to *Titanic* passengers — many were addressed to Mr. W.T. Stead.

At the time the wires were dispatched it was believed that the passengers were safe, and the telegrams contained optimistic messages of congratulation and even business news. But hours before the first news of the collision arrived in London there was no *Titanic,* and the wireless messages, sent via Cape Race, flashed across nothing but dreary icefloes and wreckage.

"The one object of the wireless operators at the land stations and on the liner has been to save life," an official of the Marconi Company told *The Daily Mirror.*

"They have been almost wholly occupied with dispatching service wires, and only during lulls have they been able to attend to private wires. At such a terrible time all purely private messages must have second place. In the ordinary way the dispatching of wireless messages to the *Carpathia* would take remarkably short time. A telegram can be handed in in London, and would be received by the wireless operator aboard the *Carpathia* within five minutes."

*(Mirror, 18 April 1912)*

## "SINKING!" — TITANIC'S CRY.

**Have been in collision with iceberg. — We are in a sinking condition and require urgent assistance.**

This was the message flashed from the *Titanic* to the Cunard liner *Caronia* in Mid-Atlantic.

But the *Caronia* was 700 miles away — too far to be of assistance, as her master, Captain Barr, sadly explained last night when the vessel arrived at Queenstown.

Captain Barr said it was on Monday morning, at half-past four, in lat. 43.45N., long. 42.20W., that he received the wireless appeal from the *Titanic,* which further stated that she had been in collision with an iceberg.

Not near enough to render assistance himself, Captain Barr sent wireless messages out indicating to steamers nearer the *Titanic* than he was aware of the nature of the accident to that vessel. The intelligence created a painful sensation on board, and Captain Barr's officers and crew deeply regretted that they were precluded from being of service to those on the sinking liner.

*(Mirror, 18 April 1912)*

## TITANIC'S LAST "GOOD—BYE".

The last known message from the *Titanic* before the disaster was received by the *Tunisian*, which yesterday reported on arrival at Liverpool, speaking to the *Titanic* by wireless on Saturday midnight, and sending a message, "Good luck." To this the *Titanic* replied: "Many thanks. Goodbye."

*(Mirror, 18 April 1912)*

## THE TITANIC'S SUBSTITUTE.

It is anticipated that the passengers who had booked for the second voyage of the *Titanic* from Southampton to New York on May 1st will suffer little inconvenience.

*New York service.*

If the *Olympic* does not arrive at Southampton in time, the *Majestic* will sail on Wednesday next.

*(Mirror, 18 April 1912)*

## VIGIL AMID ICE.

**Liner's Captain on Bridge for Two Days Among Bergs.**

**168 SEEN IN ONE DAY.**

A vivid narrative of his voyage through the huge Atlantic icebergs which wrecked the *Titanic* was given to *The Daily Mirror* last night by Dr. MacCormac, a London anethetist, who arrived at Liverpool yesterday in the Allan liner *Tunisian.*

"The *Tunisian* left St. John's (Newfoundland) last Sunday week," said Dr. MacCormac, "and we came into the ice region on the following Tuesday. It was clear, but bitterly cold, and, as sailors say, we 'smelt ice' long before we came to it. Our position on Tuesday week, when we first saw the ice, was 48N., 43W. The mass was moving southwards, and it was undoubtedly the same icefield into which the *Titanic* ran five days later in 40N., 61W."

"The ice was of two kinds—field ice and bergs. The former, composed of thousands of blocks about twelve feet square, closely packed together, was practically on a level with the sea. It was estimated to be quite sixteen miles wide, and its length can be judged from the fact that we steamed slowly alongside it all day on Tuesday."

"At times we were within a quarter of a mile of the icefield, and it almost looked as if one could step off the ship and take a walk on the packed mass. We steamed very slowly throughout Tuesday and all Wednesday morning — sometimes only just fast enough to keep 'way' on the *Tunisian*."

"So careful was Captain Fairhall that he hardly ever left the bridge, and he did not, I was told, take off his clothes for fifty-seven hours. The isolated bergs seen from the ship were far more terrible and impressive than the icefield, for they moved faster and were, of course, more dangerous. I did not count them myself, but several passengers did so, and all agreed that we passed no fewer than 168 in the twenty-four hours of Tuesday week last. They were of all shapes and sizes. One looked just like the crater of a volcano, and others were flat, jagged, pyramidal, and all kinds of fantastic shapes."

**HIGH AS BIG BEN.**

"The biggest iceberg I saw was wider than the Thames at Waterloo Bridge, and was at least as high as Big Ben. You must remember, too, that about one-ninth of an iceberg appears above water. Most of them looked as if they were coated with snow."

"As we could not find a passage through the icefield, although we did 'cut off corners' by gently forcing our way through the blocks, we had to come farther south than we intended. Consequently we are a day late in getting home. The *Titanic* was signalled as having passed us all right during the week, and we did not know of her terrible fate until the pilot came aboard off Liverpool."

*(Mirror, 18 April 1912)*

## PARENTS' MAGIC TELEGRAM.

"If only the thousands of others waiting could get the same glad tidings as I have here!"

It was the first grateful exclamation of Mr. A.J. Bride, of Shortlands, when he had the wonderful joy of learning yesterday that his son, the second wireless operator, was safe after all.

# The Daily Mirror

THE MORNING JOURNAL WITH THE SECOND LARGEST NET SALE.

No. 2,647.    Registered at the G.P.O. as a Newspaper.    THURSDAY, APRIL 18, 1912.    One Halfpenny.

## MR. W. T. STEAD, THE FRIEND OF KINGS AND THE HATER OF INJUSTICE, WHO WAS ONE OF THE MANY HUNDREDS WHO PERISHED IN THE SINKING OF THE TITANIC.

Miss Estelle Stead as Portia.

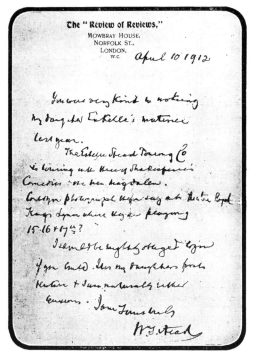

Letter written by Mr. Stead to *The Daily Mirror* on April 10.

A recent portrait of Mr. W. T. Stead.

Mr. Stead saying good-bye to his wife and daughters.

Mr. Stead wearing prison clothes.

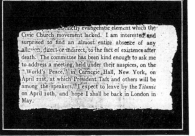

An extract from Mr. Stead's last article.

Had Mr. W. T. Stead escaped from the sinking Titanic—we say "had" because, although his fate is still uncertain, the probabilities are that he has perished—he would have written the most wonderful article of his life. He was one of the greatest journalists who ever lived. He could not only describe things, but he could *see* them, and the force of his style and the unflinching honesty of his opinions, whether they were mistaken or not, compelled the world to listen. He had interviewed Tsars and he was the friend of Kings. He knew more about foreign politics than almost any man in Europe, and his hatred of war created The Hague Peace Conference. He went to prison for his opinions, so strong were they. But the sinking of the Titanic would have been the most vivid experience of his life, and we should have known the *truth* as to why she sank. Violent as his convictions were, he was, of all things, a human man. Almost the last thing he did before he sailed on that fatal journey was to write to *The Daily Mirror* asking that his daughter's latest theatrical production might be photographed in order that publicity would help her in her artistic career. The thinking world pays a tribute to his memory.

"I could not believe my son was alive," Mr Bride told *The Daily Mirror*. "It seemed that he must be drowned with the majority of the passengers and crew. Then came this wonderful telegram. The news seemed incredible. I was quite overcome by it."

*(Mirror, 18 April 1912)*

## TWICE WARNED OF ICEBERG.

One inexplicable feature of the disaster, says a Reuter's special message, is how the *Titanic* headed into the iceberg after the ship had been warned of such a danger by the *Amerika* only a few minutes before the collision.

Nor was the *Amerika's* the only information received. The *Touraine* had radiographed to the *Titanic* on the 14th, warning her of the position of the bergs, and the *Titanic* answered the warning.

The *Etonian's* officers, who think that possibly sailing vessels may have picked up some of the survivors, believe they saw and photographed the very iceberg that sent the new liner to her grave.

*(Mirror, April 18, 1912)*

## DISASTER ITEMS

Mr. Hays, the president of the Grand Trunk Railway, his wife and daughter are safe on board the *Carpathia*.

A memorial service for those who have lost their lives on the *Titanic* will be held in St. Paul's Cathedral tomorrow at noon. No tickets will be issued or required by the general public.

Asked to show their respect for the brave men on the *Titanic,* a large crowd of seamen outside the offices of the National Sailors and Firemen's Union yesterday raised their hats and caps in reverent silence.

*(Mirror, 18 April 1912)*

## WIDOWED SOUTHAMPTON.

*(From Our Own Correspondent.)*
SOUTHAMPTON, April 17. – The gloom which settled over Southampton when confirmation of the *Titanic's* loss was received is deepening, and tonight the wives and other relatives of the crew still keep anxious vigil at the White Star offices.

# 𝔄n 𝔏oving † 𝔐emory

of the 1635 souls who perished in the

# S.S. TITANIC,

*which foundered while on her maiden voyage from Southampton to New York,*

## SUNDAY, APRIL 14th, 1912.

Nearer, my God, to Thee,
  Nearer to Thee ;
Even though it be a cross
  That raiseth me ;
Still all my song shall be,
Nearer, my God, to Thee,
  Nearer to Thee.

Till in my Father's house
  Perfectly blest,
After my journeyings
  Safe and at rest,
All my delight shall be
Ever, my God, with Thee,
  Ever with Thee.

Here, where are the homes of most of the crew, their kinsfolk have hoped and watched all day for news of survivors, news of fathers, husbands, brothers, sons. They have waited silently, anxiously, and for most the tidings came not. Tonight many of them have been waiting almost continuously for twenty-four hours for tidings of the breadwinners of many humble homes. The suspense is agonizing, and heart-rending scenes have been common.

"Will the list never come?" one poor woman exclaimed, as her fainting form was borne away.

Nothing approaching this appalling blow has ever fallen upon the port, though disasters to the local seafaring community have been by no means rare, and memories of the *Stella* and *Hilda* disasters are still recalled.

**WIDOWS IN EVERY STREET**

Here there are widows in nearly every street in certain parts, and already two deaths of bereaved people have taken place. One case was recorded yesterday, another almost as pathetic comes to light today.

A wife recently confined has died since the news was broken

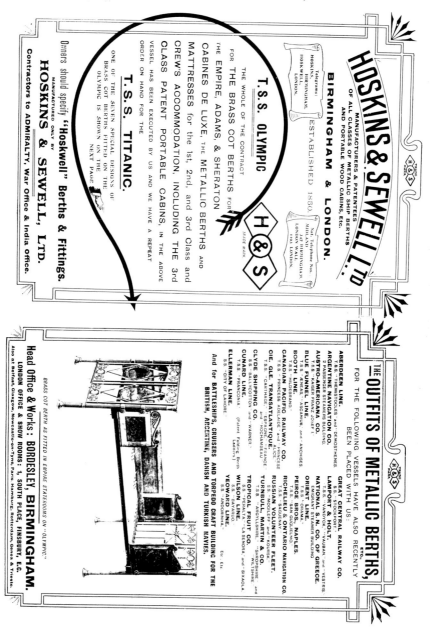
to her, and the child has died also. In two neighbouring streets in the Shirley district are two young widows, married only a few weeks since, the voyage in one case being the unfortunate husband's first. In yet another street there are three widowed women living side by side.

Crowds remained practically all last night outside the White Star Company's offices, and increased greatly in number from daybreak onwards. The company's officials granted all possible information to the bereaved inquirers, the names of the saved being posted on a notice board as soon as received.

There were pathetic scenes outside the offices as the wives in suspense learnt the worst.

Hopeless misery has cast its wing over the town, causing the wholesale cancellation of social engagements and public meetings.

*(Mirror, 18 April 1912)*

## DEATH-ROLL INCREASED BY 165.

**Only 705 Survivors of Titanic on Board Carpathia.**

**A WORLD WAITING.**

**Cable Steamer Leaves Halifax on Funeral Mission.**

**SON'S TRAGIC CRUISE.**

Pathetically slowly, the Cunard liner *Carpathia* is nearing New York with her tragic load of widowed wives and orphaned children. The eyes of the whole civilised world are following her as she ploughs her way all too draggingly along through the ocean and the icefields that cumber the track.

For on board she carries all that are left of the 2,200 souls who set sail with such high hope last week for the maiden voyage of the *Titanic*, the greatest ship the world has ever known, man's supreme challenge to the powers of nature.

Now that ship has been shattered, and all that remains is sunk in 12,000ft. of Atlantic Ocean. Of her human freight two in every three have perished, fathers, husbands, bread-winners.

And the world waits upon the *Carpathia* — waits to hear the appalling truth of that midnight crash when the 46,000 ton steamship met the mountain of ice. But meanwhile a funeral ship has left Halifax with a grim cargo of coffins, hoping to pick up the dead....

What is their number? No one yet knows for certain, but the most recent information seems to increase the death-roll by over 160. Latest wireless reports speak of but 700 or 705 survivors on the *Carpathia* — formerly it was 868.

Estimates of the number of the dead must vary between 1,400 and 1,500, for not even the precise number of those on board when the *Titanic* sailed is yet definitely established.

**CARPATHIA WITH 705 SURVIVORS.**

The following cablegram was received by the White Star Line last evening from their New York office: —

"*Carpathia* now in communication with Siasconset reports 705 survivors aboard."

These figures would seem to be the final official number of the survivors, and increase the death-roll by 163 to nearly 1,500.

The first news that came to hand concerning the terrible death-roll

### NEARER MY GOD TO THEE!

Nearer, my God, to Thee, Nearer to Thee

E'en though it be a cross That raiseth me,

Still all my song shall be, Nearer, my God, to Thee, Nearer to Thee.

Though like the wanderer, The sun gone down, Darkness comes over me, My rest a stone Yet in my dreams I'd be Nearer, my God, to Thee, Nearer to Thee.

There let my way appear Steps unto Heav'n, All that Thou sendest me In mercy given, Angels to beckon me Nearer, my God, to Thee, Nearer to Thee.

Then, with my waking thoughts Bright with Thy praise, Out of my stony griefs Bethel I'll raise; So by my woes to be Nearer, my God, to Thee, Nearer to Thee.

Hymn played by Band as the ship sank to her doom, 15th April, 1912.

of the *Titanic* put the figures of the survivors on board the *Carpathia* at 675.

**TRAGEDY IN FIGURES.**

Then came what purported to be official figures — 868. Last evening from many sources came telegrams estimating the survivors at only 700 or 705. Mere

figures, these, yet of tragic signi-
ficance to those left behind. To
you who read, 700 or 701 means
little enough. To the orphaned
child or widowed bride of that
one, left to fend for themselves,
with the tragic memory of a dear
one who is no more, that unit is
everything in the world worth
having.

**ONLY 600 PASSENGERS.**

NEW YORK, April 17 (eve-
ning). — According to the figures
published here, 700, or therea-
bouts, alone have escaped disaster, and undoubtedly among
these are 100 sailors. If these
figures turn out to be correct
there cannot be more than 600
passengers saved. The death-
roll in that case would number
over 1,500. The latest analysis
received via the cruiser *Chester*
places the number of the lost
cabin passengers at 115, and of
the second class passengers at
167.

**ELECTRICAL STORM.**

HALIFAX, April 17, (morning). —
Sable Island has been in wireless
communication with the Cunard
liner *Carpathia*, who reported
that twenty icebergs had been
sighted off the banks near the
scene of the wreck. She sent no
details of the disaster. An electrical storm interfered with the
transmission of wireless telegrams last night and this morning, and no communication was
received from the *Carpathia.* —
*Reuter.*

**SHIP THAT BRINGS THE TRUTH.**

When will the first first-hand
news of what really happened to
the *Titanic* reach England? So far
as is known at present, the only
true story is with tragic lips on
board the *Carpathia*. It does not
appear as though the *Carpathia*
is going to let any details be made
public until she lands in New
York.

Yesterday American imagina-
tive journalism took its first flight,
and stories were circulated and
telegraphed to London from New
York newspapers, purporting to
describe the actual scenes at the
wreck of the *Titanic*, and to be
based upon wireless messages
from the British steamer *Bruce*.
Subsequent inquiries showed
that the *Bruce* had not been in
touch with the *Titanic* or any
other steamer near the scene of
the disaster.

A *Reuter* message states that the *Carpathia* was 498 miles east of Ambrose Channel at 6.10 a.m. yesterday, American time. In English time this is 11.10 a.m.

Ambrose Light is twenty miles from New York, so that this extra mileage has to be added to the total of 498 miles, making the *Carpathia* 518 miles east of New York at 4 a.m. (Greenwich time) yesterday morning.

The *Carpathia*, it was officially announced by the Cunard Company yesterday, will not reach New York until eight o'clock tonight (New York time), which is one o'clock tomorrow morning (Greenwich time).

**CABLESHIP'S GRIM ERRAND.**

HALIFAX, April 17. — The cableship *Mackay-Bennett*, has been chartered by the White Star Company to go to the scene of the *Titanic* disaster. In the hope that some bodies may be picked up coffins are being taken, and several undertakers and embalmers will be on the ship.

The *Mackay-Bennett* sailed at two o'clock. In addition to the undertakers, she carries a Church of England clergyman, who will perform the last rites over any bodies that may be found. — *Reuter.*

**SON'S TRAGIC MISSION.**

HALIFAX (N.S.), April 17. — Colonel Jacob Astor's son arrived here this morning, and he is chartering a steamer for the purpose of going in search of his father's body. — *Exchange.*

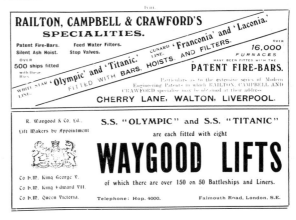
*(Daily Mail, 18th April 1912)*

# ANGUISH AT SOUTHAMPTON

Stories of bereavement were told in Bond Street, William Street, Princes Street, and Berner Street. Mrs. Gear, of 17, Bond

Street, was married a year ago yesterday. There are many babies in Northam who will never remember their fathers, and there are many who will never have been known by their fathers.

Not only in the poorer quarters are there women weeping. On the verge of the New Forest, just outside Southampton, Mrs. Smith, the wife of Captain Smith, lies in her home prostrate with grief.

At dawn today there was a large crowd of men and women outside the White Star Line offices in Canute Road.

The offices had remained open all night, and there had been watchers who had seen the sun set and the sun rise waiting and hoping throughout the night. In the afternoon the crowd increased.

As each inquirer left the office he or she did not go immediately away, but stayed with the waiting crowd as if seeking consolation in the common sorrow.

*(Daily Mail, 18 April)*

# CARPATHIA'S MESSAGE.

**ONLY 705 SURVIVORS.**

**DUE IN NEW YORK TONIGHT.**

**363 NAMES OF SAVED.**

**1,653 MISSING.**

The following cablegram was received by the White Star Line at Liverpool last night from their New York office: —

*Carpathia* now in communication with Siasconset. Reports 705 survivors aboard.

The *Carpathia* is expected by the Cunard officials to reach New York between eight o'clock and midnight tonight (1 a.m. and 5 a.m. tomorrow morning by English time).

The fast American cruiser *Chester,* which was sent to meet the *Carpathia*, has transmitted by wireless to Washington the following message: —

The *Carpathia* states that the list of the first and second class passengers and crew has been sent to shore. The *Chester* will relay list third class passengers when convenient to *Carpathia.*

This is taken to mean that the list telegraphed from the *Carpathia* to the station at Cape Race through the *Olympic* and published in yesterday's issue contained the names of all the first and second class passengers saved, and that the 342 names to come are those of steerage passengers and the crew.

The number of survivors in the *Carpathia* was officially stated in the White Star offices in New York on Tuesday to be 868. A wireless message from Mr. Winfield Thompson, a passenger in the *Franconia*, which has been in touch with the *Carpathia*, was received by the Cunard Line in New York yesterday, and stated that the *Carpathia* has only 705 survivors on board, and this is confirmed by the message printed above. No hope is left of any survivors being on board other liners than the *Carpathia*. There is just a possibility that one or two castaways may have been picked up by fishing boats near the scene of the wreck.

The position is as follows:

| | |
|---|---|
| Survivors' names received | 363 |
| Names to come | 342 |
| Number of persons on board | 2,358 |
| Number of missing | 1,653 |

Incomplete totals of the men, women, and children saved are:

| | |
|---|---|
| Men | 79 |
| Women | 233 |
| Children | 16 |

New names of survivors received yesterday included those of five officers, who were probably in charge of the boats, as follows:
C.H. Lightoller, second officer,
H.J. Pitman, third officer,
J.S. Boxhall, fourth officer,
H.F. Lowe, fifth officer.
H.S. Bride, second Marconi operator,
"and six officers" (? the sixth officer, Mr. J.P. Moody).

*(SOUTHAMPTON TIMES &*
*HAMPSHIRE EXPRESS. APRIL 20th.)*

## TITANIC INCIDENTS.

**Some Remarkable Facts.**

Four members of a Fritham family were on board the ill fated liner.

One of the *Titanic's* stewardesses, S.A.Stap, was born at sea. She was among the saved.

The loss of the *Titanic* has brought back into service the *Majestic*, Captain Smith's old command.

The North German Lloyd liner *George Washington*, from Southampton, was over a day late in arriving at New York, having been delayed by the ice floes.

The four largest ships ever built are the *Titanic, Olympic, Lusitania* and *Mauretania*. Of these only the *Lusitania* has escaped a serious accident. Mrs. Gold, a first class stewardess in the *Titanic*, was on the *Suevic* when she was stranded, and in the *Olympic* collision. She is now reported among the saved.

The White Star and American Lines were to have played a football match with Messrs. Harlands & Wolff team next Wednesday for the funds of the Seaman's Orphanage. The game has been postponed.

An unemployed greaser residing at Freemantle was offered a job on the ill-fated vessel. He accepted, but after having passed up the gangway, he turned back, saying that he would not go because "his missus would only worry".

A small boy called at our office on Wednesday and plaintively asked if we had received any news of the crew. On being answered in the negative, he sadly inquired if we thought his brother was saved. He had just left school, and begun his career as a bell-boy on the *Titanic*. (None of the bell-boys survived, and this lad was 14 years old).

Thomas Andrews one of the managing directors of Harland & Wolff was largely responsible for the construction of the *Titanic*, and was deputed to sail on the maiden voyage. With him he had eight workers from Queen's Island. One of these was Mr. Chisolm, who was chief draughtsman for the *Titanic* and *Olympic*.

The *Olympic*, which made a dash to the scene of the *Titanic's* accident, is expected at Southampton this evening, and she will sail again next Wednesday. The *Titanic* was to have sailed again on May 1st for America, but her place will be taken by the *Philadelphia*.

All later sailings assigned to the *Titanic* will be taken by the *Majestic,* and the service will be maintained by the *Majestic, Olympic* and *Oceanic.*

The Hon. J.C.Middleton, vice-president of the Akron-Canton Railway of Ohio, has made a statement to the effect that he booked a cabin in the *Titanic* on March 23, and on April 3 he dreamt that he saw the *Titanic* capsized in mid-ocean and a lot of the passengers struggling in the water.

The following night he dreamt exactly the same dream. The next day he told his wife and friends, and then he decided to cancel his passage.

Our reporter was present at the Relief Fund distribution yesterday afternoon. His impressions of the way in which the Mayor dealt with the sufferers who came before him appear to be very favourable, and we note with pleasure the remark which the Mayor made to him to the effect that as regards the "main" Relief Fund his Worship will have the assistance of a strong and representative committee.

# WOMEN PASSENGERS ON THE CARPATHIA CLOTHE AND TEND TH

# SURVIVORS OF THE TITANIC TRAGEDY.

When rescued from the Titanic lifeboats by the Carpathia many of the women were very scantily clad, as they had retired for the night when the giant liner crashed into the iceberg. This fact, of course, added tenfold to their sufferings as they drifted about in the piercing cold awaiting rescue. Once aboard the Cunarder, however, everything possible was done for their comfort, passenge giving up their cabins and ransacking their trunks for clothes. The photogra shows women passengers sewing and distributing clothes. If the garments did fit these kindly ladies took needle and thread and made the necessary alteratio

*(Mirror, 20 April 1912)*

# THE FINAL SCENES OF TRAGIC HORROR ON THE SINKING TITANIC.

**HEROES OF THE DOOMED SHIP.**

**Survivors' Accounts of the Most Terrible Experiences in the World.**

**CRIES FROM THE SEA.**

**Englishman Tells How Men Played Cards Ignorant of Their Doom.**

**MR. W. T. STEAD'S END.**

**Explosion of Boilers That Broke the Vessel in Two.**

The humble truth of the catastrophe that overwhelmed the *Titanic* and carried 1,600 souls to their deaths is revealed in the vivid and awful accounts given by the survivors. Their narratives differ in many points of detail—they saw what happened from different points of view—but in the main points there is for the most part agreement. How no one on board realised what had happened after the collision, how a party of card-players resumed their play after a moment's interruption, how the men died like heroes, how the ship was blown in two by the explosion of the boilers and sank bows first—all this is told, together with stories of unspeakable horrors and sufferings and marvellous escapes and the heart-rending sundering of brides from husbands....

The first reports that stated that Captain Smith shot himself dead on the bridge after a struggle with his brother-officers in the library is now discredited, and believed to have emanated from the hysterical imaginings of survivors overwhelmed by the horrors of the situation.

*(Mirror, 20 April 1912)*

# ENGLISHMAN'S FULL STORY.

The following account of the disaster by an Englishman, Mr. Beesley, formerly science master at Dulwich College, is given in a *Reuter's* Special Service message from New York:—

The temperature was very cold, particularly on the last day. In fact, after dinner on the Sunday evening it was almost too cold to be on the deck at all. I had been in my berth about ten minutes, when at about 10.15 I felt a slight jar. Soon afterwards there was a second shock, but not sufficient-

# SCENES ON BOARD THE CARPATHIA,

Some of the Titanic's lifeboats on board the Carpathia. It was at first reported that they had all been cut adrift.

## THE CARPATHIA.

The Carpathia, which is proceeding to New York with survivors.

Captain A. H. Rostron, R.N.R., the commander of the Carpathia, the Cunarder which brought the survivors to New York. All are united in praising his kindness.

## THE TITANIC SINKS.

New York, April 15.—The Titanic sank at 2.20 this morning. No lives were lost.—Reuter.

## VACANCIES MADE BY TITANIC.

Several important changes in the management of the firm of Messrs. Harland and Wolff are shortly to be made consequent upon the deaths of officials of the firm in the Titanic.

A brother of the late Mr. Thomas Andrews, the managing director of the firm, who was drowned in the disaster, joins the firm to-day.

Another new member of the firm will be a nephew of the late Sir Edward Harland, who has had five years' experience in shipbuilding with a Japanese firm.

## INSURED FOR £1,000,000.

The Titanic is insured at Lloyd's for £1,000,000, which of course does not include any valuables or specie that she may have been carrying at the time of the accident.

The rate of reinsurance on the Titanic at Lloyd's yesterday rose to 50 per cent.

One prominent City underwriter said that even if the vessel made port her owners would have to face a loss of at least £150,000.

ly large to cause any anxiety to anyone. The engines, however, stopped immediately afterwards. I went up on deck in my dressing-gown, and I found only a few people there who had come up in the same way to inquire why we had stopped, but there was no sort of anxiety in the mind of anyone. We saw, through the smoking-room window, that a game of cards was going on, and I went in to ask if they knew anything. They had noticed the jar a little more, and, looking through the window, had seen a huge iceberg go by close to the side of the boat.

## GAME OF CARDS RESUMED

They thought that we had just grazed it with a glancing blow, and had been to see if any damage had been done. **The game of cards was resumed, and without any thought of disaster I retired to my cabin to read until we started again. I never saw any of the players or the onlookers again.** A little later, hearing people going upstairs, I went out again, and found that everybody wanted to know why the engines had stopped. Going up on the deck again, I saw that there was an unmistakable list downwards from the stern to the

bows. Again I went down to my cabin where I put on some warmer clothing. As I dressed I heard the order shouted, "All the passengers on deck with lifebelts on."

We all walked up slowly with the lifebelts tied on over our clothing, but even then we presumed that this was merely a wise precaution the captain was taking. There was a total absence of any panic or expression of alarm. I suppose this must be accounted for by the exceeding calmness of the night and the absence of any signs of an accident. The ship was absolutely still, and except for the gentle, almost unnoticeable, tilt downwards, there were no visible signs of the approaching disaster. But, in a few moments, we saw the covers being lifted from the boats and the crews allotted to them standing by and uncoiling the ropes which were to lower them. We then began to realize that it was a more serious matter than we had at first supposed.

Presently we heard the order: "All men stand back away from the boats. All ladies retire to the next deck below," which was the smoking room or the "B" deck. The men all stood away and

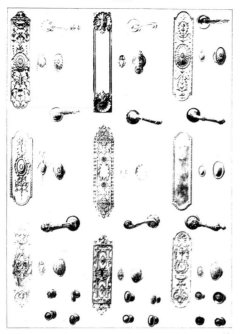

Door Furnishings of the "Olympic," "Titanic," "Mauretania," Lusitania," "Balmoral Castle," "Edinburgh Castle," Etc., Etc., Etc., supplied by

Ormoulu Electric Light Fittings of the "Olympic," "Titanic," "Mauretania," "Lusitania," "Balmoral Castle," "Edinburgh Castle," Etc., Etc., Etc., supplied by

waited in absolute silence, some leaning against the end railings of the deck, others pacing slowly up and down. The boats were then swung out and lowered from "A" deck. When they were level with "B" deck, where all the women were collected, the women got in quietly, with the exception of some, who refused to leave their husbands. **In some cases they were torn from their husbands and pushed into the boats, but in many instances they were allowed to remain, since there was no one to insist that they should go.**

Looking over the side one saw the boats from aft already in the water slipping quietly away into the darkness. Presently the boats near me were lowered with much creaking, as the new ropes slipped through the pulleys and blocks down the 90ft. which separated them from the water. An officer in uniform came up as one boat went down, and shouted out, "When you're afloat row round to the companion ladder and stand by with other boats for orders."

"Aye, aye, sir," came up the reply, but I don't think any boat was able to obey the order, for when they were afloat and had their oars at work the condition of the rapidly settling liner was much more apparent. All this time there was no trace of any disorder, no panic or rush to the boats, no scenes of women sobbing hysterically, such as one generally pictures happening at such times. Everyone seemed to realize so slowly that there was imminent danger that when realisation came it was extraordinary how calm everyone was, how completely self-controlled we were as the boats filled with women and children were lowered and rowed away into the night.

Presently word went round that men were to be put in boats on the starboard side. I was on the port side. Most of the men walked across the deck to see if this was true. I remained where I was, and shortly afterwards I heard the call, "Any more ladies?" Looking over the side of the ship, I saw boat No.13 swinging level with B deck, half-full of

women. Again the call was repeated, "Any more ladies?" I saw none coming.

Then one of the crew looked up and said, "Any ladies on your deck, sir?"

"No," I replied.

"Then you'd better jump," said he.

I dropped and fell into the bottom of the boat as they cried "Lower away!"

**BABY RESCUED JUST IN TIME.**

As the boat began to descend, two ladies were pushed hurriedly through the crowd on B deck, and a baby, ten months old, was passed down after them. Then down we went, the crew shouting out directions to those lowering us until we were some 10ft. from the water. Here occurred the only anxious moment we had during the whole of our experience from the time of our leaving the deck to our reaching the *Carpathia*. Immediately below our boat was the exhaust of the condensers, and a huge stream of water was pouring all the time from the ship's side just above the water line. It was plain that we ought to be smart away from it if we were to escape swamping when we touched the water. **We had no**

**officers on board, and no petty officers or member of the crew to take charge,** so one of the stokers shouted, "Someone find the pin which releases the boat from the ropes and pull it up!" We felt as well as we could on the floor and along the sides, but found nothing. It was difficult to move among so many people. We had sixty or seventy on board.

Down we went, and presently, what with the stream of water from the exhaust and the swell of the sea, we were carried directly under boat No.14, which had filled rapidly with men, and was coming down on us.

**ESCAPE BY SECONDS.**

"Stop lowering fourteen!" our crew shouted, and the crew of No.14, now only 20ft. above, cried out the same.

But those above could not have heard, for down she came — 15ft., 10ft., 5ft. and a stoker and I reached up and touched the bottom of the swinging boat above our heads. The next drop would have brought her on our heads, but just before she dropped another stoker sprang to the ropes with his knife open in his hand.

"One," I heard him say, and then "Two," as the knife cut through the pulley rope. The next moment the exhaust stream carried us clear, while boat No.14 dropped into the water. Our gunwales were almost touching.

Our crew seemed to me to be mostly cooks. They sat in their white jackets, two to an oar, with a stoker at the tiller. After some shouting and discussion, we elected as captain the stoker who was steering, and all agreed to obey his orders. He set to work at once to get into touch with the other boats. It was now one o'clock in the morning. The starlit night was beautiful, but, as there was no moon, it was not very light. The sea was as calm as a pond.

**LAST FLASH OF LINER'S LIGHTS.**

In the distance the *Titanic* looked enormous. Her length and her great bulk were outlined in black against the starry sky. Every porthole and saloon was blazing with light. It was impossible to think that anything could be wrong with such a leviathan were it not for that ominous tilt downward in the bows. At about 2 o'clock we observed her settling very rapidly, with the bows and the bridge completely under water.

**She slowly tilted straight on end, with the stern vertically upwards, and as she did so the lights in the cabins and saloons died out, flashed once more, and then went out altogether.**

At the same time, the machinery roared down through the vessel with a groaning rattle that could have been heard for miles. It was the weirdest sound surely that could have been heard in the middle of the ocean. It was not yet quite the end.

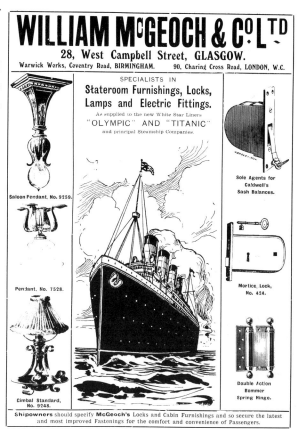
To our amazement, she remained in that upright position for a time which I estimate as five minutes.

It was certainly for some minutes that we watched at least 150ft. of the *Titanic* towering up above the level of the sea, looming black against the sky. Then with a quiet slanting dive she disappeared beneath the waters.

**Then there fell on our ears the most appalling noise that human being ever heard — the cries of hundreds of our fellow-beings struggling in the icy water, crying for help with a cry that we knew could not be answered.**

We longed to return to pick up some of those who were swimming, but this would have meant the swamping of our boat and the loss of all of us.

*(Mirror, 20 April 1912)*

# FATE OF MR. W.T. STEAD.

Of how William Thomas Stead, the great world-journalist and the greatest man on the *Titanic*, met his death there is no certain account.

It would seem that the last man now alive who spoke with him was Mr. A.H. Barkworth, of Tranby House, East Yorkshire. Mr. Barkworth himself escaped by jumping into the sea, being later picked up by one of the boats. He relates how after the collision he met Mr. Stead on deck.

The venerable journalist described to him what he had seen. He had seen the forecastle of the vessel full of powdered ice scraped off the berg.

That was a characteristic impression made upon the man with the seeing eye, one of those touches which vivified everything he wrote.

Of what happened afterwards to Mr. Stead there is no authentic account. Some of the survivors are reported as saying that he went back to bed.

*(Mirror, 20 April 1912)*

# COURAGE OF THE CREW.

The *Evening World* (says *Reuter*) publishes a story of the disaster from a staff correspondent who chanced to be on board the *Carpathia*. He speaks of the great courage of the *Titanic's* crew, which, however, could not exceed that of Mr. Astor, Mr. Harris, Mr. Futrelle, and other cabin passengers.

The crash against the iceberg, which was sighted only a quarter of a mile away, came almost simultaneously with the click of the levers operated from the bridge which stopped the engines and closed the bulkheads. Captain Smith was on the bridge at the moment. Later he summoned all on board to put on their life-preservers, and ordered the boats to be lowered. The first boat had more males, as they were the first to reach the deck, but when the rush of women and children began, the "women first" rule was strictly observed.

The officers drew revolvers, but in most cases were not called upon to use them. Many of those with life preservers on were seen to go down in spite of their preservers. The dead bodies floated to the surface. As the last boats moved away, the ship's band, which gathered in the saloon near the end, played "Nearer, my God, to Thee." Mrs. Straus refused to leave her husband's side, and both perished.

The *World's* account, which, the journal states, is testified to by several survivors, was written by Mr. Carlos F. Hurd, who places the number of lives lost at 1,700. It was the explosion of the boilers, according to Mr. Hurd, which finally finished the *Titanic's* career.

*(Mirror, 20 April 1912)*

## KISSED LOVED ONES' KNEES.

NEW YORK, April 19. – The scenes in dock as the survivors landed were full of suppressed excitement. Men were in hysterics, women fainting, children almost crushed in the arms of those welcoming them. Men fell down to kiss the knees of their beloved ones, women shrieked and wept and collapsed in the arms of their brothers and husbands.

The number of badly injured was not nearly so large as had been imagined. The cases requiring hospital attention were few, but the strain of the trial of their lives had left unmistakable signs in their faces of the arrivals. Some could barely talk, others could not refrain from shouting. What was a joyous occasion to some killed the last rays of hope in the breasts of others. Many were the affecting scenes both of joy and sorrow.

Among the most affecting scenes at the landing was the sight of the women steerage survivors as they came down from the deck, thinly clad and shivering, their eyes red with constant weeping. In their faces was the drawn, tense look of a desperate haunting fear. They were taken care of at once by members of the numerous charitable organisations who were at hand.

It was learned from the survivors that five – some said six – of the rescued died on board the *Carpathia* and were buried at sea. Three of these were sailors, the other two or three were passengers. – *Reuter*.

*(Mirror, 20 April 1912)*

## OFFICIAL FIGURES OF SAVED.

NEW YORK, April 19. — According to official figures which have been issued by the officers of the Cunard Line, 705 of the persons aboard the *Titanic* at the time of the collision were saved.

Of this number 202 were first class passengers
115 second class,
178 third.
The remaining 210 saved were members of the crew.

Many survivors were picked up from the water. In the statement the officials make no mention of the number missing. —*Exchange.*

*(Mirror, 20 April 1912)*

## SHOT WHILE TRYING TO RUSH A BOAT.

**Lady Duff Gordon's Grim Story of Her Own Escape.**

**FIFTH OFFICER'S COURAGE.**
The following stories were given by survivors, to *Reuter's* representatives at New York: —

NEW YORK, April 19. — Lady Duff Gordon, who left in one of the last boats, said that panic had begun to seize some of the remaining passengers by the time her boat was lowered.

Everyone seemed to be rushing for that boat. A few men who crowded in were turned back at the point of Captain Smith's revolver, and several of them were felled before order was restored.

"I recall being pushed towards one of the boats and being helped in," she said. "Just as we were about to clear the ship a man made a rush to get aboard our lifeboat. He was shot and apparently killed instantly. His body fell in the boat at our feet. No one made any effort to move him, and his body remained in the boat until we were picked up. I saw bodies in the water in all directions. The poor souls could not live long in the terribly cold water."

**FIFTH OFFICER'S COURAGE.**

A young Englishwoman, who requested that her name might be omitted, told a thrilling story of her experience in one of the collapsible boats, which was manned by eight of the crew and commanded by the fifth officer, Mr. Lowe, whose action she described as saving the lives of many.

Before the boat was launched he passed along the deck of the *Titanic* commanding the people not to jump into the boats, and otherwise restraining them from swamping the craft. When the collapsible boat was launched he succeeded in putting up a mast and sail. He collected other boats, and in some cases, where the boats were short of adequate crew, he did an exchange whereby each was properly manned.

Mr. Lowe threw lines to connect boats two by two, so that all moved together. Later he went back to the wreck. One boat succeeded in picking up some of those who had jumped overboard and were swimming about.

**BOAT ONE-THIRD FILLED.**

On his way back to the *Carpathia* he passed one of the collapsible boats which was on the point of sinking with thirty persons on board, most of them in scant night clothing. They were rescued in the nick of time. The relater of this account said that some of these people died on the way to the *Carpathia.*

One of the *Carpathia's* stewards gave an interesting account of how the first boatload of passengers was rescued. He said: —

"Just as it was about half-day we came upon a boat with eighteen men in it, but no women. It was not more than a third filled. All the men were able to climb up a Jacob's ladder which we threw over the port side. Every one of them was given a glass of brandy, or as much coffee as he wanted."

"Between 8.15 and 8.30," continued the steward, "we got the last two boats, crowded to the gunwale, almost all the occupants of which were women. After we had got the last load on board the *Californian* came alongside. The captains arranged that we should make straight for New York, while the *Californian* looked around for more boats. We circled round and round and saw all kinds of wreckage."

**"THEN BEDLAM CAME."**

"While we were pulling in the boatloads the women were quiet

# The Daily Mirror

### THE MORNING JOURNAL WITH THE SECOND LARGEST NET SALE.

No. 2,649.  Registered at the G.P.O. as a Newspaper.  SATURDAY, APRIL 20, 1912  One Halfpenny.

## ONE OF THE THOUSANDS OF TRAGEDIES WHICH MADE THE TITANIC WRECK THE MOST HORRIBLE IN THE WORLD'S HISTORY.

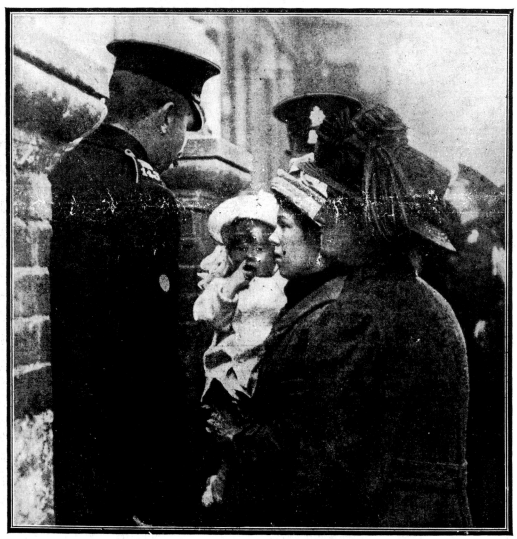

Of the 903 members of the crew of the Titanic, only 210 have been saved. This means tragedy upon tragedy for Southampton, where the majority of the men lived, for by this appalling disaster mothers have been robbed of sons, wives of husbands and young girls of sweethearts. Yesterday was a terrible day in the history of the town, though it put an end to all suspense. A list of the saved was posted outside the White Star offices, and mothers and wives who had been hoping against hope eagerly read the names, only to find that their worst fears were realised. For some, of course, the list contained glorious news, but they hushed their joy in the presence of the terrible grief of their friends and neighbours. The photograph illustrates one of the many tragedies, and shows two women anxiously awaiting the posting of the list, and what happened in Southampton yesterday has been happening in New York and London for five days.—*Daily Mirror* photograph.

98

## CAPTAIN SMITH DIES LIKE A BRITISH SAILOR.

### THE SHIP'S MASTER.

#### MYSTERY OF CAPTAIN E. J. SMITH'S DEATH.

How did Captain Smith die? Did he die by his own hand at the moment when the Titanic prepared for her last plunge below the waves or did he remain on the bridge, silent, immovable, until the ocean that had known him all his life drew him to her breast? The cables as yet do not say.

So contradictory are the stories bearing on the point that it would be as well for the public to reserve judgment and wait for a definite pronouncement. The story of the disaster published by the " Evening World " and quoted by Reuter seems to be the most plausible :—

Revolver shots were heard just before the Titanic went down. Many rumours were in circulation in consequence, one being to the effect that Captain Smith had shot himself and another that the first officer, Mr. Murdoch, had ended his life, but members of the crew discredited these reports.

Captain Smith was last seen on the bridge just before the ship sank, leaping into the sea only after the decks were awash.

Captain E. J. Smith, R.N.R., the veteran commander of the Titanic, who, it was at first reported, shot himself on the bridge. It now appears that he met his death like a true British sailor. In the words of a survivor, he " stuck to the bridge and behaved like a hero . . . He continued directing his men right up to the moment when the bridge was level with the water."—(*Daily Mirror* photograph.)

# MRS. ELEANOR SMITH, WIFE OF THE TITANIC'S COMMANDER, WHOSE HUSBAN WENT DOWN WITH HIS VESSEL SHOUTING "BE BRITISH."

" To My Poor Fellow Sufferers.
    " My heart overflows with grief for you all, and is laden with sorrow that you are weighed down with this terrible bur-
den that has been thrust upon us.
    " May God be with us and comfort us all.
" April 18, 1912."

    "Yours in deep sympathy,
        (Signed)        " ELEANOR SMITH."

The sympathy of the whole world goes out to Mrs. Smith, the widow of Captain E. J. Smith, the heroic commander of the Titanic. Though no woman could have lost her husband in more tragic circumstances, she has borne her overwhelming grief with a bravery which compels admiration. In the midst of her distress her thoughts have been as much for others as for herself. This is proved by the heartbroken message which she sent to her fellow-sufferers. The message which is reproduced above, was posted outside the White Star offices in Southampton. The above photograph is said to be the only one in existence of Mrs. Smith It was taken ten years ago, and shows her with her daughter Melville, now four teen years of age.

enough, but when it seemed sure that we should not find any more persons alive, then bedlam came. I hope never to go through it again. The way those women took on for the folk they had lost was awful. We could not do anything to quiet them until they cried themselves out."

Major Arthur Peuchen, of Toronto, an experienced yachtsman, after assisting members of the crew to fill the first five boats, was assigned by the second mate to take charge of boat 6. Just as he entered the boat Mr. Hays, president of the Grand Trunk Railway, who went down with the ship, came to wish him God-speed. None of the passengers thought the ship would sink so soon. Mr. Hays predicted that she would keep afloat for at least eight hours, during which time help was sure to arrive, according to Major Peuchen.

**REFUSED TO ENTER A LIFEBOAT.**

Mr. Jacques Futrelle, the novelist, says a *Reuter's* special message, was one of those who parted from his wife and steadfastly refused to accept a chance to enter a lifeboat when he knew that the *Titanic* was sinking under

him. How he went to his death is told by Mrs. Futrelle, who said: —

"Jacques is dead, but he died like a hero, that I know. Three or four times after the crash I rushed up to him and clasped him in my arms, begging him to get into one of the lifeboats. "For God's sake, go!" he fairly screamed, and tried to push me towards the lifeboat. I could see how he suffered. "It's your last chance; go," he pleaded. "Then one of the ship's officers forced me into a lifeboat, and I gave up all hope that he could be saved."

*(Mirror, 20 April 1912)*

# HOW THE HEROES OF THE TITANIC DIED ON BOARD THE DOOMED LINER.

**MAN WHO WENT DOWN WITH 'TITANIC.**

**Terrible Experience of Colonel Gracie, the Last Saved.**

**NIGHT ON A RAFT.**

Of all the recitals of personal adventure in the *Titanic* disaster, that of Colonel Gracie, of the United States Army, who jumped from the top-most deck of the *Titanic* when she sank, and was sucked down with her, is (says *Reuter*) the most extraordinary. Colonel Gracie, on reaching the surface again swam until he found a cork raft, and then helped to rescue others. He gives the exact time of the sinking of the *Titanic* as 2.22 a.m., which was the hour at which his watch was stopped by his leap into the sea.

"After sinking with the ship," he said, "it appeared to me as if I was propelled by some great force through the water. This might have been occasioned by explosions under the water, and I remembered fearful stories of people being boiled to death. The second officer has told me that he has had a similar experience. Innumerable thoughts of a personal nature having relation to mental telepathy flashed through my brain. I thought of those at home as if my spirit might go to them to say 'Goodbye' for ever. Again and again I prayed for deliverance, although I felt sure that the end had come. I had the greatest difficulty in holding my breath until I came to the surface. I knew that once I inhaled, the water would suffocate me. When I got under water I struck out with all my strength for the surface. I got

to air again after a time, which seemed to me to be unending."

"There was nothing in sight save the ocean, dotted with ice and strewn with large masses of wreckage. Dying men and women all about me were groaning and crying piteously. Colonel Gracie relates how, by moving from one piece of wreckage to another, he at last reached a cork raft."

"Soon," he continued "the raft became so full that it seemed as if she would sink if more came on board her. The crew for self-preservation had therefore to refuse to permit any others to climb on board."

**"GOOD LUCK-GOD BLESS YOU!"**

"This was the most pathetic and horrible scene of all. The piteous cries of those around us still ring in my ears, and I will remember them to my dying day. 'Hold on to what you have, old boy!' we shouted to each man who tried to get on board. 'One more of you would sink us all!' Many of those whom we refused answered as they went to their death: "Good luck-God bless you!"

"So we passed the night, with the waves washing over and burying the raft deep in water. We prayed through all the weary night, and there never was a moment when our prayers did not rise above the waves. Men who seemed long ago to have forgotten how to address their Creator recalled the prayers of their childhood and murmured them over and over again. Together we said the Lord's Prayer again and again."

*(Mirror, 20 April 1912)*

## EXHAUSTED WIRELESS OPERATORS.

NEW YORK, April 19. — The refusal of the operators on board the *Carpathia* to answer questions concerning the disaster is now explained. It was due to the physical exhaustion of both the men. They sent a large number of personal messages from survivors to friends ashore, and received replies from the latter. — *Reuter.*

Mr. Harold Cotton, the Marconi operator on the *Carpathia*, did not go to bed at his usual time on Sunday night, and as a result he caught the first message of the *Titanic*. This was responsible for saving hundreds of lives.

*(Mirror, 20 April 1912)*

## FATHER'S PRIDE IN HIS SON.

The proudest father in London sat in a City office yesterday afternoon. He was Mr. J.A. Bride, the father of Mr. Harold Bride, the junior Marconi operator of the *Titanic*, who after a thrilling rescue and with injured feet, calmly took over the Marconi operator's work on the *Carpathia*.

"Am I proud?" said Mr. Bride to *The Daily Mirror*. "I cannot express how glad I am — not so much at my son being safe and sound as the fact that he seems to have done the right thing. He acted, I believe, as an Englishman should. I know my boy — he takes things pretty quietly and never makes a fuss about anything."

*(Mirror, 20 April 1912)*

## "YOU GO. I WILL STAY."

**Heartbreaking Partings Between Husbands and Wives — Two of the Heroes.**

NEW YORK, April 19. — On landing from the *Carpathia*, Mrs. J.J. Astor told the members of her family what she could recall of the disaster. She had no very definite idea as to how her husband, Colonel Astor, met his death. She recalled that in the confusion, as she was about to be put into one of the boats Colonel Astor was standing at her side. From other narratives it appears that the conduct of Colonel Astor was deserving of the highest praise. He devoted all his energies to saving his young bride, who was in delicate health. He helped to get her into the boat and as she took her place he requested the permission of the second officer to go with her for her own protection. "No, sir," replied the officer, "no men shall go in the boat until the women are all off." Colonel Astor then inquired the number of the boat and turned to work clearing the other boats and reassuring frightened and nervous women.

Mrs. Churchill Candee, of Washington, was taken from the *Carpathia* with both her legs broken. She received her injuries while getting into the lifeboat. "Major Archibald Butt and Colo-

nel Astor died like heroes," she said.

*(Mirror, 20 April 1912)*

## WOMEN AT THE OARS.

Mrs. Edgar J. Meyer, of New York, said that after the first shock she and Mr. Meyer ran to the lifeboats. She pleaded with her husband to be allowed to remain with him. He finally threw her into the lifeboat, reminding her of their nine year-old child at home. Mrs. Meyer, with an English girl, rowed in her boat for four and a half hours. "We were well away from the steamer when it sank," she said. "There were about seventy of us widows on board the *Carpathia*."

Mrs. W.D. Marvin, of New York, who was on her honeymoon trip, was almost prostrated when she learned on reaching the dock that her husband had not been picked up. "As I was put into the boat he cried to me," she said, "It's all right, little girl. You go. I will stay.' As our boat shoved off he threw me a kiss, and that was the last I saw of him."

George Rheims, of New York, who was on the *Titanic* with his brother-in-law, Mr. Joseph Hol-

# DISASTER TO TITANIC

## Giant Iceberg

ONE OF THE PERILS OF THE NORTH ATLANTIC:

A HUGE ICEBERG, THREE HUNDRED FEET HIGH ABOVE THE WATER LINE AND TWO THOUSAND FEET HIGH OVER ALL.

### THE TITANIC

THE HUGE GANTRIES UNDER WHICH THE "OLYMPIC" AND "TITANIC" WERE BUILT

# 1,635 LIVES LOST.

### The Ship that Never Came Home.

They listened to wondrous music, in
  rooms that were planned for kings ;
Beautiful notes from beautiful throats,
  sung as a songbird sings :
They revelled in baths of marble, like the
  baths of ancient Rome,
'Twas a wondrous trip on a wondrous
  ship,
    The ship that never came home.

Music and baths and splendour, but
  where are the noble men,
Saying good-byes with glistening eyes—
  that never shall glisten again?
They called it a floating palace, and they
  found it a funeral urn ;
Crowded by fate with a hero freight,
    The ship that can never return.

**W. F. Kirk, in the New York 'Evening
Journal.'**

HER FIANCE SAVED.

Miss Mabel Ludlow, a nurse, who is one of the happiest
girls in England to-day. She is engaged to be married
to Mr. Harold Bride, the junior wireless operator on
board the Titanic, who is among the rescued.

land, a London resident, said that many of the passengers stood round for hours with their lifebelts on. When all the boats had gone he shook hands with his brother-in-law, who would not jump, and leaped over the side of the boat. He swam for a quarter of an hour, and reached a lifeboat. It had eighteen occupants, and was half under water. The people were in the water up to their knees. Seven of them died during the night. Only those who stood all the time remained alive. — *Reuter's Special Service.*

*(Mirror, 20 April 1912)*

## OUT TO SMASH RECORD?

NEW YORK, April 19. — Mr. Hugh Woolner, of London, the son of the late Mr. Thomas Woolner, the sculptor, said that after the collision he saw what seemed to be a continent of ice.

"It was not thought at first," he said, "that the liner had been dealt a dangerous blow. Some of the men were in the gymnasium taking exercise, and for some minutes they remained there, not knowing what was going on above their heads. After a while there was an explosion, then a moment later a second explo-

sion. It was the second which did most damage. It blew away the funnels, and tore a big hole in the steamer's side. The ship rocked like a rowing boat, and then careened over on one side to such an extent that the passengers making for the boats slid into the water. The ship filled rapidly, There is abundance of evidence that the shock of the collision with the iceberg was scarcely noticeable. Many people seem to have slept through it." — *Reuter.*

*(Mirror, 20 April 1912)*

## SLOWLY KILLED HOPES.

**Man Faints and Women Break Down After Waiting in Vain for Names.**

Once again, for the fifth dreadful day, the London offices of the White Star Line were thronged yesterday with hundreds of sad-faced, silent men and women, waiting and watching for the name, the word or two, which meant the difference between life and death.

It was perhaps the most dreadful day of all. Previously there had been the chance — a slender chance, it is true, of some wonderful unexpected news being flashed across the wires. There had been just the hope that other ships than the *Carpathia* might have picked up survivors from the *Titanic.* But yesterday that hope was dead. It was known that only comparatively few fresh names of saved ones could be expected. Every hour that passed uneventfully hammered its growing message of despair firmer and firmer into many already torn, aching hearts.

One man, probably a father or a brother, was so affected by the fact that the name he sought never came that he at last lost control of himself, and, staggering from the office, fell insensible on the steps. A policeman rendered first aid, and succeeded in restoring the poor fellow to consciousness. And then the awful, gaunt-eyed tragedy of it all would be thrown out into relief by the one thrice fortunate watcher who found that eagerly-sought name.

The clerks knew her well. They had seen her come each day, garbed in mourning clothes, to sit there, weary and listless, ever since that awful morning—how many ages ago!—when the news came through. They posted a list again yesterday, and

there was a flutter of hopeless hope in the hearts of those who waited. The lady in black reached the list and scanned the names, and suddenly:—"Saved, my God, saved!" she cried, half-hysterically, and ran towards the door.

A poor woman, a relative of one of the crew from her appearance, completely broke down in the early afternoon. Sitting alone, hope ebbing from her soul as the cruel, silent minutes sped on, her tears suddenly began to fall fast. With a great effort she managed to control her emotion for a moment and, rising, passed swiftly from the building out into the sun-flooded streets—anywhere.

*(Mirror, 20 April 1912)*

## GIRL'S JOY AT LOVER'S RESCUE.

*(From Our Special Correspondent).*
SOUTHAMPTON, April 19.— Hundreds of people were this afternoon wearing mourning for those for whom all hope has been abandoned. I have visited several homes which are plunged in the deepest grief. One poor woman lost her first husband in the wreck of the *Stella,*

and now her second in the *Titanic.*

Three young girls, who reluctantly left the White Star office at 2 a.m., when it was announced that no further names could be received till 6 a.m., returned at 2.30 a.m., and stood shivering in the street till, for sheer pity, they were asked to come inside and sit by the manager's office fire. One of them was in a hysterical state of fear for the life of her sweetheart, a young fellow named Johnstone, and the other two girls were faithful friends who would not leave her. Her sobs were heart-rending till her lover's name appeared in the list of survivors, and then she swooned with joy.

A White Star official informed me that he thinks they can identify from the passenger and crew lists in the office all except about fifty of the 728 names received. The approximate figures and the analysis so far as it goes shows roughly 350 men and 378 women and children saved. These figures include 190 men of the crew and fifteen women employed as stewardesses or in the ship's laundry.

"I cannot understand that awful wicked lie from America about Captain Smith shooting himself," he said afterwards. "Nobody who knew him as I did could possibly believe he would do such a thing. He was one of the best men God ever made, and one of the bravest and truest."

It has been heartbreaking to witness the agony of the women at the White Star office since 7.15 this morning, when the first list of the crew survivors was put up. They stuffed handkerchiefs and gloves in their mouths to deaden the sound of the sobs they could not withhold. A little invalid girl in a perambulator hugged her mother's arm as the poor woman bent over her, wailing amid her sobs. She stretched up her face to kiss, with the words in a baby lisp: "Let me love you, mama. Daddy will come back soon." The mother could not speak.

*(Mirror, 20 April 1912)*

## FACED DEATH ALONE.

**Captain Smith's Fate on the Deck of His Ship.**

**BANDSMEN'S LAST HYMN.**

Sublime in its supreme unselfishness, the death of Captain

E.J. Smith was the death of an English captain — he perished with his ship.

Face to face with certain disaster, he was calm and self-possessed, thinking only of the lives of those in his charge. He ignored his own peril.

And then, when all that human foresight could do and had been done unavailingly to save the *Titanic*, he still remembered his quiet little band of hard-working officers, and released them from duty. "It's every man for himself at such a time as this," he said. "I release you. Look out for yourselves."

But for Captain Smith there was no one to give the word of release. His place was with his riven vessel to the end. Standing on the deck of his ship, alone, a solitary and heroic figure, Captain Smith faced death in the swirling, ice-cold sea with all the calm, death-defying heroism that is the tradition of the men of the British Navy.

**FACED DEATH ALONE.**

Poignantly sad in its realism is the word picture of the passing of the *Titanic's* captain given by Mr. George A. Braden, of California.

He states: —

"I saw Captain Smith while I was in the water. He was standing on the deck all alone. Once he was swept down by a wave, but managed to get to his feet again. Then, as the boat sank, he was again knocked down by a wave and then disappeared from view."

Extraordinary rumours cabled from America were to the effect that Captain Smith shot himself as the *Titanic* was sinking, but this picturesque version was generally discredited yesterday. Captain E.J. Smith, R.N.R., of the *Titanic*, had been in the service of the White Star Company for thirty-eight years, and was sixty years of age. Until last year, at the time of the *Olympic* collision, when he was in command of the liner, he had met with no serious accident.

He was a native of Staffordshire, and served his apprenticeship to the sea with Gibson and Co., of Liverpool. During the South African war he twice carried troops to the Cape in the *Majestic*, and was decorated by the Government for his work as a transport officer. He held an extra master's certificate, and was honorary commander of the R.N.R. He leaves a wife and a thirteen year-old daughter.

Not the least of the heroes of the catastrophe were the *Titanic's* bandsmen. In the whole history of the sea there is little equal to the wonderful behaviour of these humble players. In the last moments of the great ship's doom, when all was plainly lost, when presumably braver and hardier men might almost have been excused for doing practically anything to save themselves, they stood responsive to their conductor's baton and played a hymn, "Nearer, My God, to Thee."

There were two bands on board the *Titanic,* one, a saloon orchestra, comprising five men, the other, a deck band, numbering three, so Mr. Black, of the Liverpool firm which controlled the band, yesterday told *The Daily Mirror.*

"Probably," he said, "they all massed together under their leader, Mr. Wallace Hartley, as the ship sank. Five of the eight, Mr. Hartley, P.C. Taylor, J.W. Woodward, F. Clark and W.T. Brailey, were Englishmen; one, J.

Hume, was a Scotsman, and the remaining two, Bricoux and Krins, were French and German respectively."

Mr. Wallace Hartley, the man who got his men together and played the tune which must have given blessed consolation to hundreds in their last moments of life, was a young Yorkshireman. Only thirty-four, he was well known and popular in Bridlington, Harrogate and Leeds musical circles. He was to have been married shortly, his fiance being a Boston girl, whose bereavement is double, for she only lost her father a few weeks ago.

It is a coincidence revealed yesterday that Mr. W.T. Stead, when issuing a special book of hymns, was the first to reveal the fact that "Nearer, My God, to Thee" was a favourite hymn with King Edward. The author of the hymn was Mrs. Sarah Flower Adams, of Great Harlow, Essex, who died in 1848.

*(Daily Graphic, 20 April 1912)*

# THE OCEAN GRAVE OF THE TITANIC.

**THE NOBLE ELEMENT IN THE OCEAN TRAGEDY.**

No element of tragedy seems to have failed to contribute its share to the overwhelming catastrophe of the *Titanic*. The forces of nature shook themselves free from the chains with which Man would bind them, burst in all their power from the limits in which he has sought to confine them, and dealt him a blow that has sent mourning through two nations. His last word in ship construction, equipped with every last device making for safety, or for aid in case of need, met at her maiden issue with the sea a challenge that broke her utterly and took her in toll with over twelve hundred of the lives she carried.

The magnitude of such a disaster leaves the mind as incapable of expressing the emotions aroused in it as its agencies were powerless to avert the catastrophe. For years we take our eager, heedless way, demanding more and more of life, increasingly impatient of its hindrances to our pleasure and our business, increasingly bold and cunning in

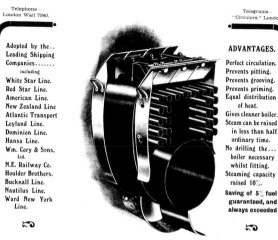
overcoming them, and never pausing but to congratulate ourselves upon our triumphs. Every now and then comes some cataclysmic reminder that, if it is not possible to go too far and too fast, it is very possible to congratulate ourselves too well. For a brief moment we are brought to a full stop.

We trust the relatives of those who have perished may find some solace in the thought that though they have been called upon to suffer a grief almost

the saved, that in this dire emergency the imperilled rose to supreme heights of courage and devotion. Millionaire and steerage emigrant alike were called upon: alike they have presented us with that most inspiring of all spectacles — the inherent nobility of mankind.

*(Daily Graphic, 20 April 1912)*

# LOST LINER'S TRAGEDY.

### THE SAILING AND — THE END.

The largest ship in the world went to sea from Southampton harbour on the tenth of April, 1912. People spoke of the tenth of April as a great day in the history of Southampton, for many fathers of families had found employment on the *Titanic*, many women's faces were lightened because the shadow of need and poverty had been banished from their homes.

It was a day that no one who stood upon the quayside will ever forget. We who saw it saw a sight that will be unforgettable until our eyes are turned to dust. We saw the start of the mightiest vessel in the world upon her solitary and uncompleted voyage. She was

unendurable to bear, they suffer it amidst that deepest sympathy which only when we are brought to face the realities of life can be aroused. For us, as for them, moreover, there is heartening thought in one thing that can be read into the disaster from the facts that have come to light. It is terribly clear that scenes of most dreadful horror must have taken place in the few hours between the *Titanic's* striking and her disappearance. And it is clear, from the fact that women and children form by far the greater majority of

named *Titanic* and she has been *Titanic* in her sorrow. We saw her, the mightiest, finest product of human brains in the matter of ships to sail the sea, a gigantic vessel that realized in her being a floating city of treasured glories, riches, and luxury, as she first ploughed the grey fields of the ocean.

And her displacement of water, the foam, and the rush of her passage, was so tremendous that the stern ropes of another mighty liner parted and the *New York*, but for the ready aid of holding tugs, would have swung out aimlessly into the fairway.

**THE HAPPY START.**

We paused in our cheering then, chilled to a sudden silence at this first evidence of the great ship's untested powers for evil as for good. And our cheering now is hushed into sobbing, for within a week of her majestic passage from Southampton Harbour, the displacement of the *Titanic* has been so tremendous that she has drenched the bosom of the world in an ocean of tears.

Those of us who had come to wish the vessel "Good speed" —

in the dark wisdom of Providence to wish "Good speed" and "a fair journey" to those loved ones who were going out upon the longest and loneliest voyage in Eternity — were up "by times" on that pleasant Wednesday morning, long before the stroke of noon when we knew Captain Smith would climb into his lofty perch on the navigating bridge and give the order to "let go" from the Trafalgar landing stage.

The air was busy with chatter, with "good bye for the present" and good wishes. We lived that morning in an atmosphere of pride. All these happy-faced Southampton women were proud that their men had entered into service on the greatest vessel ever built by man. They prattled of the *Titanic* with a sort of suggestion of proprietorship.

Rumours and legends and tales of her glories and luxuries and powers were bandied about in every street in Southampton. She was a caravanserai of marvels; a mighty treasure house of beauty and luxurious ease. In the phrase of the people, she was "the last word." The phrases of the people are often true, because they are double edged.

## "FAITHFUL UNTO DEATH": "NO MAN JOSTLED A WOMAN (

Mr. John Harper, pastor of the Walworth-road Baptist Chapel, who was drowned. He is seen with Miss Leitch, his niece, and his daughter Nana, who were both rescued by the Carpathia.

Mr. H. J. Pitman, third officer on the Titanic, who was one of the four officers saved from the wreck. Mr. Pitman, who is thirty-four years of age, is a native of Castle Cary, Somersetshire.

Mr. H. F. Lowe, the fifth officer, who is among the rescued. Mr. Lowe, who is twenty-nine years old, comes from Llandudno.

Dr. J. Edward Simpson, assistant ship's surgeon, who went down with Dr. W. F. N. O'Loughlin, the senior surgeon.

Mr Burke, one of the crew. A steward of that name appears on the list of those who have been rescued.

Sailors from the ships in port arriving for the Southampton memorial service.

Mrs. Hurst, of 15, Chapel-road, Southam that both her husband and father were lo surprise she received a telegram from Mrs. Hurst, who is seen with a baby i door. The portrait

POST OF

Mrs. Hurst's telegram. Scores of

"No American man jostled a woman or child as the weaker ones were hurried to the boats." This was the proud boast of Senator Smith, who is conducting the T

# ILD AS THE WEAKER ONES WERE HURRIED TO THE BOATS"

Saturday was bowed down with grief, believing
nto mourning for them. To her great joy and
rday saying "Walt safe, father gone." Above,
wn reading the telegram to her aunt at her front
—(*Daily Mirror* photograph.)

Mr. Dyer, one of the engineers on board the
Titanic, who perished in the disaster to the
giant liner. In the event of a ship going
down the engineers have a very poor chance
of being rescued.

Mr. H. F. Wilde, the chief mate on board
the Titanic, who went down with his captain. Mr. Wilde, who was thirty-eight years
of age, belonged to Walton, Liverpool.

Mr. J. Wesley Woodward, 'cellist, and Mr. F. Clarke (double bass), who is seen
in the circle. Their heroism in playing as the ship went to her doom is an incident which will live in history. Both belonged to Liverpool.

Salvation Army band playing a hymn outside the White Star's London offices yesterday

Senator William Alden Smith,
the chairman of the committee
which is investigating the disaster
in New York.

Mr. Frank Carlson, who was
drowned. Formerly a ship's
officer, he was returning to the
States to settle

the headline above we purposely omit the word "American" because it is equally true of the Britishers aboard. The Anglo-Saxon race was triumphantly heroic to the last.

Another phrase sticks now in the puzzle of a darkening mind: "They're breaking all records this time." And so they were. It had been determined that the *Titanic* should excel in luxury and equipment her sister vessel, the *Olympic*, which had sailed for New York a week before.

And in a sort of desperate endeavour to achieve this we who had come to take temporary parting from dear ones and friends were shown a new and latest marvel on the promenade deck of the *Titanic*. It was called the Cafe Parisienne. Its walls were covered with a delicate trellis work around which trailed cool foliage. We looked at the soft-cushioned chairs, we regarded the comfort of the whole scene, and, feeling the suggestive atmosphere of the place, thought of those who would be taking coffee there after dinner with music lulling every sense, melting into the gentle roll and rhythm of the open sea.What a place in which to dream! — perhaps if one were young to hold a little romantic dalliance — what a place in which to forget the trials and harass of the world! What a place in which to sleep!

Some of us looked into the private suites that were to cost a mere trifle of £870 a voyage, and here we found snug dining-rooms, bedrooms that looked in themselves like little enchanted palaces of slumberous rest, and private promenade decks.

Let us note that everyone spoke of "dining rooms" and "bedrooms." The word "cabin" would have been an anachronism in this floating citadel of luxurious beauty. We examined the delicate glass and napery, the flowers and the fruit, the baths and the playing-courts, and the innumerable mechanical appliances that seemed to make personal effort or discomfort the only human impossibility on board.

There was one thing that no one looking even for a brief half-hour on this cushioned lap of luxury ever thought of giving a cursory glance or a thought. No one looked at the boats.

Punctually at noon Captain E.J. Smith, a typical figure of an English sailor as we knew him and imagined him in tougher, pre-*Titanic* days, took up his post of captainship on the navigating

# CHILD'S SACRIFICE FOR TITANIC SURVIVORS.

These photographs were taken on board the Carpathia, the liner which rescued the Titanic survivors, while she was travelling between Gibraltar and Naples (1) The Rev. Roger Anderson, an American, who conducted the burial service for those who were buried at sea. (2) Captain Rostron, with Marjory Sweetheart, who gave all her spare clothes to the little survivors.—(*Daily Mirror* photographs.)

# THE TITANIC

THE TITANIC'S PASSENGERS TAKING THEIR LAST LOOK AT HOME.

A photograph taken as the boat was leaving Southampton on April 10th, showing, on the deck, some of the passengers who are probably among the missing.

# The Daily Mirror

### THE MORNING JOURNAL WITH THE SECOND LARGEST NET SALE.

No. 2,649.    Registered at the G.P.O. as a Newspaper.    SATURDAY, APRIL 20, 1912    One Halfpenny.

## BANDSMEN HEROES ON THE SINKING TITANIC PLAY "NEARER, MY GOD, TO THEE!" AS THE LINER GOES DOWN TO HER DOOM.

N EARER, my GOD, to Thee,
    Nearer to Thee ;
E'en though it be a cross
    That raiseth me ;
Still all my song shall be,
Nearer, my GOD, to Thee,
    Nearer to Thee.

Though, like the wanderer,
    The sun gone down,
Darkness comes over me,
    My rest a stone ;
Yet in my dreams I'd be
Nearer, my GOD, to Thee,
    Nearer to Thee.

There let my way appear
    Steps unto Heav'n,
All that Thou sendest me
    In mercy given,
Angels to beckon me
Nearer, my GOD, to Thee,
    Nearer to Thee.

Then, with my waking thoughts
    Bright with Thy praise,
Out of my stony griefs
    Beth-el I'll raise ;
So by my woes to be
Nearer, my GOD, to Thee,
    Nearer to Thee.

When the historians chronicle the terrible disaster to the Titanic for the generations that have yet to be born, they will of a surety give the members of the orchestra a prominent place in the list of heroes. Though they knew that their minutes on earth were numbered, these brave men assembled on deck as the liner was going down and played "Nearer, My God, to Thee!" and it is easy to imagine the comfort that the music of this beautiful hymn must have brought to the unfortunate people who had to remain on the vessel. Miss Bonnell, an American survivor, relates this touching incident, and says that "by that time most of the lifeboats were some distance away, and only a faint sound of the strains of the hymn could be heard." Above are the words and music.

bridge. And as the bells sounded, the cheers of the multitudes went upward and hands and handkerchiefs were waved from quay and ship's side, and kisses were blown across and last familiar greetings exchanged.

So she went away with her human freight of two thousand two hundred and eight souls. We cheered to the last and waved our salutations, and that night I think there was not an unhappy woman in all Southampton. And tonight — who is to count the tear-stained faces or to cast a reckoning over the travail of these broken hearts, some here, some two thousand miles away, but all united beyond the cleavage of the pitiless seas, by the sacred companionship of sorrow!

**WHAT WE THOUGHT —**

So the *Titanic* went her way, and we went ours, and thought perhaps little about her, save thoughts of remembered joy in her strength and beauty, until on Tuesday morning came the news that smote upon our hearts with the thunder of doom. These were, of course, the first indefinite rumblings that woke fear in every human breast.

She had struck an iceberg; she had been rent; but she was unsinkable. She was heading slowly for shore, a great giant wounded thing in the wake of the *Virginian.* How our hopes died down until it seemed that the heart was burnt into a heap of dead cold ashes, only to rise, Phoenix-like, in jubilant and hopeful expectancy. Human lips have sobbed out strange prayers before today, but what volume of prayer went up to heaven in thankfulness to the Lord of Hosts who had brought the new wonder of wireless telegraphy out of the slow womb of time.

We thought of that unforgettable message speeding through the viewless air that is marked upon the chart sheets SOS We picked up the common phrase of the operator and repeated to ourselves: "Save Our Souls," and thanked Providence for their salvation.

We pictured the scene. The lonely operator, composed with that old English valiance that has turned the blood of history into wine, calmly tapping out the cry of help. We saw the realisation of that message in the operator's cabin on other vessels. We saw

# Titanic Survivors Rescued by the Carpathia.

Titanic lifeboats on board the Carpathia and some of the survivors from the wreck.

Lowering the Titanic's lifeboats from the Carpathia after she docked at New York.

## TWO GREATEST LINERS' PERIL.

Twice within eight months the two most colossal vessels that the world has ever seen have met with disaster. It is as though Nature grudged man his triumph over the nation-sundering ocean and revenged herself upon his puny presumption.

Last year it was the Olympic whose mass of 45,000 tons collided with a warship that tore a hole in her side.

Yesterday it was the Titanic, mightier still in weight, yet for all her mammoth proportions a mere tub in the face of the overwhelming ice-mountain of the Atlantic.

So disaster crashed upon her, threatening 3,000 lives and the destruction in one blow of a floating township valued in gold at over 2¼ millions.

But the inventions of man proved mightier than the brute force of the inanimate elements. The unsinkable ship builded by all the resources of centuries of science withstood the shock, messages carried by the harnessed waves of the air brought speedy help, and every life, it seems, was saved, and the ship herself proceeded unaided to port.

## *"Rest Eternal Grant to Them, O Lord"*

## THE PLIGHT OF THE SHIPWRECKED WOMEN.

The Titanic survivors huddled together on the deck of the Carpathia as the latter turned back with them to New York. They had to borrow clothes, and were helped by the other passengers.

the wonderful chain composed of those three words, stronger than wind or sea, suddenly dragging all the vessels within the sphere of hearing away from their allotted course, and sending them on the great adventure of succour and mercy. We pictured them racing along the railless roads of the open sea, rushing with insensate speed towards the spot of the catastrophe. We had leisure to imagine the scene, because we were told there had been a great deliverance; because we felt that man had fought his battle with the ocean and had won.

Then we knew that we had lost.

— AND WHAT WE LEARNT.

All the world knows how slowly those confessions of defeat came in upon us, how slowly the last flicker of an expiring hope was beaten down within our breasts, with what dilatory hands the veils were drawn from the implacable face of doom. Gradually the hush laid hold upon us, gradually a realisation of what had happened sank into our souls.

We knew that nothing but a miserable residue of the great human freightage had been saved to us. We knew that the enchanted floating palace, conceived by the brain of man and wrought by his hands, with all its mighty scheme of luxurious ease, health, and comfort, lay somewhere tangled in an old sea forest, two miles beneath the quiet surface of the sea. Little more do we know as I write. We can only hear the sobbing of the women at the street corners of Southampton, and find in them an eternal echo of the cheers with which we sent the *Titanic* out on her first, her last, her only voyage.

*(Daily Graphic, 20 April 1912)*

# THE OCEAN GRAVE OF THE 'TITANIC'

**THE LINER DE LUXE.**

**SPLENDOUR THAT NOW LIES IN THE DEPTHS.**

**A MILLION AND A HALF.**

**RESTAURANT, RACQUET COURT AND PARISIENNE CAFE.**

Sister to the *Olympic*, the *Titanic* was the last word in ocean liners and the largest ship in the world. Her fittings were the most luxurious of any vessel afloat, in-

"Oh, hear us, when we cry to Thee
For those in peril on the sea."

The above photograph (No. 2) shows the crowd assembling at St. Paul's Cathedral for the "Titanic" memorial service.

The White Star flag at half-mast. The above photograph (No. 1), shows one of the many marks of mourning at the London office of the owners of the "Titanic."

❦   ❦   ❦

Photograph No. 2 shows children dropping their coppers into the collecting box outside the Mansion House, London, towards the Lord Mayor's Fund for the relief of "Titanic" sufferers.

❦   ❦   ❦

The bottom photograph shows officers and men of the White Star Company marching from Southampton docks to the memorial service at the parish church.

cluding a restaurant, furnished in the Louis XVI. style, a reception-room of Jacobean style, and a squash racquet court.

The *Titanic's* displacement was 46,328 tons, 1,004 tons more than that of the *Olympic*. She cost over a million and a half. She was built by Messrs. Harland and Wolff at Belfast, and launched on May 31st, 1911. Her building took over a year, and her fitting-out nearly another year.

The ship was fitted with electri-cally-controlled watertight doors, and those giving communication between the various boiler-rooms and engine-rooms were arranged, as usual in White Star Line steamers, on the "drop sys-tem." They were of Messrs. Har-land and Wolff's special design, of massive construction, and provided with oil cataracts.

Each door, according to the of-ficial description, was held in the open position by a friction clutch, which could instantly be released by means of a powerful electric magnet controlled from the cap-tain's bridge, so that in the event of accident the captain, by simply moving an electric switch, could instantly close the doors

throughout, thus, it was believed, practically making the vessel un-sinkable.

As a further precaution, floats were provided beneath the floor level, which, in the event of water accidentally entering any of the compartments, would automat-ically lift and thereby close the doors opening into that compart-ment if they had not already been dropped by those in charge of the vessel.

The lifeboats attached to the liner were 30ft. long, and mounted on special davits on the boat deck. For purposes of wire-less telegraphy the *Titanic* had two masts 205ft. above the aver-age draught-line.

**UNPARALLELED LUXURY.**

Among the features of the *Ti-tanic* may be mentioned the first-class promenades on the three top decks, which were excep-tionally fine. In keeping with the public rooms were the large and beautiful first class staterooms, perhaps the most striking of these being the suite rooms dec-orated in several different styles and periods, including the follow-ing: – Louis Seize, Empire, Adams, Italian Renaissance,

THE DAILY GRAPHIC, SATURDAY, APRIL 20, 1912.   [Registered as a Newspaper.]   No. 6979A

# THE·DAILY·GRAPHIC

# TITANIC
## ·IN·MEMORIAM·NUMBER·

ONE PENNY

# TITANIC From Rare Historical Reports

HOW THE TITANIC MET WITH DISASTER ON HER MAIDEN VOYAGE.

The Titanic sailed from Southampton on Wednesday, April 10th, and she struck the iceberg on Sunday, April 14th, at 10.25 p.m. (American time), in the neighbourhood of the Newfoundland banks to the south of Cape Race. After the collision the Titanic sent out wireless appeals for immediate assistance, which were recorded on the Virginian, the Baltic, the Carpathia, and her sister ship the Olympic. All these vessels proceeded at once to the scene of the disaster, but apparently only the Carpathia was in time to render assistance. Our diagram illustrates the position of the Titanic at the time of the catastrophe, and shows the locality of the first boats to receive the distress signals. Inset portraits (left): Lord Pirrie, chairman of Messrs. Harland and Wolff, the builders of the Titanic; (right) Captain Smith, the commander of the Titanic, who went down with the ship.

THE CUNARD LINER CARPATHIA WHICH RESCUED THE SURVIVORS OF THE DISASTER.

Louis Quinze, Louis Quartorze, Georgian, Regency, Queen Anne, Modern Dutch, Old Dutch.

The second and third class accommodation was also on a scale of unparalleled luxury for those classes.

The *Titanic's* special features were the two promenade deck suites, with private promenades about fifty feet long—an absolutely novel feature—and the open-air Parisienne cafe which adjoined the restaurant. The rates for these two suites during the busy season was to be £870 each.

The following is the official account of the Titanic's first class dining saloon: —
"It is an immense room decorated in a style peculiarly English, reminiscent of early Jacobean times; but instead of the sombre oak of the sixteenth and seventeenth centuries, it is painted a soft, rich, white, which, with the coved and richly-moulded ceilings and the spacious character of the apartment, would satisfy the most aesthetic critic. The furniture is of oak designed to harmonise with its surroundings."

*(Daily Graphic, 20 April 1912)*

## SURVIVORS' THRILLING STORIES.

### "NEARER MY GOD TO THEE" PLAYED BY ORCHESTRA AS TITANIC SETTLED.

Mr. W.C. Chambers, one of the Titanic's survivors, interviewed by a Central News reporter, said the *Titanic* struck the iceberg head on. The passengers came running out on deck, but believing that the ship could not sink, and being assured that this was so by the liner's officers, they went back to their staterooms again.

After about two hours, however, the alarm was sent round, and the passengers started to enter the lifeboats. There was nothing in the way of a panic at first, as everybody believed there were plenty of lifeboats to go around.

After the lifeboat in which he was seated had gone about four hundred yards from the ship they saw the *Titanic* begin to settle down very quickly. It was then that there was a rush for the remaining boats, and one was swamped.

## THE DEATHLESS STORY OF THE "TITANIC."

### SOME FACTS OF THE DISASTER.

The iceberg, from 50 to 100 feet high, was struck at 11.35 p.m.

The blow was a glancing one on the starboard side, which was ripped open, rendering useless the essential water-tight compartments.

The "Titanic" sank in two miles of water, two hours and forty-five minutes after she struck.

Jack Phillips, the "Titanic's" wireless operator, remained at his post flashing out signals for assistance until the deck was awash.

Captain Smith, indifferent to his own safety, worked till the very last moment to save as many as possible. "Be British" was his word to one and all.

The "Carpathia's" wireless operator, by a lucky chance, was up late, and heard the "Titanic's" call for help.

The White Star liner "Olympic," on hearing the "Titanic's" wireless call for assistance, covered 400 miles at twenty-four knots, the highest speed the liner has ever attained.

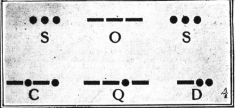

How the wireless call for help was sent.

(1.) Jack Phillips, the chief Marconi operator on the "Titanic," who flashed out his messages till the ship went down.

(2.) The wireless cabin on an ocean liner, the operator receiving a message.

(3.) Harold Bride, the second Marconi operator on the "Titanic," who was saved.

(4.) The wireless signal of distress, "S. O. S." in the Morse code. Formerly the signal "C. Q. D." was used.

"Going up on the deck again, I saw that there was an unmistakable list downwards from the stern to the bows, but knowing nothing of what had happened I concluded that some of the front compartments had filled and had weighed her down.

"Again I went down to my cabin, where I put on some warmer clothing. As I dressed I heard the order shouted, 'All the passengers on deck with lifebelts on.'"

Before this order was given Captain Smith had gone to the "wireless" room. He had ascertained by that time that the damage to the "Titanic" was very grave, and that, in spite of all her water-tight compartments, she was filling rapidly. There was but one thing to do: to call for help across the sea in the hope that the appeal might be heard and answered by ships within reach of those wireless words. Never before had Captain Smith sent such a message out into the darkness. But now he must make use of that modern miracle invented by Marconi, by which ships may speak across the great silence of the sea.

There were two men in the wireless cabin—Phillips, the first operator, and Bride, the second operator. It was but a little room, yet large enough for heroic virtues. And Phillips was a hero great as any on the roll-call of honour. His name is imperishable; his death a glorious tradition. As will be seen later in this narrative, he did his duty to the uttermost and

heroism and of all that happened in that wireless cabin has been told by Harold Bride, who shares the honour of his comrade:—

"On the night of the accident I was not 'sending,' but was asleep. There were three rooms in the wireless cabin: one was the sleeping room, one the dynamo room, and the other the operating room.

"I took off my clothes and went to sleep in bed. I was conscious of waking up and hearing Phillips sending to Cape Race. I read what he sent; it was traffic matter. I remembered how tired he was, and got out of bed without my clothes on to relieve him.

"I did not even feel a shock. I hardly knew anything had happened. I was standing by Phillips telling him to go to bed when the captain put his head in the cabin.

"'We've struck an iceberg,' he said, 'and I'm having an inspection made to tell what it's done to us. You'd better get ready to send out a call for assistance; but don't send it until I tell you.'

*TITANIC From Rare Historical Reports*

4    THE DAILY GRAPHIC SPECIAL TITANIC IN MEMORIAM NUMBER, APRIL 20, 1912.

# SOME OF THE TITANIC'S NOTABLE PASSENGERS.

Lady Duff-Gordon ("Lucile").—She is known to be saved.
(Photographed by Bassano, Old Bond Street.)

Mr. and Mrs. Daniel Marvin, who were returning to New York from their honeymoon. Mr. Marvin is only nineteen years of age, and his bride is a year younger. Their parents are prominent New York people. Mrs. Marvin was saved.    (Photographed at the Dover Street Studios.)

Mrs. J. J. Astor, wife of Colonel J. J. Astor, the well-known millionaire.—She is known to be saved.

Mr. Isidor Straus, formerly a member of the United States Congress, and a partner in the New York firm of L. Straus and Son.

Mr. James Carleton Young, a prominent citizen of Minneapolis.

Mr. Cardeza, a partner in the firm of Cardeza Brothers, of Rio de Janeiro and New York.—Known to be saved.

Mrs. F. J. Swift, a New York society hostess—Known to be saved.

Mr. J. J. Borebank, a well-known Californian horticulturist.

Major Archibald W. Butt, aide-de-camp to President Taft.

Mr. Charles Williams, the racquets champion, who was on his way to New York to meet G. Standing.

Mr. C. M. Hays, the president of the Grand Trunk Railway.

Mrs. H. B. Harris, daughter-in-law of an American theatre owner.—Known to be saved.

Mrs. C. E. H. Stengel, an American society hostess and wife of a well-known racehorse owner.—Known to be saved.

Miss Margaret Graham, a well-known Californian actress.—Known to be saved.

Mrs. G. M. Stone, well known in American society—Known to be saved.

# SOME OF THE TITANIC'S NOTABLE PASSENGERS.

Mr. Herbert Parsons, formerly Congressman for New York City.

Mr. Francis M. Warren, formerly United States Senator for Wyoming.

Mr. W. Van der Hoef, a prominent citizen of Minneapolis.

Mr. P. Marechal, a well-known resident of Washington.—Known to be saved.

Miss E. M. Eustis, well known in New York society.—Known to be saved.

Mrs. J. Snyder, well known in New York society.

Mrs. Figler, well known in New York society.

Mrs. Ettlinger, well known in New York society.

Mr. Christopher Head, ex-Mayor of Chelsea.

Colonel Archibald Gracie, a large cotton grower, of Jefferson County, Arkansas.

Mr. George Eastman.

Mr. J. H. Ross, a professor of Wisconsin University.

The Countess of Rothes.—Known to be saved. (Photographed by Lafayette, Bond Street.)

Miss Gladys Cherry, daughter of Lady Emily Cherry.—Known to be saved. (Photographed by Kate Pragnell.)

Mrs. F. M. Hoyt, wife of an ex-Governor of Washington.—Known to be saved.

Mrs. W. E. Carter, of Pennsylvania.

So far as his own boat was concerned, she created no suction. No shots were fired. There was nothing of that kind. Of those who were rescued from the *Titanic,* seven were subsequently buried at sea, four being sailors and three passengers. Two rescued women had gone insane.

As the liner continued to gradually recede into the trough of the sea the passengers marched towards the stern. The orchestra belonging to the first cabin assembled on deck as the liner was going down and played "Nearer my God to Thee."

Mr. and Mrs. Isidor Straus were drowned together, Mrs. Straus refusing to leave her husband's side. They went to their deaths together, standing arm in arm on the first cabin deck of the *Titanic.*

Mr. C.H. Stengel, a first class passenger, said that when the *Titanic* struck the iceberg the impact was terrific, and great blocks of ice were thrown on the deck, killing a number of people. The stern of the vessel rose in the air, and people ran shrieking from their berths below.

Women and children, some of the former naturally hysterical, having been rapidly separated from husbands, brothers, and fathers, were quickly placed in boats by the sailors, who, like their officers, it was stated, were heard by some survivors to threaten that they would shoot if male passengers attempted to get into the boats ahead of the women.

Mr. Stengel added that a number of men threw themselves into the sea when they saw that there was no chance of their reaching the boats. He himself dropped overboard, caught hold of the gunwale of a boat, and was pulled in because there were not enough sailors to handle her. In some of the boats women were shrieking for their husbands, others were weeping, but many bravely took a turn with the oars.

Mrs. Dickinson Bishop, of Detroit, Mich., said: — "I was in my bed when the crash came. I got up and dressed quickly, but being assured that there was no danger I went back to bed. There were few people on deck when I got there, and there was little or no panic."

# TITANIC From Rare Historical Reports

## FEATURES WHICH CONTRIBUTED TO THE SPLENDOURS OF THE TITANIC.

A SINGLE BERTH STATE-ROOM.

A DECK STATE ROOM.

THE SWIMMING BATH, A POPULAR FEATURE WHICH IS POSSESSED BY VERY FEW VESSELS AFLOAT.

THE TURKISH BATH COOLING ROOM, WHICH, WITH ITS SUGGESTION OF THE "MYSTERIOUS EAST," IS ONE OF THE SHIP'S MOST INTERESTING ROOMS.

THE VERANDAH CAFE ADJOINING THE SMOKE ROOM. IT IS SURROUNDED BY GREEN TRELLIS-WORK, OVER WHICH GROW CLIMBING PLANTS.

THE MAIN STAIRCASE FROM THE GREAT HALL.—FROM THIS HALL LIFTS GO UP AND DOWN TO EVERY FLOOR OF THE SHIP.

THE GEORGIAN SMOKE ROOM, PANELLED IN THE FINEST MAHOGANY AND RELIEVED EVERYWHERE WITH MOTHER-O'-PEARL INLAID WORK.

THE RESTAURANT. DECORATED IN LOUIS XVI. STYLE, AND PANELLED FROM FLOOR TO CEILING IN FRENCH WALNUT.

# TITANIC From Rare Historical Reports

**BREAKING THE NEWS OF THE TITANIC'S LOSS WITH OVER TWELVE HUNDRED LIVES TO LONDON.**

Consternation reigned in London when the news of the Titanic's awful fate became known. All day long the City and West End offices of the White Star Company, over which the White Star flag floated at half-mast, were besieged by anxious relations and friends of those who sailed in the liner. The photograph on the left shows the flag at half-mast over Oceanic House, Cockspur Street. At the top, on the right, the scene inside the Cockspur Street offices is depicted, and below an anxious crowd is seen outside the City offices of the company.

**THE ALLAN LINER VIRGINIAN, THE FIRST VESSEL TO RECEIVE THE TITANIC'S WIRELESS MESSAGE OF DISTRESS. UNFORTUNATELY SHE ARRIVED TOO LATE TO BE OF SERVICE.**

# TITANIC From Rare Historical Reports

Mr. Guggenheim, one of the millionaire passengers.

AN ARTIST'S IMPRESSION OF THE DISASTER.

Colonel J. J. Astor, the famous millionaire.—His wife is among the saved.

Colonel May.

Senator Carter, of the United States.

Mr. W. T. Sloper, a prominent business man of Seattle.—Known to be saved.

Mr. W. T. Stead, editor of the "Review of Reviews."

Mr. E. W. King, chief clerk to the Titanic's purser.

## THE AWFUL NEWS AT LLOYD'S.

Unprecedented scenes were witnessed at Lloyd's when the news of the total loss of the Titanic was made known. During the morning the "floor" was quite deserted and no business was done, as everybody was anxiously awaiting tidings of the great liner. Directly the telegram with the dreaded particulars was received three copies were posted instead of the usual one, and the boys, whose duty it was to post the notices, were so hampered by the anxious underwriters that they had much difficulty in reaching the boards. The total loss book, shown on the right of our sketch, had not long contained the particulars of the sinking of the Titanic before another total loss—one which is not exciting public interest—was recorded below it.

Master Harry Widener, son of the traction magnate who recently bought Rembrandt's "The Mill."

Master Spedden, son of Mr. John Spedden, of
New York.

Mr. Harry Rogers, of Tavistock.

Mr. Thomas Andrews.

Mrs. W. D. Douglas, well known in American
society.—Known to be saved.

### THE AGONISING WAIT FOR THE LIST OF THE LOST AT SOUTHAMPTON.

The majority of the Titanic's crew belonged to Southampton, and day after day the relations swarmed round the offices of the White Star Company in Canute Road anxiously awaiting tidings. As hour after hour passed and no list of the lost, or additions to the list of the saved, were forthcoming, the distress of the people was pitiable to witness. The company erected a great board in readiness to receive the list as soon as it should come, and though repeatedly told that delay was inevitable, nothing could persuade the sufferers to leave this board.

("Daily Graphic" photograph.)

# TITANIC From Rare Historical Reports

### THE ICEBERG ABOVE AND BELOW THE WATER.

The iceberg is one of those dangers to shipping against which the ingenuity of man cannot guard. It often rises from 150 to 300 feet above the sea level, and seven or eight times as much lies under the surface of the water.

### THE UPPER DECK OF THE TITANIC.

A view showing some of the lifeboats by which many of the survivors left the ship. Most of the boats were filled with women and children, and all these boats have been accounted for.

("Daily Graphic" photograph.)

### MANSION HOUSE FUND OPENED FOR THE WIDOWS AND CHILDREN OF TITANIC SAILORS.

The Lord Mayor very promptly opened a fund at the Mansion House for the relief of the widows and orphans of those sailors of the Titanic who have gone down in the ship. In this picture the Lord Mayor's servants are seen fixing a public collecting box outside the Mansion House. The King and Queen, and Queen Alexandra were among the first to send donations to the fund.

Mr. Robert Davill, of Richmond, Virginia, said: — "I jumped overboard, and I reckon that over a thousand did likewise. I swam about in the icy water for an hour before being picked up by a boat. At that moment I saw the *Titanic* take her final plunge. It was awful."

"Colonel Astor has gone down. So has Major Butt and Mr. W.T. Stead. I believe they jumped into the sea. I was in a state of collapse when picked up, and there are scores of survivors seriously ill. Captain Smith stuck to the bridge and behaved like a hero."

William Jones, a fireman, of Southampton, who was making his first trip, said that when the *Titanic* sank four of her lifeboats were swamped. He also declared that her boilers exploded, and that ice from the berg falling on her decks killed many people.

Mrs. Andrews, an elderly lady, interviewed by the Exchange representative, said the crash occurred at 11.35 p.m. on Sunday night. The women and children got off in the lifeboats at 12.45 a.m. The *Titanic* sank at 2 a.m., and the *Carpathia* picked up the boats at 8.30 a.m.

*(Daily Graphic, 20 April 1912)*

## SOME OF THE MISSING.

**MEN FAMOUS ON BOTH SIDES OF THE ATLANTIC.**

**CAPTAINS OF INDUSTRY.**

Among those well-known passengers on the *Titanic* who have not been heard of are the following: —

Colonel John Jacob Astor. — Eldest son of Mr. William Astor, who had five children, four daughters and one son. His father was an uncle of Mr. William Waldorf Astor, and great-uncle of Mr. Waldorf Astor, M.P. Colonel Astor, who was born in 1864, served in the Spanish-American war, and presented a mountain battery to the Government for use in the campaign. His surviving sisters are Mrs. George Ogilvie Hay, of London, and Mrs. Orme Wilson. The dead body of Colonel John Jacob Astor — whose marriage last year created a considerable sensation — is to be searched for. His young wife is among those saved.

Mr. Benjamin Guggenheim — A member of the famous Guggenheim family of capitalists, associ-

# TITANIC From Rare Historical Reports

THE DAILY GRAPHIC SPECIAL TITANIC IN MEMORIAM NUMBER, APRIL 20, 1912.

19

### THE FINANCIAL SIDE OF THE GREAT DISASTER: EXCITEMENT AT LLOYD'S CONTINUES.

The underwriters at Lloyd's will suffer financially by the loss of the Titanic, which was insured for a million pounds. The state of excitement, which was so very acute on Tuesday, continued in a more modified form on Wednesday, and during the business hours the entrance to the "house" at the back of the Royal Exchange was the scene of a great deal of activity. Our photograph shows the constant stream of underwriters entering and leaving the building, or standing in little groups discussing the terrible event.

### THE CHEFS OF THE LOST TITANIC: VISITORS TO THE WHITE STAR OFFICES.

The centre pictures show above the Titanic's chef and his assistants, and below is a view of one of the ship's kitchens. On the left is a picture showing the Right Hon. Alexander Montgomery Carlisle, the designer of the Titanic, leaving the White Star office. On the right is a picture of two ladies waiting at the office for fuller details.

# LIONISING A BABY.

## SON OF MILLIONAIRE TITANIC VICTIM.

### TRAGIC LIFE-STORY OF COLONEL J. J. ASTOR'S WIDOW.

All New York is rejoicing over the birth of a son to the widowed bride of Colonel John Jacob Astor, who perished in the Titanic disaster. The event marks a tragic incident in the life of the young widow—the beautiful Madeline Force, as he was—who has become bride, widow, and mother all within a year. She was returning from a honeymoon trip round Europe with her husband four months ago when the Titanic sank and she was rescued in one of the lifeboats, whilst her husband went down with the ship. The terrible sufferings that she then underwent, combined with her youth and beauty, served to make her popular with Americans in spite of the storm of protest raised at the time of the marriage. When Colonel Astor met her she was living with her parents in humble circumstances. She was 18 and the Colonel 47. It was a case of love at first sight, but Miss Madeline Force was not destined to become the wife of the man who had gained some notoriety in the Divorce Court without a protest being made. There was much difficulty in finding a clergyman, but eventually the ceremony was performed. For a week past eager crowds

gathered daily outside the famous £4,000,000 Astor mansion in Fifth Avenue and awaited the arrival of the new "three million dollar baby," to give it its popular sobriquet derived from the amount of fortune specially set aside in Colonel Astor's will for a posthumous member of the Astor family. Throughout all this time Mrs. Madeline Force Astor bore with the utmost patience the peculiar attentions showered upon her by the millionaire-loving public. Sight-seeing motor-cars daily paused in front of her windows, into which the curious passengers gazed intently, while guides expatiated on the cost of the mansion, its art treasures, and, above all, on the sumptuous

# HEIR TO £2,000,000.

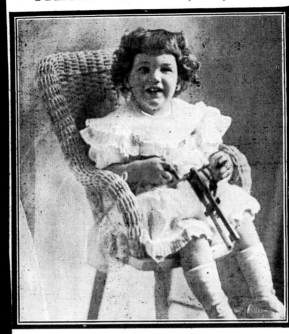

First published portrait of the eighteen-months-old heir of Colonel Astor, who perished in the Titanic disaster. He will inherit about £2,000,000 when he comes of age.—(Copyright by Lillian Baynes Griffin.)

### NURSERY PROVIDED AT A COST OF £2,000

for the prospective heir. Every afternoon Mrs. Astor drove with her mother through Central Park, avoiding the streets where were displayed in shop windows enormous photographs of herself surmounting the announcement in large print: "Mrs. Astor, whom the stork is about to visit" (a German method of announcing the approaching birth of a child). She permitted nothing to disturb her equanimity, though the newspapers devoted columns describing recent incidents in the Astor mansion—incidents which included the smashing of the Astor railings by a too eager motor-omnibus, and the resulting exciting chase in which the Astor servants joined. One day Mrs. Astor for the first time omitted to drive out, and next morning, shortly after eight, the butler opened the door and beckoned the crowd, to whom he made the joyful announcement: "It's a fine boy. We had feared that it would be a girl, but it isn't." A few moments later the following bulletin was issued:

A son was born to Mrs. Astor at 8.15. His name will be John Jacob Astor.

This was followed by a second bulletin setting forth:

The baby weighs 7¾lb. Both mother and son are doing well. No other doctor is present but Dr Cragin.

The last sentence was due to the fact that a rumour had circulated that the Astor mansion was inhabited by an army of special physicians and nurses, whereas only one doctor and two nurses had taken up their residence with Mrs. Astor. With incredible swiftness the news was flashed far and wide. Monster headlines scarcely left room for the news to be printed in the papers, and every hotel and club posted huge bulletins, while enthusiasts who generally spend their time cursing the "idle rich,"

### MEGAPHONED THE NEWS ACROSS THE RIVER

and from the housetops. A great crowd gathered outside the Astor mansion and cheered for the baby, his mother and father and the Titanic heroes, so that a strong force of police had to be drafted to the scene to regulate the traffic. The mansion in fact, quickly became the Mecca of all tourists and visitors, and enterprising tourist agents ran "rubber-neck," or sight-seeing, cars past it all the morning, while guides regaled their curious passengers with stories of the Astor millions, the amount of land owned by the family in New York, the tragic manner in which Colonel Astor met his death, the story of his first marriage and divorce, how he married the young widowed mother, and, in fact, everything connected with the history of the Astor family. Sensational reports were afterwards current that the parents of the widowed mother intend to dispute the will of the late Colonel Astor, as they consider that the posthumous son ought to have £4,000,000 instead of only £600,000. These reports are probably invention. Young John Jacob has literally been born with a golden spoon in his mouth, for he will have the absolute disposal of his fortune, which, however, will revert to Mr Vincent Astor (Colonel Astor's heir by his first wife) if he should die intestate. To Vincent Astor comes of age and attains full possession of £60,000,000 in November. Under the will executed on Sept. 18 last, a few days after the multi-millionaire married Miss Force, the widow was left £1,000,000, which she forfeits if she marries again, and another £20,000 to which no conditions were attached. The colonel's first wife, Mrs Ava Willing Astor, was not mentioned

# A PRETTY MULTI-MILLIONAIRE.

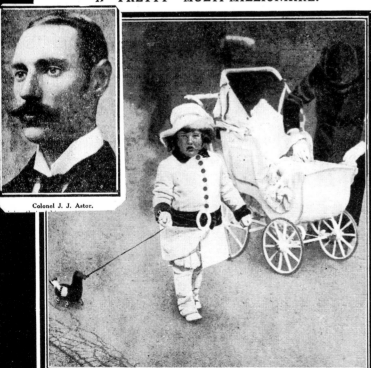

Colonel J. J. Astor.

MRS. MADELINE ASTOR.

This is little John Jacob Astor, the young son of the late Colonel John Jacob Astor who lost his life in the Titanic disaster, when returning from his honeymoon with his young bride. The little multi-millionaire loves nothing so much as the open air.

ates of Mr. Pierpont Morgan, and world-famous in connection with Alaskan development and copper production.

Major Archibald Butt. — Aide-de-Camp to President Taft, returning to Washington after visiting the Pope.

Mr. George D. Widener. Well-known Philadelphia capitalist, and son of Peter A. Widener, who bought Rembrandt's "The Mill" for £100,000. Some of the exhibit's in the London Museum, recently opened, were presented by Mrs. George Widener, who has been visiting London with her husband.

**Twice Wrecked.**

Mr. C.M. Hays — President of the Grand Trunk Railway, and one of the best-known railwaymen in Canada. He, with Mrs. Hays and Miss Hays, both on board, had recently been on a short visit to London. Mr. Hays had also been shipwrecked in the Pacific Ocean.

Mr. J.B. Thayer — President of the Pennsylvania Railroad.

Mr. Washington Roebling. Millionaire president and director of

John A. Roebling's Sons Company, iron and steel wire and wire-rope manufacturers. He directed the construction of Brooklyn Bridge.

Jonkheer von Reuchlin — Joint managing director of the Holland America Line.

Mr. Frank D. Millet — An American artist, who has a house at Broadway, Worcestershire.

Mr. Isidor Straus — Member of Congress. He lives in Broadway, New York, is a merchant, a member of the firm of L. Straus and Sons, and director of various banks.

Mr. C. Clarence Jones — New York stockbroker, who has been visiting European capitals in connection with the purchase of American Embassy sites.

Mr. J. Futrelle — The noted story writer, author of "The Thinking Machine."

Mr. W.T. Stead — Editor of the "Review of Reviews," on his way to attend the convention to close the "Man and Religion Forward Movement," which has been operating in America for some

# *TITANIC From Rare Historical Reports*

**THE TITANIC'S PASSENGERS TAKING THEIR LAST LOOK AT HOME.**

A photograph taken as the boat was leaving Southampton on April 10th, showing, on the deck, some of the passengers who are probably among the missing.

**THE SCENE ROUND THE FATEFUL BOARD AT SOUTHAMPTON.**

The board erected by the White Star Company outside their Southampton offices was watched day after day by the crowd of grief-stricken wives and other relatives of the Titanic's crew. One list of members of the crew known to be on the Carpathia was posted, but it only contained about half a dozen names.     ("Daily Graphic" photograph.)

Printed and Published by the Proprietors, Messrs. H. R. BAINES and Company, Ltd., at Tallis House, Whitefriars in the City of London.—Saturday, April 20, 1912.

months with the object of inducing business men to take an active part in religious movements. Several messages were sent to Mr. W.T. Stead in the hope that as a practised journalist he might be able to give a reliable account of the disaster, but no reply has been received.

Mr. Thomas Andrews — Managing director of Messrs. Harland and Wolff, builders of the *Titanic.*

Mr. Christopher Head — Former Mayor of Chelsea, who was much interested in art matters and took a prominent part in the discussions at the Mansion House regarding the King Edward Memorial.

**SOME OF THE SAVED.**

**LADY DUFF-GORDON, COUNTESS OF ROTHES, WHITE STAR CHAIRMAN.**

The *Titanic's* saved include: —

Lady Duff-Gordon — who carries on the famous firm of "Madame Lucile" — and her husband, Sir Cosmo Duff-Gordon. They sailed incognito as Mr. and Mrs. Morgan.

The Countess of Rothes — On her way to New York to join her husband. They have planned a trip through the States to the West, returning via Canada. The Earl has been some months on the American Continent, as it is his intention to settle down there fruit farming.

Mr. J.B. Ismay — Chairman and managing director of the White Star Line, and president of the International Mercantile Marine Company. He was carrying out his usual custom of sailing on the maiden voyage of the company's liners.

Also among the saved are Mr. and Mrs. Henry S. Harper. He is a grandson of the founder of the famous publishing house.

*(Mail, April 20)*

# GRIEF AND JOY.

**SOUTHAMPTON'S MIXED EMOTIONS.**

*FROM OUR OWN CORRESPONDENT.*
*SOUTHAMPTON, Friday.*

Joy and sorrow met in the crowd which saw the last list of the survivors of the Titanic posted up outside the White Star Line offices here early this morning. Name after name was recog-

# THE FIRST AND LAST VOYAGE OF THE TITANIC
## HOW SHE ENCOUNTERED THE DEADLY ICEBERG

Mr. G. F. Morrell has here summarised the disaster, showing where the ice which wrecked the Titanic came from. She knew there was danger, because the French liner Touraine warned her by wireless, having encountered the ice on the day the Titanic sailed from Southampton. The Titanic thanked her, and then steamed westward at eighteen knots an hour. In consequence of the phenomenal quantity of ice in the North Atlantic, the White Star Line, in conjunction with other companies, have instructed their vessels to take a more southerly course.

# THE BRIEF CAREER OF THE LARGEST LINER
## DESCRIBED IN THREE TABLEAUX

DEPARTURE —THE LEVIATHAN (AND HER COMMANDER, CAPTAIN SMITH) LEAVING SOUTHAMPTON— APRIL 10

DOOM —THE FATE OF THE TITANIC, ILLUSTRATED BY ICEBERGS FLOATING IN THE ATLANTIC— APRIL 14, 10.25 P.M.

**DAILY GRAPHIC**
ACCIDENT **£1,000** INSURANCE
TUESDAY, APRIL 16, 1912
# TITANIC SUNK: APPALLING LOSS of LIFE

DISTRESS —SCENES AT THE WHITE STAR OFFICES IN COCKSPUR STREET AND THE CITY— APRIL 15

The Titanic's first and last voyage was ill-fated from the very first, for as she was leaving Southampton the displacement of so much water caused the New York to break away from the quayside, and a collision nearly resulted. Her commander, Captain E. J. Smith, R.N., who is reported to have gone down with the liner, was captain of the Olympic when, last September, she collided with the cruiser Hawke off the Isle of Wight. Two of our pictures show a battleship in peril amid icebergs, which are submerged to the extent of seven-eighths of their bulk.

nized and joyfully shouted from one to another, and name after name was sought and found missing. Smiles and tears, shouts and sobs. Here a woman fainting with the weight of despair; there a woman in hysterics with the shock of sudden joy.

Well-dressed women, poverty-stained women, old women, and young girls rubbed shoulders in the craving for names. It was a painful contrast between warm joy and grey despair; fate juggling with the masks of grief and laughter. Soon the happy ones went away, and there were left only those who could not believe in the finality of the posted lists and those who were left in a maddening state of uncertainty owing to the absence of initials to the firemen's names. For instance, there were 5 Olivers, 3 Blakes, 2 Cunninghams, 3 Moores, and 2 Barretts on the boat, and of the 1 or 2 saved none could say who was who.

**FRANTIC WITH SUSPENSE.**

The wives of those and other men of the same name were frantic with suspense, and throughout the day they were appealing for further information. "Is it my Jack or is it her George?"

was the pathetic request uttered again and again by a woman who wore widow's weeds. Many names were duplicated and others wrongly spelt.

Now that the mayor is administering the distress fund destitution is vanishing from the stricken quarters. Well-known Southampton women are visiting and relieving the cases I mentioned yesterday, but there still remain bedridden women who cannot get to the town hall, and unless they are sought out they will starve amid plenty.

This afternoon I met Sister Frances Magdalen in a tramway-car on her way to an isolated case. She had just come away from a woman whose baby was two hours old. "Many of these women are lying helpless." she said, "and unless neighbours bring us information they will be left to lie in their poverty." There is another class of women who are in danger of starving; the women who do not live with their husbands, but whose men have gone down in the *Titanic.* These women will not go to the town hall for relief, but there are children to be considered.

## SHIPS WITHIN CALL OF THE TITANIC.

The plan shows the relative position of the many ships fitted with the Marconi apparatus in the radius of the call for help from the ill-fated Titanic in mid-ocean on Sunday night. The chart is based on information supplied by the Marconi Wireless Telegraphic Company.

# HEROES OF THE ENGINE-ROOM.

## Names of 34 Brave Men Who Died Like Rats in a Trap.

## AT THEIR POSTS BELOW.

**(From Our Own Correspondent.)**

SOUTHAMPTON, April 22.—At last the list of survivors from the Titanic is approximately complete and corrected, and it is possible to proceed with some certainty in enumerating the terrible roll of dead.

One fact that stands out in glowing brilliance is the established heroism of the thirty-four engineers who stayed at their posts to the end, and not one of whom has survived.

The duties which kept the heroic engineers of the Titanic at their posts till death were threefold.

They had to keep the ship afloat if possible, to maintain pumping operations, and to keep the dynamos at work generating the electric light.

Their plight in the stokehold after it was flooded and the boilers burst or were flooded causing clouds of scalding steam is terrible to think of, and this applies also, of course, to the firemen and coal trimmers.

The majority were Southampton men, and because their splendid heroism has hitherto been scarcely mentioned I give the full list of the thirty-four names, with their addresses.

"The bravery of the captain and other officers on deck deserves the highest respect, of course," said one of the officers of the Olympic to me to-day, "but it must not be forgotten that the engineers showed equal heroism, and their chance of ever seeing the sky again was almost nothing."

CAPT. E. J. SMITH.

Mr. Dyer, one of the engineers on board the Titanic, who perished in the disaster to the giant liner. In the event of a ship going down the engineers have a very poor chance of being rescued.

## SAVED BY "WIRELESS."

### Valuable Record of Service to Life and Shipping.

Wireless telegraphy has a long record of valuable service in life-saving at sea and the salving of distressed ships since its adoption by the Mercantile Marine.

On March 3, 1899, the s.s. R. F. Matthews ran into the East Goodwin lightship. The accident was reported by wireless to the South Foreland lighthouse and lifeboats were promptly dispatched.

On January 1, 1901, the barque Medora, of Stockholm, was waterlogged on the Ratal Bank. The mail steamer Princess Clementine notified the Marconi station near Ostend and a tug was sent out and towed the barque off. Some days later the Princess Clementine herself ran ashore at Mariakerke during a thick fog, intelligence of the accident being conveyed to Ostend by wireless.

Towards the end of 1905 the liner Kroonland disabled her steering-gear 130 miles W. of the Fastnet and had to put back to Queenstown. The captain within an hour and a half of the receipt of the news by the agent at Antwerp had been instructed as to the measures to be taken. Passengers on board communicated with their friends in all parts of the world, and in some cases obtained money supplies from the purser on the authority of the replies.

In 1904 two accidents—a stranding and a collision to the liner New York—were reported by wireless, and the Friesland was also located with a broken propeller shaft by the same means.

On January 23, 1909, the liner Republic sank after a collision. Communication was established with the Marconi station at Siasconset and the news was telegraphed to several other vessels, which immediately proceeded to the scene and the whole of the crew and passengers were saved.

On June 10, 1909, the whole of the passengers, numbering 410, and the crew of the Slavonia were saved. The vessel was wrecked on Flores Island, Azores, and was able to communicate with two liners, which went to her assistance.

**MONEY RETURNED.**

The Mayor of Southampton's fund is growing every hour. This evening the total was well over 6,000. One woman who had received relief promptly returned the money to the mayor when she found her husband's name among the survivors.

The National Union of Ships' Stewards, Butchers, and Bakers last night decided to start a fund for the distressed relatives of the members through the *Titanic* disaster, and instructed the Southampton secretary to grant meantime two per member to meet immediate needs.

*(Mail, April 20)*

# INCIDENTS.

### "I WENT ON DICTATING."

Mr. Robert E. Daniel, a young cotton broker, of Philadelphia, said: "I was in my cabin dictating to the typist when the ship struck the berg."

"The officers who survived told me afterwards the *Titanic* slipped up on the iceberg and tore her bottom out. No one seemed to be alarmed at first. I went on dic-tating until somebody knocked at my door and cried out that the ship was sinking. There was no panic." Mr. Daniel leaped overboard (says *Reuter*) and was picked up by one of the boats.

### SAD HOMECOMING.

There was an impressive scene at Montreal Railway Station yesterday when Mrs. Hays, whose husband, the president of the Grand Trunk Railway, was one of the drowned, and Mrs. Davidson, whose husband was also drowned, arrived by special train.

The bell of the locomotive was tolled, and the station flag was at half-mast. Every head was uncovered as Mrs. Hays and Mrs. Davidson stepped from the train.

### HALF-FULL BOATS.

A passenger in the *Carpathia* said:

"Ropes were tied round the waists of the adult survivors to help them in climbing up the rope ladders from the boats to the *Carpathia*. The little children and babies were hoisted on to our deck in bags. Some of the boats were crowded, but a few were not half-full."

## MEETING WITH LOVED ONES.

When the survivors landed there were affecting scenes at the dock. Men were in hysterics and fell down to kiss the knees of beloved ones; women shrieked and wept and collapsed in the arms of husbands and brothers; children were almost crushed in the arms of those welcoming them.

## A LUCKY DELAY.

Dr. J.F. Kemp, the *Carpathia's* physician, says that their wireless operator happened by chance to have delayed turning in on Sunday night for ten minutes, and so, being at his post, he got the *Titanic's* call for help. Had he gone to rest as usual, there would have been no survivors.

## FOREIGNER SHOT.

Mr. Brayton, one of the *Titanic's* passengers, has stated that he saw a steward shoot a foreigner who tried to press past a number of women in order to gain a place in the lifeboats.

*(Daily Mail, 20 April)*

# THE LAST SCENES.

*From Our Own Correspondent.*

*NEW YORK, Friday.*

The narrative of the greatest coherence by the survivors is that of Mr. Robert W. Daniel, of Philadelphia. Not until two minutes before the *Titanic* went down did he leap from her rail, clad only in a bath robe. For an hour he swam through the icy water naked, the robe having drifted off. He was picked up by a lifeboat frozen and semi-conscious. When he revived he was in the steerage of the *Carpathia*, where he lay between two sailors with both feet frozen.

Mr. Daniel is a Philadelphia banker and went to London on business in August. He was in the Carlton Hotel at the time of the fire there...

The *Titanic* was running along at twenty knots, he said, as he rested after being assisted from the *Carpathia* by two stewards. The night was clear and the stars shining brilliantly. Danger was far from our thoughts, even when we entered the icefield. I was in my room when the shock came, and it did not seem great.

I ran on deck. A huge iceberg was floating by. It was at least 150 feet in the air and towered far above the *Titanic.* Beneath I heard it tearing into the sides of the vessel. From stem to stern the *Titanic* was ripped. We had not struck bow on but diagonally.

The ship pounded along the ice, her side being torn to shreds and the air compartments and bulkheads being pierced or smashed as the steel plates were ripped. The ship was doomed at once.

No one knew it, however. That was the real tragedy. There was no panic. People rushed on deck, of course, all in their nightclothes, but they were calm. The officers went among the passengers assuring them that nothing was wrong and that the ship was unsinkable. They said it over and over again, and they repeated it — "unsinkable!" My friends and I myself even then thought the *Titanic* was as unsinkable as a railway station.

The iceberg swept astern like a mist-wraith. On and on we went, our momentum carrying us forward. Not until we were a mile from the scene of the shock did the Titanic come to a stop. The decks were coated with snowy splinters of ice. Assured that the accident would mean nothing

more than a short delay I returned to my room. Half an hour later the alarm was sounded, voices crying through the ship: "All hands on deck. Adjust life-preservers."

This and the sound of hurrying feet roused me from bed. Throwing on a bathrobe I again hurried on deck. Still nothing appeared to be wrong. The sea was perfectly calm and the *Titanic* lay motionless. Men and women were on the decks, apparently unexcited. There was absolutely no panic even then, but the crew had begun to swing out the lifeboats, and rafts were being lowered. I stood watching, unafraid, like the majority of others, because of my conviction that the *Titanic* could not go down.

I learned later that there was a conflict of orders given. When the boats were filled on the starboard side husbands were ordered to enter the smaller craft with their wives on the port side.

The husbands were then driven back, the order being, "Women and children first." That explains why so many men survived.

In many instances within the range of my vision wives refused point-blank to leave their husbands. I saw members of the crew literally pull the women from the arms of the men and throw them over the side into the boats.

Mrs. Isidor Straus clung to her husband, and none could force her from his side. Not until the last five minutes did the awful realisation come that the end was at hand. The lights became dim and went out, but we could see. Slowly, ever so slowly, the surface of the water seemed to come up towards us. So gradual was it that even after I had adjusted the lifejacket about my body it seemed a dream.

Deck after deck was submerged. There was no lurching or grinding or crunching. The *Titanic* simply settled.

I was far up on one of the top decks when I jumped. About me were many others in the water. My bath-robe floated away, and it was icily cold. I struck out at once. I turned my head, and my first glance took in the people swarming on the *Titanic's* deck. Hundreds were standing there helpless to ward off approaching death.

I saw Captain Smith on the bridge. My eyes seemingly clung to him. The deck from which I had leaped was immersed. The water had risen slowly, and was now to the floor of the bridge. Then it was to Captain Smith's waist. I saw him no more. He died a hero.

The bows of the *Titanic* were far beneath the surface, and to me only the four monster funnels and the two masts were now visible.

It was all over in an instant. The *Titanic's* stern rose completely out of the water and went up thirty, forty, sixty feet into the air. Then, with her body slanting at an angle of 45deg., slowly the *Titanic* slipped out of sight.

*(Daily Mail, 20 April)*

## "ONE SUPREME CRY."

**LAST VIEW OF THE 'TITANIC' FROM A LIFEBOAT.**
*PARIS, Friday.*
The *Matin* publishes the following narrative of three French survivors, M. Pierre Marchal, an airman: M. Omout, a manufacturer, of Havre, and M. Chevre, a sculptor: —

## SURPASSING THE GREATEST BUILDINGS AND MEMORIALS OF EARTH

### The White Star Line's New Triple-screw Steamers
### "OLYMPIC" ☆ "TITANIC"
LARGEST AND FINEST IN THE WORLD
(SEE OVER)

We were quietly playing auction bridge with a Mr. Smith, of Philadelphia, when we heard a noise similar to that produced by the screw racing. We did not think for a moment of a catastrophe. We rushed on deck and saw that the *Titanic* had a tremendous list. There was everywhere a momentary panic, but it speedily subsided.

To the inquiries of a lady one of the ship's officers caustically replied, "Don't be afraid; we are only cutting a whale in two." Confidence was quickly restored, all being convinced that the *Titanic* could not founder.

Captain Smith appeared nervous; he came down on deck chewing a toothpick. "Let everyone," he said, "put on a lifebelt; it is more prudent." He then ordered the boats to be got out.

The band continued to play popular airs in order to reassure the passengers. Nobody wanted to go in the boats, everyone saying, "What's the use?" and firmly believing there was no risk in remaining on board. In these circumstances some of the boats went away with very few passengers; we saw boats with only about fifteen persons in them.

When our boat had rowed about half a mile from the vessel the spectacle was quite fairylike. The *Titanic,* which was illuminated from stem to stern, was stationery, like some fantastic piece of stage scenery. The night was clear and the sea smooth, but it was intensely cold. Presently the gigantic ship began to sink by the bows, and then those who had remained on board realized the horror of their situation.

Suddenly the lights went out and an immense clamour filled the air in one supreme cry for help. Little by little the *Titanic* settled down, and for three hours cries of anguish were heard. At moments the cries of terror were lulled and we thought it was all over, but the next instant they were renewed in still keener accents. As for us we did nothing but row, row, row to escape from the death cries.

In our little boat we were frozen with cold, having left the ship without overcoats or rugs. We shouted from time to time to attract attention, but obtained no reply. A German baron who was with us fired off all the cartridges in his revolver. This agonizing suspense lasted for many hours until at last the *Carpathia* appeared. We shouted "Hurrah!" and all the boats scattered on the sea made towards her.

Some of the passengers who had remained on the ship launched a collapsible boat and some fifty got into it. It was soon half full of water and the occupants, one after another, either were drowned or perished with cold, the bodies of those who died being thrown out. Of the original fifty only fifteen were picked up by the *Carpathia*, on board which we joined them.

We bear sorrowful tribute to the brave dead of the *Titanic.* Colonel Astor and others were admirable in their heroism, and the crew fulfilled with sublime self-sacrifice all the dictates of humanity. Much useless sacrifice of life would have been avoided but for the blind faith in the unsinkableness of the ship, and if all the places in the boats had been taken in time. *Reuter.*

(Daily Mail, 20 April)

## CAPTAIN SMITH.

**HOW HE WENT DOWN WITH HIS SHIP.**

### "BE BRITISH!"

The reports circulated in New York immediately after the *Carpathia's* arrival that Captain E.J. Smith, the *Titanic's* commander, committed suicide on the bridge were baseless slanders on a brave man dead. Our New York correspondent's prompt information enabled us to suppress the story almost as soon as it was published.

The fuller reports available today combine to show that the captain was on the bridge at the time of or immediately after the slight shock caused by the collision with the iceberg. He took all steps humanly possible to minimize the consequences.

His first act was to send for the carpenters to sound the ship and report the extent of the damage. While they were doing so he told the wireless operators to prepare to send out the call for help. Ten minutes later he knew the ship was sinking and ordered the call to be sent. At the same moment the captain's order was being shouted through the ship for all passengers to put on lifebelts and come on deck. The boats were lowered under the captain's orders, and the women and children saved. When all the boats had gone Captain Smith still stood on the bridge. On this point all the narratives are clear.

"Captain Smith's unparalleled self-sacrifice and heroism," says one account "are commended by high and low. Before he was washed off the bridge he called through his megaphone "Be British" to the mass on the decks below. Later he was seen helping those struggling in the water, refusing an opportunity to save himself. Other officers followed this noble example. The bravery of the whole ship's company is a matter to record."

One lady has stated that Captain Smith shot down a man who tried to get into a lifeboat and that the body fell at her feet, but Colonel Gracie, who survives, states emphatically that no shots were fired. The captain went down with his ship, though the actual manner of his drowning can only be judged from the confused accounts of the survivors. One of these says that as the *Titanic* began to plunge the captain leapt from the bridge and was seen no more; another that a wave swept him from the bridge into the icy water; and a third that an effort was made to drag him into a lifeboat, but that he cried, "Let me go!" and jerked himself free and went down.

Mr. George A. Braden states: "I saw Captain Smith while I was in the water. He was standing on the bridge all alone. Once he was swept down by a wave, but managed to get to his feet again. Then as the boat sank he was again knocked down by a wave, and then disappeared from view."

All accounts agree that he did his duty to the last, and died with the traditional heroism of the British captain.

*(Daily Mail, 20 April)*

## MR. ISMAY.

**HOW HE LEFT THE TITANIC.**

**WHISPERED REPLY.**

**"THERE WERE NO WOMEN."**

**AMERICAN SENATE INVESTIGATION.**

Mr. Bruce Ismay, the chairman of the White Star Line, was questioned by the Investigating Committee of the United States Senate in New York yesterday. When asked (according to a *Reuter* telegram) to state the circumstances in which he left the *Titanic,* Mr. Bruce Ismay replied almost in a whisper:

One of the boats was being filled and the officers called out to know if there were any more women to go. There were none, and no passengers were on the deck. As the boat was being lowered I got into it.

The following statement by Mr. Ismay after landing from the Carpathia is reported by the Exchange Telegraph Company's New York correspondent: —
"The *Titanic*, after striking the iceberg, remained above the water for two hours and twenty-five minutes. She then sank. Whether there were enough lifeboats to care for all her passengers I do not care to say."

Mr. Ismay was asked in which lifeboat in the order of their leaving the *Titanic* he made his escape. He replied:

"I took the last lifeboat which pulled out from the *Titanic*."

Mr. Ismay was asked: "Were there any women or children on board when you left the *Titanic*?"

Mr. Ismay: I am sure I cannot say.

Mr. Ismay said he sent a statement of the wreck to the White Star offices at New York on Monday. Mr. Franklin, vice-president of the line, said this statement was not received by the White Star offices in New York until Wednesday afternoon. It was not given out then because "the whole of the accident" was known.

**STATEMENT ON LANDING.**

Mr. Bruce Ismay gave out the following prepared statement (according to a *Reuter* telegram) on the pier after landing from the *Carpathia*: —

"In the presence and under the shadow of this catastrophe of the sea, which overwhelms my feelings too deeply for expression in words, I can only say that the White Star officers and employs will do everything humanly possible to alleviate the sufferings and sorrow of relations and friends of those who perished."

"The *Titanic* was the last word in ship-building. Every regulation prescribed by the British Board of Trade had been strictly complied with. The master, officers, and crew were the most experienced and skilful in the British service. I am informed that a committee of the United States Senate has been appointed to investigate the circumstances of the accident. I heartily welcome a most complete and exhaustive inquiry, and any aid which I and my associates and our builders and navigators can render is at the service of the public and the Government both in the United States and Great Britain. Under these circumstances I must defer making any further statement at this hour."

Mr. Ismay said informally before giving out this statement that he left the ship in the last boat, one of the collapsible boats on the starboard side. "I do not know the speed at which the *Titanic* was going," said Mr. Ismay in reply to a question; "she hit the iceberg a glancing blow."

Mr. Ismay then went to his rooms at the Ritz-Carlton Hotel.

According to another story of the rescue Mr. Ismay was pulled on board the *Carpathia* from the lifeboat clad only in pyjamas. He collapsed on reaching the deck, and lay in a semi-conscious condition for some time afterwards.

Senator Smith, of Michigan, the chairman of the Investigating Committee, had a conference with Mr. Ismay and Mr. Franklin during Thursday night. Senator Smith afterwards said that Mr. Ismay made a very frank statement, but he preferred that the public should hear Mr. Ismay's story from his own lips, when he appeared before the committee.

The rescued officers of the *Titanic* were placed on board the Red Star liner *Lapland* for the night after the *Carpathia's* arrival. They refused to say anything, declaring that they were under instructions to give no information except to the Senate Committee.

*(Daily Mail, 20 April)*

## MR. ISMAY'S TELEGRAM.

The managers of the White Star Line at Liverpool have received the following telegram from New York: —

Press here today comment most favourably on the behaviour of the officers and crew of the *Titanic* under extraordinary and trying circumstances, and we are satisfied that the discipline was everything that we could desire. —*ISMAY.*

*(Daily Mail, 20 April)*

## OFFICERS ISOLATED.

*NEW YORK, Friday.*

The officers and sailors saved from the *Titanic* are being kept practically isolated on board the Red Star liner *Lapland.* —*Reuter's* Special.

*(Daily Mail, 20 April)*

## THE LAST OF MR. STEAD.

*NEW YORK. Friday.*

Mr. A.H. Barkworth, of Tranby House, East Yorkshire, one of the Titanic's passengers, says he saw Mr. W.T. Stead on deck after the collision.

Mr. Stead described to him how the forecastle of the vessel was full of powdered ice scraped off the berg. Mr. Barkworth himself escaped by jumping into the sea, from which he was picked up later by one of the boats.

## SURVIVORS OF TITANIC'S CREW RETURN

# FIRST SURVIVORS OF TITANIC TO REACH ENGLAND.

the Lapland,

### THE TITANIC'S SWAN-SONG.

Nearer, my God, to Thee,
 Nearer to Thee !
E'en though it be a cross
 That raiseth me :
Still all my song would be,
 "Nearer, my God, to Thee,—
 Nearer to Thee !"

Though, like the wanderer,
 The sun gone down,
Darkness be over me,
 My rest a stone;
Yet in my dreams I'd be
Nearer, my God, to Thee,
 Nearer to Thee !

There let the way appear,
 Steps unto Heaven;'
All that thou send'st to me
 In mercy given.
Angels to beckon me
Nearer, my God, to Thee,
 Nearer to Thee !

### DRIFT OF THIRTY-FOUR MILES BEFORE SHE SANK AFTER STRIKING THE ICEBERG.

## DISASTER ITEMS

**Liner "Ripped as if by a Gigantic Tin Opener."**

"Ripped from her stem to the engine-room by the great mass of ice which she struck amidships, the Titanic's side was laid open as if by a gigantic tin-opener. She quickly listed to starboard. A shower of ice fell on deck. Shortly before she sank she broke in two abaft the engine room, and as she disappeared beneath the water two explosions were heard. A moment more," says Reuter, " and the Titanic had gone, with doomed hundreds grouped on her after-deck."

**Died After Rescue.**
Five of the rescued passengers are said to have died afterwards on the Carpathia.

**79 Widows on Board.**
There were about 70 widows on board the Carpathia when it reached New York.

**Woman with Both Legs Broken.**
While getting into one of the lifeboats Mrs. Churchill Candee, of Washington, had both her legs broken.

**"Full of Powdered Ice."**
After the collision the forecastle was full of powdered ice, says Mr. A. H. Barkworth, of Tranby House, East Yorkshire.

**Calmly went to Bed.**
In some parts of the monster vessel the extent of the calamity was not realised, and some of the passengers, says Reuter, even went back to bed.

**Bridegroom's Farewell to His Bride.**
" It's all right, little girl. You go. I will stay," said Mr. W. D. Marvin, of New York, to his wife, who was on her honeymoon trip. As the boat pushed off he threw her a farewell kiss.

**Lifeboats to the Rescue.**
After the disappearance of the Titanic those in the lifeboats rowed about searching for any survivors, and those who had embarked in the collapsible boats were picked up in this way.

## LIFE STORY OF THE TITANIC

Keel-plate laid at Belfast on March 31, 1909.

Vessel fully framed May, 1910.

Launched on May 31, 1911.

Taken to Southampton for maiden voyage on April 10, 1912.

Sunk after collision with iceberg, April 14, 1912.

Some of the survivors are reported as saying that Mr. Stead came to the door of his stateroom and then went back to his bed. He is not mentioned in any of the other survivors' narratives. — *Reuter.*

(*Daily Mail, 20 April*)

## GALLANT ENGINEERS.

**WHAT HAPPENED BELOW AFTER THE COLLISION.**

We are indebted to a passenger in the *Lapland*, which brought home the surviving members of the *Titanic's* crew, for the story of what happened in the ship's engine-rooms and stokeholds after the collision.

It is a tale of surpassing heroism — of the thirty-six engineers who went calmly to their doom under the orders of Chief Engineer Bell in a desperate effort to save the ship, of the oilers and stokers who remained unflinchingly at their posts in a moment of mortal peril.

There was no panic among the "black squad." All did their duty to the last, like Englishmen. All the watertight doors were in perfect order at the collision. Not one jammed.

Two people on board must have known from the moment the *Titanic* struck that she was doomed — Mr. Andrews, the constructor, and Chief Engineer Bell. Both went down with her.

Leading Stoker Threlfall states that after the collision his stokehold, No.4, was dry. "The fires were burning as usual." The watertight doors were closed, but they were opened to bring through an engineer with a broken leg, and were closed after him again. Nos. 1, 2, and 3 stokeholds were also dry. Up to shortly before 2 a.m. "everything was going on just as usual below; the lights were burning and all pumps were working as if nothing had happened."

It was then that the order was given by the chief engineer to the men to go on deck. They found the boats gone, the ship down by the head, her stern up in the air, and her hull with a heavy list to port. The captain ordered all articles that would float to be thrown overboard and gave the command, "Every man for himself."

157

Threlfall adds that shortly after he took to the water he gained a raft and climbed upon it. There were several firemen standing on it. Chief Engineer Bell swam up, and they called to him: "Come on, Mr. Bell, we'll pull you on board." He shouted back: "No, men, your raft might capsize. I'll be all right and find something else. Good-bye, men, God bless you."

Oiler A. Whyte states that shortly after the accident the emergency dynamos were started to run the electric light in case the engine-room should be flooded. He was sent on deck by the engineers at 1.40 a.m., saw the last boat leaving, and slid down the falls to her. The engineers were still in the turbine-room.

Leading-Stoker F. Barrett states that at the order of Engineer Harvey he drew thirty-six fires in the boilers. Engineer Shepherd broke his leg by falling in a manhole. His only sorrow was that he could render no aid to save the ship. Barrett was sent on deck at 1.30 and was ordered to take charge of No.13 boat. Out of ninety-one men in his watch only sixteen were saved.

"When the water came pouring in," said one of the firemen, "one of the engineers shouted 'You chaps have done your best; get up on deck.' I was the last man to go up the ladder, and when half-way up I turned to look at the engineer, who had just shouted, 'Goodbye.' Even as I looked the steel floor of the engine-room passages buckled and broke. A great hole appeared and the engineer was shot down the hole clean through the bottom of the ship."

*(Daily Mail, 20 April)*

# MR. ISMAY AND THE WOMEN.

*From Our Special Correspondent.*
*PLYMOUTH, Monday.*

Today the stewardesses and stewards of the *Titanic* told the stories of their escape. Being more amenable to official control than the trade unionist firemen and sailors, the men had spent the night at the dock station and the women at an hotel, and they were permitted to tell their experience only after making formal depositions of their evidence.

Their statements show very clearly how little the imminence of danger was realized until the ship

158

actually began to tilt downwards for the plunge. The first boats left the ship's side half empty because the passengers said they would not leave the *Titanic* to go in a cockleshell, said Mrs. Gould, a first-class stewardess on B deck. "Mrs. Wallace, the steerage matron, even went back to her cabin after seeing her passengers into their boats and locked herself in, remarking 'I am going to stay where I am safe.' She was a nervous little woman."

"Mrs. Snape, too, a second cabin stewardess, a woman of twenty-one, who had left a baby behind in Southampton, shook hands with her passengers as they got in, but would not go in a boat herself."

Among the passengers in Mrs. Gould's section was Mr. Bruce Ismay. She saw him on deck when she went up and he put her into a boat. He was wearing an overcoat over pyjamas. "I saw him again in a boat near to ours when we were rowing up to the *Carpathia*," said Mrs. Gould. "He was sitting on the gunwale at the stern of the boat. His face was blue with cold and he sat perfectly still, staring straight in front of him, expressionless like a statue."

Mrs. Maclaren was another stewardess whom Mr. Ismay put in a boat. When Mr. Ismay told them to get in the boat they said, "We are not passengers; we are members of the crew." "It doesn't matter," Mr. Ismay replied. "You are women, and I wish you to get in."

Mrs. Martin, a tall, graceful woman, who was a first stewardess, told how, when the steward came to call them to get up and put on lifebelts, they thought it was a practical joke. Curious traits of character were instanced in the story told me by a steward. He told of a woman in his boat who complained that she was unduly crowded and appealed to the officer in charge to prevent her from being crushed. There was a sad tale of a Portuguese bride on her honeymoon who knew no English, and when she saw the *Carpathia* thought that the boats were returning to the *Titanic*, in which she had left her husband. An Italian waiter jumped from the top deck into one boat as it was lowered and broke the ankle of a lady, Mrs. Parish.

# THE SPHERE

AN ILLUSTRATED NEWSPAPER FOR THE HOME

With which is incorporated
"BLACK & WHITE"

Volume XLIX.  No. 639.  | REGISTERED AT THE GENERAL | POST OFFICE AS A NEWSPAPER | London, April 20, 1912.  [WITH SUPPLEMENT]  Price Sixpence.

### THE GREATEST WRECK IN THE WORLD'S MARITIME HISTORY—THE LOSS OF THE "TITANIC"

The above composite picture is given not as an actual document but as some realisation of essential factors in the loss of the great White Star liner.  Seeing that she sank at 2.20 a.m. on Sunday night no actual records of the vessel's meeting with the ice are likely to be forthcoming.  The icebergs shown here are reproduced from photographs obtained off Newfoundland.  The size of them of course varies very considerably according to the season.  The height of the vessel's bow above water-line would be about 60 ft.  The opening shown near the top was a cable socket for a bow hawser, used when entering harbours

# THE GREATEST SHIPWRECK IN THE WORLD

THE SUMPTUOUS APPOINTMENTS OF THE "TITANIC"—THE PARISIAN CAFE WITH ITS TRELLISWORK AND CLIMBING PLANTS

**A Sitting-room of a Private Suite on the "Titanic"**

Showing marble fireplace and costly electrical fittings

# History : The Loss of the "Titanic."

BOATS WHICH RESCUED SOME OF THE PASSENGERS—SEEN TO THE LEFT OF PROMENADE DECK

**The Swimming Bath on the "Titanic"**

The biggest of its kind on any vessel

*(LLOYDS WEEKLY NEWS. APRIL 21st.)*

## PET DOGS SAVED.

Five women survivors saved their pet dogs, and another has saved a little pig, which she regards as her mascot.

*(Mirror, 22 April 1912)*

## STRONG FEELING AGAINST MR. ISMAY.

**White Star Chairman Resents "Brutal Unfairness" of Inquiry.**

**ORDERED TO STAY.**

**Thrilling Evidence of Titanic's Junior Wireless Operator.**

**SECOND OFFICER'S ESCAPE.**

**Steward's Strange Story of Conversation Between Two Look-Outs.**

The United States Senate inquiry into the causes of the loss of the *Titanic* will be resumed today at Washington, the New York inquiry having terminated.

The seriousness of the Senatorial investigation into the loss of the *Titanic* was disclosed on Friday evening (says *Reuter*), when Senator Smith at first flatly refused to permit any of the officers or crew of the *Titanic* to sail on the Red Star liner *Lapland* despite the protests of Mr. Burlingham, counsel for the White Star Line.

Later, as the result of a conference, it was decided to permit all but twelve of the crew and the four rescued officers — Messrs. Lightoller, Pitman, Boxhall and Lowe — to depart, but not to allow Mr. Bruce Ismay to leave.

Although Mr. Ismay urged that he should be allowed to go for the present, pleading that he was on the verge of a collapse, his request was not granted. Mr. Ismay, discussing the work of the investigating committee with interviewers today, described it as "brutally unfair." He said: —

"I cannot understand this inquiry. They're going at it in a manner that seems unjust, and the injustice lies the heaviest on me. Why, I cannot even protect myself by having my counsel to ask questions. Don't misunderstand me by thinking I mean questions calculated to upset witnesses — on the contrary, questions intended simply to evolve meanings."

## "MY CONSCIENCE IS CLEAR."

"I have searched my mind with the deepest care. I am sure I did nothing I should not have done. My conscience is clear. I took a chance of escape when it came to me. I did not seek it. Every woman and child had been cared for before I left the boat, and more, all the men within reach had been cared for before I took my turn."

"It is true, I'm president of the company, but I didn't consider myself any different from the rest of the passengers. I took no other man's place."

During the debate in the Senate at Washington today on the resolution concerning the regulation of ocean traffic, Mr. McCumber took occasion to register a protest against "the trial, conviction, sentencing and execution of one who is connected with the *Titanic* on the floor of the Senate yesterday without fair, honest and full consideration."

Mr. McCumber was evidently referring to the speech of Mr. Raynor, in which he made a violent attack on Mr. Bruce Ismay. — *Reuter.*

## SENATOR SMITH AND MR. ISMAY.

NEW YORK, April 20. — The investigation here concluded today, and Mr. Bruce Ismay and other White Star officials have been subpnaed by the Senate Committee to appear in Washington on Monday.

Mr. *Cottam,* the wireless operator of the *Carpathia,* who appeared before the committee yesterday, was further examined. He stated that after picking up the *Titanic's* boats, the *Carpathia* at first made towards Halifax, but afterwards changed her course for New York.

He denied having sent any message stating that all the passengers were safe, or that the *Titanic* was in tow.

Owing to the constant dispatch of messages he had had less than ten hours' sleep in three days. He gave full details of the disaster to the *Baltic,* which was then steaming toward the scene of the wreck. This was round about half-past ten on the Monday morning.

Mr. Bride, the assistant wireless operator of the *Titanic,* who was wheeled in a chair, both feet having been injured in the course of his escape, was also called.

Perhaps the most interesting part of his evidence related to the steamer *Frankfurt*. He said that twenty minutes after Phillips, the chief operator, had sent out the C.Q.D. signal, the *Frankfurt* operator interrupted to ask what was the matter.

By that time the *Carpathia* was on her way to the rescue, and although, judging by the strength of the signals, the *Frankfurt* was the nearer of the two vessels, Phillips, remarking that the man was a fool, replied, telling him to keep out.

Bride explained that Phillips' idea was that he preferred to trust to the *Carpathia* than to send out a message accepting the help of a vessel which had been so much slower in responding, and thus, perhaps, lead the *Carpathia* to think she was not wanted.

"He preferred to hang on to the certainty."

Mr. Bride, in concluding his evidence, said that he saw the captain, who had not donned a life preserver, on the bridge until just before the *Titanic* went down.

The water had reached the bridge and the captain jumped into the sea.

*(Mirror, 22 April 1912)*

# CAPTAIN SMITH'S LAST ORDER.

In his evidence Mr. Lightoller, second officer (says a *Reuter's* special message), said he was in the sea with a lifebelt an hour and a half.

When the *Titanic* sank he was in the officers' quarters. All but one of the lifeboats were gone. Mr. Murdoch (the first officer) was trying to launch it.

Did you see Mr. Ismay then? — No.

When did you see him? — When he was uncovering the boats. He was standing on the boat-deck.

When you saw Mr. Ismay twenty minutes after the collision, were any other passengers near him? — I did not see anyone in particular, but there might have been.

"Although ice had been reported," he added, "I was not anxious about it."

You did not post an additional look – out? – No.

Mr. Murdoch relieved him at ten o'clock. The weather was calm and clear, and stars on the horizon were observable.

After the crash he found Mr. Murdoch and Captain Smith on the bridge. He last saw Captain Smith walking the bridge.

What was the last order of Captain Smith? – "Put the women and children into the boats and lower away."

What did you do? – I obeyed the order.

How were the passengers selected to fill the boats? – By sex.

Who determined who should go? – I did. Whenever I saw a woman I put her in, except the stewardesses. I turned those back.

**SUCKED UNDER AND BLOWN UPWARDS.**

In accounting for the saving of so many of the crew, Mr. Lightoller declared that he had especially inquired and had ascertained that out of every six persons picked up from the water five were either firemen or stewards.

In describing his own escape, the officer recounted how he stood in the officers' quarters and dived as the ship sank. He was sucked under and held fast against a blower.

Then came a terrific gust up through the blower, due probably to a boiler explosion. He was blown clear, and came to the surface near a boat.

*(Mirror, 22 April 1912)*

## "WARNED OF ICEBERG."

NEW YORK. April 21. – Mr. Whiteley, a first class steward of the *Titanic*, lying in St. Vincent's Hospital with frozen feet, tells of extraordinary experiences.

He says he overheard a conversation between two of the crow's nest lookouts on the lifeboat in which he had taken refuge.

He heard one of them say that fifteen minutes before the *Titanic* struck he had reported to Mr. Murdoch on the bridge that he fancied he saw an iceberg, and twice afterwards the lookout warned the first officer.

They were most indignant that no attention was paid. "No wonder Mr. Murdoch shot himself," said one of the lookouts. —*Reuter's* Special Service.

*(Mirror, 22 April 1912)*

## BRITISH WOMEN'S NOBLE SYMPATHY.

**£13,000 Already Subscribed to "Daily Mail" Fund.**

**REPAYING A DEBT.**

**Rich and Poor Alike Help Relatives of 'Titanic' Heroes.**

**ORPHANS' PENNIES.**

**Money from Continent as Well as from All Over the United Kingdom.**

The women of England have been touched to the heart by the quiet, self-sacrificing heroism of men on the *Titanic,* and they have subscribed the magnificent sum of over £12,000 in response to The Daily Mail's appeal on behalf of the widows, orphans and relatives of those dependent upon the heroes.

Directly it was known that the *Titanic's* boats contained "mainly women and children," the heroism of her crew was impressed on every mind. It was proof positive that the men on board had stood quietly aside, and had willingly embraced death that the women and children might live.

Now that the full story of the catastrophe is known, we learn of nothing that mars the magnificence of the dead or lessens the greatness of the sacrifice.

It is ever the same heroic tale of the men, quietly, but as the natural thing to do, remaining on the riven liner to die that the women and children might live.

Who can read of their heroism without a lump in the throat or a thrill of pride? Certainly not members of that sex for whom these heroes died, and it is to them that The Daily Mail makes an especial appeal.

They that can show their appreciation of this supreme sacrifice by seeing to it that the

# IMPRESSIVE MEMORIAL SERVICE FOR THE TITANIC VICTIM

The scene outside St. Paul's as the Lord Mayor was leaving. The Lord Mayor's coach and the other civic carriages are seen waiting

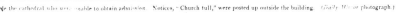

de the cathedral who were unable to obtain admission. Notices, " Church full," were posted up outside the building. *(Daily Mirror photograph.)*

Waiting for

# T ST. PAUL'S WHILE SOUTHAMPTON MOURNS HER DEAD.

of the cathedral. The photograph gives a good idea of the crowd which gathered outside the building. *(Daily Mirror photograph.)*

outhampton.

Anxious faces watch the names of the crew who have been rescued being posted outside the White Star

outhampton yesterday.

kindred of such men do not suffer want, and by making ample pecuniary provision for the needs of their widows and families.

All those who can afford it, let them give a contribution, large or small, in honour of the illustrious dead, and to show their practical and needed sympathy. It is needed. No matter how small, it will be heartily welcome.

And that the women of England do appreciate the superb self-sacrifice of these heroes of the *Titanic* is borne out by their instant and noble response to The Daily Mail appeal.

**8,000 CONTRIBUTORS.**

Money is not only coming in from all over the kingdom, but from the Continent as well now. It is a splendid tribute to a splendid deed.

The total number of contributors is 8,000 odd, 4,000 of whom sent money on Saturday. Although the amounts received are somewhat smaller, the number of contributors daily increases, and Saturday's number almost doubles that of Friday.

The anonymous gifts received range from £500 to 6d.

The letters which pour in show that the response to the appeal is a national one. They come from all classes. A few extracts will show the genuine feeling and sympathy which have been aroused.

One letter came from the Infant Orphan Asylum, Wanstead, and enclosed £1.14s. 6d. The headmistress added: —

"Fourteen and sixpence of this is the joint offering of the orphan girls of this institution. Their ages vary from four to fifteen, and they were all so anxious to show their sympathy with these newly made orphans that I had to restrain their generosity."

"Some of them have very few pennies of their own, and I could not allow anything to be given by those who had less than 3d., because they have to pay for the postage of their letters to their mothers and relations."

"Their contribution, you will understand, was made up chiefly of halfpennies, pennies, and two-pences."

Another letter, which enclosed 10s., shows how much the simple heroism has touched the hearts of all women.

"It is," says the writer, "a very tiny sum to send, and in no way expresses the heartfelt grief and sympathy for the distressed and needy ones left to fight life's battle, nor can it express the admiration felt for the noble men who faced their fate so bravely."

"We are needy ourselves, and in ill-health, and so not able to earn just now. If we could, we would do more. It comes from a widow and two daughters (the youngest of whom is just on fifty years old), who know what earning daily bread means, and who know what sorrow and sickness and need mean."

A special message from the sea was: —
"Please add £36, which we send with deepest sympathy from captain, officers and crew of steam yacht *Doris*, Monaco."

Mrs. Ernest J. Thal, who the previous day had sent twenty-five guineas, wired yesterday saying "Please make it fifty guineas."

An American, Mr. Edward J. Price, of Chicago, wrote: —
"As an American traveller who has crossed the Atlantic many times, I fully realize and appreciate the sacrifice made by the officers and crew of the *Titanic* in the discharge of their duty. I enclose cheque for £50."

Several sums of money subscribing to this fund have been received by The Daily Mirror. They have been forwarded to The Daily Mail, in which paper they will be acknowledged.

Boy scouts worked hard at Hyde Park Corner yesterday collecting money towards the *Titanic* fund, awaiting the fashionable throng which flowed through the gates.

Dogs were being used as collectors for the fund, and one appeared to be doing good business yesterday in the charge of a little girl. He wore his collecting box on his back.

*(Mirror, 22 April 1912)*

RESCUERS OF THE TITANIC SURVIVORS TO HELP THE WIDOWS AND ORPHANS.

After rescuing the survivors of the Titanic, the officers and crew of the Cunarder Carpathia thought out schemes for helping the bereaved, and a match has been arranged between the liner's football team and a Hungarian eleven after the liner's arrival at Trieste. (1) The Carpathia team. (2) Captain Rostron (the centre figure seated) and his officers. Both groups were taken on the liner by a *Daily Mirror* staff photographer.

## THE PRINCE'S GIFT.

The Mansion House Fund for the relief of the *Titanic* sufferers now totals upwards of £72,000.

The latest contributions include 250 guineas from the Prince of Wales, £500 from the Gackwar of Baroda, fifty guineas from the Attorney-General, £500 each from Messrs. John Brown and Co. and William P. Bonbright and Co. and 250 guineas from Messrs. Barnato Brothers.

A big City firm which has contributed liberally to the fund suggests that in its distribution the circumstances of first and second class passengers should be considered as well as those of the crew and third class. They say: —

There must undoubtedly be some among the two former who

# "We Slammed-to the Watertight Door Quick."

CYLINDER SUPPLYING POWER

DOOR

HAND GEAR WITH LONG VERTICAL SHAFT FOR CLOSING DOOR AS DEMANDED BY THE BOARD OF TRADE

DOOR OPEN SO GREAT IS THE POWER FOR CLOSING THAT ANY OBSTRUCTION CAN BE FORCED OUT OF THE WAY

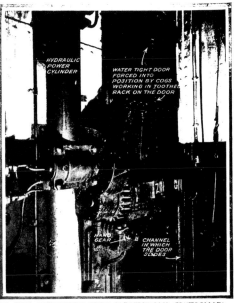

HYDRAULIC POWER CYLINDER

WATER TIGHT DOOR FORCED INTO POSITION BY COGS WORKING IN TOOTHED RACK ON THE DOOR

HAND GEAR

CHANNEL IN WHICH THE DOOR SLIDES

TWO VIEWS OF A HYDRAULIC TYPE OF COMPARTMENT DOOR (THE "TITANIC'S" WERE ELECTRICALLY CONTROLLED)

## WHAT HAPPENED DOWN BELOW : *An Eye-witness's Story.*

¶ "*The Morning Post*" printed in its issue of the 29th ult. one of the most interesting narratives yet obtained. It describes what happened to a foreman of the firemen.

"We were working away and thinking our watch was nearly up when all of a sudden the starboard side of the ship came in on us. It burst in like a big gun going off, and the water came pouring in. It swilled our legs, and we made a dash into the next section and slammed-to the watertight door quick. There was no time to waste. My section was about one-third of the ship's length from the bows, and we found that the whole of the starboard side was smashed in as far aft as our section. Well, we got into the next section aft and there we stayed, for, being on watch, it was our business to stay. I did not think, and nobody thought at the time, that

the *Titanic* could sink. There was a poor fellow named Shepherd, an engineer, who joined at Southampton, whose leg was broken when the side was stove in. We carried him into the pump-room near our section, and there he lay with his broken leg, wild because he was unable to be of any further assistance. There would have been time at first to carry him up if we had thought the ship would sink. I don't know whether he was carried up afterwards, but at any rate we know he was not saved, for there were thirty-six engineers aboard and not a man of them was saved.

"They talked in America of millionaire heroes, but what of the engineers? They stuck to their work to the last, and went down with the ship. They kept the engines going until three minutes before the *Titanic* went out of sight. They were the heroes I think. Those who in the ordinary way would have gone off duty stayed on the couple of extra hours, and they died like men. Some time after I and my chaps got in to the next section most of the stokers were sent up on deck, but I went up and brought twenty of them down again to keep the boilers going. Afterwards they were sent up again, and three engineers and I had orders to stop where we were. The engineers were there to work the section pumps to try and pump the water out of the section from which we had been driven. Harvey was the engineer in charge of us, Wilson was the second, and Shepherd was the third. While we were there the electric light went out, and I was watching, groping along the alleyway to fetch some lamps. When I got back the lights were on again, and we found they had been switched over from

dynamos to the emergency dynamos, which were situated in the fourth funnel—a dummy funnel—so we had light again and we stuck to the job. Then all of a sudden the water came with a rush into where we were. How it came I don't know, but in it came, and Harvey, the engineer, said to me, 'Get up on deck.' I was nearly swilled off my feet but I managed to get out and I reached the deck beneath the boat deck. I knew then that the ship must sink, for the forecastle head was under water, but men were leaning up against the saloon walls smoking cigarettes, and no one seemed alarmed. I dare not say what I believed for fear of causing a panic. A lifeboat was hanging from the davits, and the boatswain, who knew me as I had sailed with him in other ships, said to me, 'You go in this boat and pull an oar.'

**The Small Starboard Light on the "Titanic"**

The starboard light occupies a corner of the grey-painted space on the side of the captain's bridge.

**How the Captain Makes Himself Heard**

A megaphone becomes more than ever necessary as the height of the bridge adds to the din.

have perished — travelling, probably, on business and with appearances to keep up — whose loss brings nearly as great destitution to homes and families as those others towards whom public sympathy naturally turns first.

Among the numerous entertainments, the proceeds of which will be devoted to the sufferers, are: —

Miss Marie George's Anglo-American concert at the Aeolian Hall — May 3.

Matinee at Covent Garden — May 14.

Alhambra matinee, at which the Lord Mayor* and Sheriffs will attend — This afternoon.

Coliseum matinee — May 1.

Hippodrome matinee — April 30.

About £80 will be handed over to the fund as the result of the special matinee performance of "The Military Girl" by Charles and Muriel Scott-Gatty at the Savoy Theatre on Saturday.

*(Mirror, April 22)*
*(From Our Special Correspondent.)*

SOUTHAMPTON, April 21. — Sister ship to the ill-fated *Titanic*, the White Star liner *Olympic* entered Southampton docks at 2 a.m. She is a day late in arriving through having had to go far out of her course in the effort to take help to the *Titanic.*

The *Olympic* is due to leave again at noon on Wednesday, and a small army of men must work night and day to get her ready for the voyage.

The very first business undertaken was the stowing and fitting up on the top deck of no fewer than forty new lifeboats and collapsible boats and about a dozen rafts, which are an addition to the sixteen lifeboats she has hitherto carried.

One squad of men was busily engaged today unloading boats from trucks on a siding. Other men were testing, stretching and soaking the new collapsible boats in the water, and yet a third squad was measuring and fitting up the allotted places for the boats on the top deck.

*(Mirror, 22 April 1912)*

## SAVED BY TEN MINUTES.

If the *Titanic* had received the fatal blow from the iceberg at 11.50 p.m. instead of 11.40 p.m. not a single soul would have been saved!

BOATS FOR EVERYONE ON THE OLYMPIC: SHIPS' OFFICERS LAST TRIBUTE TO TITANIC HEROES

A barge load of collapsible boats ready to be placed on board the Olympic. When that vessel next sails from England for the States she will have enough boats for everyone on board.

"The disaster is a mighty lesson against over security and confidence and trust in the strength of machinery and money," said the Bishop of Winchester in preaching at the memorial service for the victims at St. Mary's Church, Southampton, on Saturday. Above, ships' officers are seen arriving at the church.—(*Daily Mirror* photograph.)

*Sheet music was the most popular and affordable entertainment for most people. With the Titanic sinking, music publishers had a ready market.*

No. 172

WITH TONIC SOL-FA.

This Song may be Sung in Public without Fee or License except at Theatres or Music Halls.

# THE SHIP THAT WILL NEVER RETURN

## (The Loss of the "Titanic.")

SONG

AND

POEM

Written & Composed

by

# F. V. S⊤. CLAIR.

LONDON,

E. MARKS & SON,

125, MARE STREET, HACKNEY, N.E.

Ten minutes more and the wireless operator on board the *Carpathia* would have been in bed, the *Titanic's* call for help would not have been heard, and the 705 passengers who went away in lifeboats would have perished

It was solely because the *Carpathia's* wireless operator happened by chance to have delayed for ten minutes turning in on the fateful Sunday night that he was at his post and received the *Titanic's* urgent signal for help.

"Had he gone to rest, as usual," said Dr. Kemp, the *Carpathia's* physician, "there would have been no survivors."

Most people will be amazed to learn that on many ships only one wireless operator is carried, and consequently during several hours of each day there is no one in charge of the apparatus to receive messages.

"It is nothing less than a public scandal," a Marconi expert said to The Daily Mirror yesterday. "Wireless telegraphy is installed in a ship primarily for the purpose of saving life, but, as a matter of fact, the apparatus is regarded as more of a luxury for passengers.

**WHEN SHIPS CANNOT HEAR.**

"Only on the long-distance boats — the boats fitted with the most powerful apparatus — are two operators employed.

"They take turns at the apparatus in four-hour watches, so that there is always one man on duty to send or receive messages. But on the short-distance boats — those fitted with apparatus carrying up to 200 miles — there is only one operator, and therefore when he retires to rest, there is no one to take his place. The ship might be within ten miles of a sinking vessel and yet the distress signal would not be heard."

"Clearly this is a matter sufficiently grave to call for the strictest investigation."

"Every vessel fitted with wireless ought to be compelled by the Board of Trade regulations to carry two operators, so that there should always be somebody on duty in case of emergency."

*(Mirror, 22 April 1912)*

# PASSENGERS WHO WERE SAVED.

The following is an alphabetical list of "Titanic" passengers who were picked up by the "Carpathia" a taken to New York, as cabled to the White Star Company's London office:

Abbott, Mrs. Rose
Abelseth, Olans
Abelseth, Koran
Abelson, Mrs. Hanna
Abrahamson, August
Ajal, Bemora
Akelseph, Alous
Aks, Filly
Aks, Leah
Allen, Miss Elizabeth Walton
Allison, Master, and Nurse
Aloum, Badmoura
Anderson, Corla
Anderson, Mr. Harry
Andrews, Miss Cornlia I.
Angle, Mrs. Florence
Anton, Louisa
Appleton, Mrs. E. D.
Argenia, Mrs. Genova, and two children
Artonon, V.
Asplund, William
Assim, Marriam
Astlund, Selma
Astlund, Felix
Astor, Mrs. J. J., and Maid
Aubert, Mrs. N., and Maid
Balls, Mrs. Ada A.
Barawich, George
Barawich, Harren
Barawich, Marian
Barkworth, Mr. A. H.
Barlson, Rinat
Bassette, Miss
Batman, Emily
Paxter, Mrs. James
Beane, Mr. Edward
Beane, Mrs. Ethel
Becker, Mrs. A. O., and Three Children
Beckwith, Mr. R. L.
Beckwith, Mrs. R. L.
Beesley, Mr. Laurence
Bentham, Miss Lillian W.
Billa, Maggie
Bing, Lee
Bishop, Mr. D. H.
Bishop, Mrs. D. H.
Blank, Mr. Henry
Bockstrom, Masy
Behr, Mr. K. H.
Boklin, Marie
Boklin, Eugene

Boklin, Helena
Boklin, Latifa
Bolos, Monthora
Bonnell, Miss Caroline
Bonnell, Miss Elizabeth
Boias, John
Bowen, Miss
Bowerman, Miss Elsie
Bradley, Bridget
Bridgett, Ros
Brayton, Mr. George
Brown, Miss E.
Brown, Miss Mildred
Brown, Mrs. J. J.
Brown, Mrs. J. M.
Bryhl, Miss Dagmar
Buckley, Daniel
Bucknell, Mrs. W. and maid
Burns, Miss O. M.
Bury, Mr. Richard
Buss, Miss Kate
Bystrom, Mr. Karolina
Calderhead, Mr. E. P.
Caldwell, Mr. Albert F.
Caldwell, Mrs. Sylvia
Caldwell, Master Alden G.
Cameron, Miss Clear
Cardell, Mrs. Churchill
Cardeza, Mrs. J. W. M.
Cardeza, Mr. T. D. M.
Carr, Ellen
Carter, Mr. Wm. E.
Carter, Mrs. Wm. E.
Carter, Miss Lucile
Carter, Master Wm. C. T.
Casem, Boyan
Cassen, Masef
Cassebeer, Mrs. H. A.
Cavendish, Mrs. T. W. and maid
Chaffee, Mrs. Herbert F.
Chambers, Mr. N. C.
Chambers, Mrs. N. C.
Chandanson, Miss Victorine
Charles, Mr. Wm. E.
Charters, John
Cheang, Foo
Cherry, Miss Gladys
Chevré, Mr. Paul
Chibnall, Mrs. E. M. Bowerman
Chip, Chang

Choonsson, John
Christy, Mrs. Alice
Christy, Miss Juli
Clark, Mrs. Walter M.
Clarke, Miss Ada Maria
Cohen, Gust
Collett, Mr. D.
Collett, Mrs. Stuart
Collier, Gosham
Collyer, Mrs. Charlotte
Collyer, Miss Marjorie
Compton, Miss S. R.
Compton, Master A. T.
Connolly, Kate
Coutts, Neville
Coutts, Will
Coutts, Winne
Cornell, Mrs. R. C.
Cribb, L. M.
Crosby, Mrs. Edward G.
Crosby, Miss Harriett
Cummings, Mrs. John Bradley
Dahl, Charles
Daly, Chas.
Daly, Eugene
Daly, Marsella
Daly, P. B.
Daniel, Mr. Robert W.
Daniel, Sara
Darnell, Elizabeth
Davidson, Mary
Davidson, Mrs. Thornton
Davis, Mrs. Agnes
Davis, Master John M.
Davis, Miss Mary
Dean, Ettie, and two children
Deanodelman, Delia
Devany, Margaret
de Villiers, Mrs. B.
Dick, Mr. A. A.
Dick, Mrs. A. A.
Dodge, Mr. Washington
Dodge, Mrs. Washington
Dodge, Master Washington
Doling, Mrs. Ada
Doling, Miss Elsie
Domunder, Theodore
Dorking, Edward
Douglas, Mrs. F. C.
Douglas, Mrs. W. D.
Doyt, Agnes (or Mrs. A. A. Dick)

Drachstedt, Baron von
Draplin, Jennie
Drew, Mrs. Lulu
Drew, Master M.
Driscoll, Miss Bridget
Dugenon, Joseph
Duran, Miss Florentina
Duran, Miss Asimcion
Dyker, Elizabeth
Earnshew, Mrs. Boulton
Eldegrek, Leonek
Eliass, Nicola
Emanuel, Ethel
Emearmaslon, Mr. Renardo
Endres, Miss Caroline
Eustis, Miss E. M.
Falnai, Ermaulman
Fastman, Daniel
Faunthorpe, Mrs. Lizzie
Ferole, Luigi
Flegenhein, Mrs. A.
Flynn, Mr. J. I.
Fortune, Mrs. Mark
Fortune, Miss Ethel
Fortune, Miss Alice
Fortune, Miss Mabel
Frauenthal, Mr. T. G.
Frauenthal, Dr. Henry W.
Frauenthal, Mrs. Henry W.
Frolicher, Max
Frolicher, Mrs.
Frolicher, Miss Marguerite
Fulwell, Mrs. J.
Gallenagh, Kate
Garside, Miss Ethel
Gibson, Mrs. L.
Gibson, Miss D.
Glynn, Mary
Goldenberg, Mr. Samuel
Goldenberg, Mrs. Samuel
Goldsmith, Emily
Goldsmith, Frank
Gracie, Colonel Archibald
Graham, Mrs. Wm. G.
Graham, Miss Margaret
Greenfield, Mrs. L. D.
Greenfield, Mr. W. B.
Hakaonen, Line
Hamalainer, Mrs. Anna and infant
Hamann, Maria
Hankonen, Elina
Hanson, Jenny

THE DEATHLESS STORY OF THE "TITANIC."

The following, who had "signed on," did not go on the voyage by the vessel:—
A. Haveling,
W. Sims,
V. Penny,
C. Blake,
A. Slade,
Thos. Slade,
D. Slade,
W. Burrows,
J. Shaw,
F. Holden,
B. Brewer,
E. di Napoli,

B. Fish,
P. Kilford,
W. W. Dawes,
P. Ettlinger,
R. Fisher,
A. Manley,
W. J. Mewe,
P. Dawkins,
F T. Bowman,
J. Coffey.

The following were taken on as substitutes :—

Renny Dodds, Queen's Park Terrace.

L. Kinsella, Canal Walk.
A. Geer, Stamford Street, Chapel.
E. Hosgood, Wooley Road, Euston.
W. Lloyd, Orchard Place.
H. Witt, Lower Cottage Street.
D. Black, Sailors' Home.
A. Windebank, Wyndham Place.
A. Locke, Portswood Road.
J. Brown, Desborough Road, Eastleigh.
F. O'Connor, Tower Place, Bargate Street.
W. Dickson, Oriental Terrace.
T. Gordon, Sailors' Home.

Hanson, Miss Jeannie
Harder, Mr. George A.
Harder, Mrs. George A.
Harper, Mr. Henry Sleeper
  and Manservant
Harper, Mrs. Henry Sleeper
Harper, Miss Nina
Harris, Mr. George
Harris, Mrs. Henry B.
Hart, Mrs. Esther
Hart, Miss Eva
Haven, Mr. H.
Hawksford, Mr. W. J.
Hays, Mrs. Charles M.

Hokkronen, Ellen
Hold, Mrs. Annie
Holverson, Mrs. A. O.
Hosono, Mr. Masabumi
Howard, Mary
Hoyt, Mr. Frederick M.
Hoyt, Mrs. Frederick M.
Hyman, Abraham
Ilett, Miss Bertha
Ismay, Mr.
Jacobson, Mrs. Amy F.
Jacques, Mrs.
Jansen, Carl
Jap, Jules

Jousef, Hannah
Jousef, Mariam
Jousef, Thamine
Jusefa, Carl
Jusefa, Manera
Karlson, Einar
Keane, Miss Nora A.
Kelly, Annie
Kelly, Mary
Kelly, Mrs. F.
Kennedy, John
Kenton, Miriam
Kenyon, Mrs. F. R.
Kesorny, Florence

Laroche, Miss Louise
Leach, Miss Jessie
Leader, Mrs. F. A.
Lehman, Miss Bertha
Lesneur, Mrs. Gustav
Lines, Mrs. Ernest H.
Lines, Miss Mary C.
Lindstroem, Mrs. J.
Lindquist, Eihar
Longley, Miss Gretchen F.
Louch, Mrs. Alice
Ludgais, Amo
Lulu, Nella
Lundegreen, Aurora

**BOAT DRILL ON A WHITE STAR LINER.**

The first photograph shows a boat being lowered away, with the officers and crew in cork jackets. The second photograph gives a general view of the boat deck, with the boats at the davits ready for lowering. The bottom photograph is that of the crew at quarters swinging out a lifeboat.

Hays, Miss Margaret
Hedman, Oscar
Hemvig, Croft
Herman, Mrs. Jane
Herman, Miss Kate
Herman, Miss Alice
Herronen, Hilda
Hewlett, Mrs. Mary D.
Hillsfrom, Hilda
Hip, Ching
Hippach, Mrs. Ida S.
Hippach, Miss Jean
Hocking, Mrs. Elizabeth
Hocking, Miss Nellie
Hoffman, Mr. Lolo
Hoffman, Mr. Lones
Hogeboom, Mrs. John C.

Joblom, S.
Jenson, Carl
Jermyn, Miss Mary
Jermyn, Annie
Jerserac, Inav
Johannson, Oscar
Johanson, Verendt
Johnnanson, Alice
Johnnanson, Elenora
Johnnanson, Oscar L.
Johnsen, Harold
Johnsila, Eric
Josburg, Siline
Joseph, Katherine
Joseph, Mary
Joseph, Nigel
Jousef, George

Kimball, Mr. E. N.
Kimball, Mrs. E. N.
Kink, Louisa
Kinorn, Krikoraen
Kockovean, Erickau
Kolsbottel, Anna
Koucher, Miss Emile
Krigesne, Jos
Kuram, Anna
Kuram, Frans
Lam, Hah (Ali)
Lamore, Mrs. Amelia
Lang, Fang
Lang, Hee
Lare, Eleoneh
Laroche, Mrs.
Laroche, Miss Simonne

Lunden, Olga
Lundstrom, Imrie
Madigan, Maggie
Madill, Mrs. Georgette Alexandra
Maioni, Miss Ruberta
Mallet, Mrs.
Mallet, Master A.
Mallie, Bertha
Maloney, Mrs. R.
Manga, Margaret
Manga, Mr. Paula
Manv, Juvio
Maran, Bertha
Massey, Marion
Marechal, Pierre
Marlkarl, Hauwakan

Marrigan, Margaret
Marrion (Mannión), Margaret
Marshall, Mr.
Marshall, Mrs.
Marshall, Miss Katey
Marson, Adele
Marvin, Mrs. D. W.
Matheson, Frithiof
Mathgo, Karl
Mauman, Hanne
Meyer, Mrs. Edgar G.
McCarthy, Katie
McCoy, Bernard
McCoy, Agnes
McCoy, Alice
McCoy, Ernest
McDearmont, Miss Leila
McDermott, Delia
McCormick, Thomas
McGovan, Mary
McGovan, Anna
McGowan, Miss A.
McGough, Mr. J. R.
McKaren, John
Mellers, Mr. William
Mellinger, Mrs. Elizabeth, and Child
Merigan (Harrigan)
Messelmolk, Anna
Messelmolk, G. D.
Messewacker, Guilliam
Messewacker, Arcina
Midtago, Carl
Minahan, Mrs. W. E.
Minahan, Miss Daisy
Missulmona, Amina
Mock, Mrs. Philippe
Mocklaire, Ellen
Modelmot, Celia
Montharck, Annie
Montharck, Gurio
Montharck, Halim
Moran, Bertha
Moore, Belle
Moore, Neciman
Morgan, Mr.
Morgan, Mrs., and Maid (Miss Francatelli)
Moss, Albert
Moubarck, Burns
Muhun, Erikorian
Mullen, Kate
Mulder, Theodore
Mulvehill, Bertha
Murphy, Kate
Murphy, Maggie J.
Murphy, Nora
Naseraill, Miss Adelia
Neckard, Said
Neket, Marin

Nelso, Helmina J.
Nelson, Bertha
Nelson, Carlo
Nern, Hannah
Newell, Miss Alice
Newell, Miss Madeline
Nevatey, Margaret
Newsom, Miss Helen
Nicolo, Jancoli
Nicolo, Elias
Niskenen, John
Nouberek, Halin
Noubarek, Jiron
Nubulaket, Samula
Nye, Mrs. Elizabeth
Nyhan, Anna
Nysten, Anna
Oamb, Nicola
O'Brien, Hanna
O'Dwyer, Nelly
O'Keefe, Patrick
O'Leary, Nora
Olivia, Miss
Ollmson, Sourly
Olman, Virma
Olsen, Arthur
Ongalen, Helena
Ornout, Mr. Alfred F.
Osman, Mara
Osplund, C. Anderson
Oumson,
Oxenham, Mr. Thomas
Padro, Mr. Julian
Pallas, Mr. Emilo
Parrish, Mrs. L. Davis
Parsons, Ernest
Patos, Coterina
Patro, Hobesa
Penasco, Mrs. Victor
Pears, Mrs. Thos.
Person, Eames
Pericault, Miss A.
Peuchen, Major Arthur
Phillips, Miss Alice
Picard, Benoit
Pinksy, Miss Rosa
Portaluppi, Mr. Emilio
Potter, Mrs. Thomas, jun.
Quick, Mrs. Jane
Quick, Miss Phyllis
Quick, Miss Vera W.
Ranelt, Miss Appie
Reardon, Hannah
Reibon, Anna
Renago, Mrs. Naman J.
Renouf, Mrs. Lillie
Rheims, Mr. George
Richards, Mrs. Emily
Richards, Master William
Richards, Master George
Ridsdale, Miss Lucy
Robert, Mrs. Edward S.

Rogers, Miss Selina
Rolmane, Mr. C.
Rosenbaum, Miss
Roth, Sarah
Rothes, the Countess of, and Maid (Miss Mayoni)
Rothschild, Mrs. M.
Rugg, Miss Emily
Ryan, Edward
Ryerson, Mrs. Arthur
Ryerson, Miss
Ryerson, Miss Susan
Ryerson, Master
Saalfield, Mr. Adolph
Saleman, Mr. A. L.
Salkjelsock, Anna
Sandstrom, Agnes
Sandstrom, Beatrice
Sandstrom, Margaret
Sap, Jules
Schabert, Mrs. Paul
Schurbint, John
Schurlinch, Jane
Scunda, Assed
Scunda, Famine
Segisser, Miss Emma
Serepeca, Miss Augusta
Seward, Mr. Frederick K.
Shelley, Miss Imanita
Shine, Axel
Shine, Ellen
Shutes, Miss E. W.
Sibelrome, Agnes
Sibelrome, Rose
Silven, Miss Lyyli
Silverthorne, Mr.
Silvey, Mrs. Wm. B.
Simmonius, Mr. Oberst Alfons
Simpson, Miss Anna
Sincock, Miss Maud
Sindo, Beatrice
Sinkkonen, Miss Anna
Sjablom, Annie
Slayter, Miss H. M.
Sloper, Mr. Wm. T.
Smith, Miss Marion
Smythe, Salia
Snyder, Mr. John
Snyder, Mrs. John
Sofia, Anna
Spedden, Mr. Frederick O.
Spedden, Mrs. Frederick O.
Spedden, Master R. Douglas
Spencer, Mrs. W. A., and Maid
Stahelin, Dr. Max
Stanley, Amy
Steffanson, Mr. H. B.
Stengel, Mr. C. E. H.
Stengel, Mrs. C. E. H.
Stephenson, Mrs. W. B.

Stone, Mrs. George M., and Maid
Strander, Julo
Strauss, Maid of Mrs.
Strinder, Juho
Smith, Mrs. L. P.
Submaket, Fituasa
Sulici, Nicola
Sunderland, Victor
Sundman, Julian
Svenson, Severin
Swift, Mrs. Frederick Joel
Taussig, Mrs. Emil
Taussig, Miss Ruth
Taylor, Mr. E. Z.
Taylor, Mrs.
Thayer, Mrs. J. B. and Maid
Thayer, Mr. J. B., jun.
Thorneycroft, Florence
Tonglin, Gunner
Toomey, Miss Ellen
Trant, Mrs. Jessie
Trenobisky, Berk
Troutt, Miss E.
Tucker, Mr. G. M., jun.
Turgen, Anna
Tukula, Hedvig
Turnguist, H.
Vagil, Adele J.
Walcroff, Miss Nellie
Ware, Mrs. Florence
Warren, Mrs. F. M.
Waters, Miss Nellie
Watt, Mrs. Bessie
Watt, Miss Bertha
Webber, Miss Susie
Weisz, Mrs. Matilda
Wells, Miss Addie
Wells, Miss J.
Wells, Master Ralph
West, Mrs. Ada
West, Miss Barbara
West, Miss Constance
White, Mrs. J. Stuart and Maid
Wick, Miss Mary
Wilhems, Mr. Chas.
Wilkes, Ellen
Widener, Mrs. George D. and Maid
Willard, Miss Constance
Williams, Mr. C.
Williams, Mr. R. M., jun.
Wilson, Miss Helen
Wimhormstrom, Amy E.
Woolner, Mr. Hugh
Wright, Miss Marion
Yazlick, Salamy
Young, Miss Marie
Zenn, Phillip
Zuni, Fabin

*.* *This list, issued by the White Star Company on April 20, shows many discrepancies with the Board of Trade's official figures.*

## Officers and Members of Crew who were saved:

C. H. Lightoller (2nd officer)
H. Pitman (3rd officer)
J. Boxhall (4th officer)
G. Lowe (5th officer)
J. Haines (boatswain's mate)
H. Bailey (master-at-arms)

**Stewardesses, etc.**

Miss S. Strap
Mrs. K. Gold
Mrs. E. Leather
Mrs. A. Martin
Miss M. Sloan
Miss V. Jessop
Miss M. Gregson
Miss Smith
Mrs. K. Bennett
Mrs. McLaren

Miss E. Marsden
Mrs. A. Pritchard
Mrs. Roberts
Mrs. N. Robinson
Miss B. Lavington
Mrs. E. Bliss
Mrs. M. Slocombe
Miss A. Caton.

J. Foley (storekeeper)
S. Hennings (lamps)
W. Winnie, A.B.
J. Perks
R. Bright
G. Rome
J. Poing Derstoc
G. McGough

W. Meiles
W. Peters
P. Hogg
T. Jones
E. Archer
F. Flett
G. Symons
A. Jewell
F. Church
R. Hitchens
Cavell
Priest
Blake
W. White
Lindsey
Pearce
Noss

Hunt
Godley
Thrasher
Beacha
Combes
Clark
Mansea
Pinsted
Pelboun
Casper
Nutlearn
Podesta
F. Oliver
C. Hascoe
Avery (fireman)
Doel (fireman)
F. A. R. Mason

Striet
Dore
Sparkman
Fryer
Crummins
Kerrish
Oliver
Dymond

J. Piggott
L. Moore
F. Orman
J. Bewley
P. McCarthy
F. O. Evans
V. Hopkins
J. Forward

F. Louis
H. A. Etches
A. Tessinger
H. Crawford
C. Cullen
A. Cunningham
J. Johnstone
W. Ward

S. H. Nichols
H. Phillamore
F. Tirrel
J. G. Willgery
J. Whitter
J. Hart
A. Pearcey
H. J. Prior
L. Hyland
F. Port
W. S. Halford
A. E. R. Lewis
P. J. Savage
C. Foley
A. Pugh
J. Maynard
J. Ellis
A. Windbank
A. Simmons
Barrett
Hendrieksen
Puen ( ? )
Threllfall
Collins
Moore

Anxious crowds at London and Southampton : 1. Reading the lists of survivors outside the White Star Offices in London ; 2. Awaiting news inside the office ; 3, Relatives of the crew studying the lists at Southampton.

Triggs
Cooper
Harty
Harris
Rue
Dilley
Draper
Knowles
Panger
A. White
Scott
Judd
Thompson
Self
Hogan
W. Wright (plate washer)
G. Whiteman (barber)
W. Fitzpatrick (steward)
Miss R. Bowker (restaurant)
Miss M. Martin (restaurant)
Paul Mange (kitchen clerk)
F. Marten
H. Rose
J. Colgan
R. Hardrick
J. Joughin (chief baker)
H. Neal (baker)
C. Burgess (baker)
C. Mills (butcher)
P. Bull

Perry
Sheath
J. Taylor
W. H. Taylor
Shears
Fredericks
S. Humphreys
J. Lee
J. Horsewell

S. Evans
W. Brice
W. Lucas
J. Anderson
J. Scarrott
W. Horder
A. McMicken
E. Brown
F. Ray

E. J. Gay
R. P. Fropper
W. E. Eyerson
J. W. Gibbons
W. J. Williams
W. Seward
J. Chapman
C. Andrews
A. Burrage

## Officers and Crew of the "Titanic."

The following is a complete official list of the officers and crew who sailed on the "Titanic." Unless otherwise stated, they resided at Southampton :—

Edward J. Smith, Winn Road, Southampton, captain.

H. F. Wilde, Grey Road, Walton, Liverpool, chief mate.

W. M. Murdoch, Belmont Road, first mate.

C. H. Lughloller, Netley Abbey, second mate.

H. J. Pitman, Castle Cary, Somerset, third mate.

J. S. Poxhall, Westbourne Avenue, Hull, fourth mate.

H. J. Lowe, fifth mate.

James Pelloody, St. James' House, Grimsby, sixth mate.

William F. N. O'Loughton, Polygan House, Southampton, surgeon.

J. Edward Simpson, Pakenham Road, Belfast, surgeon.

J. Bell, Canute Road, chief engineer.

W. Farquharson, Wilton Avenue, senior second engineer.

J. H. Hesketh, Garrett Avenue, Liverpool, junior second engineer.

N. Harrison, Coventry Road, junior second engineer.

G. F. Hosking, Avenue Road, Itchen, senior third engineer.

E C. Dodd, Queen's Parade, junior third engineer.

L Hodgkinson, Arthur Road, senior fourth engineer.

J. N. Smith, Millars Road, Itchen, junior fourth engineer.

B Wilson, Richmond Road, Shirley, senior assistant engineer.

H. G. Harvey, Obelisk Road, Woolston, junior assistant second engineer.

J. Shepherd, Bellevue Terrace, junior assistant second engineer.

C. Hodge, Ivy Road, Woolston, senior assistant third engineer.

F E. G. Coy, Portswood Road.

James Fraser, Tennyson Road, junior assistant third engineer.

H. R. Dyer, Middle Street, senior assistant fourth engineer.

A. Haveling, South Front, junior assistant fourth engineer.

A. Ward, Manor House, Romsey, junior assistant fourth engineer.

Thomas Kemp, Cedar Road, assistant fourth engineer.

F. A. Parsons, Bugle Street, senior fifth engineer.

W. D. Mackie, Margery Park Road, Forest Gate, E., junior fifth engineer.

R. Millar, North Street, Alloa, fifth engineer.

W. Moyes, Douglas Terrace, Stirling, senior sixth engineer.

W. M. E. Reynolds, Lagon Villas, Belfast, junior sixth engineer.

H. Creese, Enfield Grove, Woolston, deck engineer.

T. Millar, Meadow Street, Belfast, assistant deck engineer.

G. Chiswall, High Street, Itchen, boilermaker.

H. Fitzpatrick, Nelson Street, Belfast, junior boilermaker.

Peter Sloan, Clovelly Road, chief electrician.

A. S. Alsopp, Malmesbury Road, second electrician.

H. Jupe, Bullar Road, assistant electrician.

Alfred Middleton, Sligo, assistant electrician.

A. W. May, York Street, Northampton.

J. Hutchinson, Onslow Road, joiner and carpenter.

A. Nicholls, St. Cloud, Oak Tree Road, 'bosun.

J. Maxwell, Leighton Road, carpenter.

A. Haines, Grove Street, boatswain's mate.

T. King, Middlemarket Road, master-at-arms.

H. Bailey, Oswood Road, master-at-arms.

J. Foley, Queen's Road, storekeeper.

S. Hemming, Kingsley Road, lamp trimmer.

C. Proctor, Southview Road, chef.

A. Bocketay, Oakbank Road, assistant chef.

H. Stubbings, Onslow Road, cook.

H. Maynard, Earls Road, cook.

H. W. McElroy, Polygon House, purser.

R. L. Barker, Mayhaith, Old Shirley, purser.

C. Holcroft, Canterbury Road, Seacombe, clerk.

E. W. King, Currin Rectory, Clones, clerk.

F. R. Rice, Kimberley Drive, Crosby, clerk.

G. F. Turner, Hedley Gardens, Chiswick, stenographer.

F. G. Phillips, Farncombe, Godalming, telegraphist.

H. St. Bride, Bannister's Hotel, telegraphist.

L. Gatti, Harbour Road, Southampton, manager of restaurant.

Francisco Nanni, Aubert Road, Finsbury Park, N., head waiter.

Giuseppi Bochet, London, second head waiter.

R. Boroker, Little Sutton, Cheshire, first cashier.

M. E. Martin, Apsley Villa, Acton, second cashier.

W. A. Jeffrey, Apsley Villa, Acton, controller.

H. Vine, Apsley Villa, Acton, assistant controller.

Albert Ervine, Maryfield, Belfast, assistant electrician.

William Kelly, Claude Road, Dublin, writer.

William Duffy, Garton Road, Itchen, writer.

A. Rous, Ratcliffe Road, writer.

R. J. Sawyer, Bevois Street, window cleaner.

W. Hardie, Winton Street, window cleaner.

### Mess Stewards.

W. A. Makeson, Western Esplanade.

John Coleman, Mortimer Road, Itchen.

S. Blake, Holyrood House.

George Gumery, Canute Road.

C. W. N. Fitzpatrick, Millbrook Road.

### Quartermasters.

S. Humphreys, Duke's Road.

W. Wynn, Church Street.

A. Olliver, Anderson's Road.

R. Hickens, St. James's Street, Dongola.

G. Rowe, Henry Street.

A. Bright, Firgrove Road.

W. Perkis, Victoria Road, Bitterne.

### Look-Out Men.

S. Symons, Fanshaw Street.

F. Fleet, Norman Road.

J. A. Hoff, High Street.

F. Evans, Deal Street.

A. Jewell, College Street.

R. R. Lee, Threefield Lane.

### Able Seamen.

W. Weller, Holyrood House, Southampton.

W. Lucas, Corporation Flats.

F. Bradley, Threefield Lane.

G. Moore, Graham Road.

W. H. Lyons, Orchard Lane.

J. Forward, Sailors' Home.

A. Horswick, Derby Road.

E. Archer, Pitswood Road.

F. Osman, High Street.

Stephen J. Davis, Duncan Street, Landport.

C. Taylor, High Street.

F. Crouch, Port Isaac, Cornwall.

B. Terrell, Trinity House Street.

W. McCarthy, Gratton Hill Road, Cork.

T. Jones, Nesbitt Street, Liverpool.

E. Buley, Cliff Road, Woolston.

C. H. Pascoe, High Street.

H. Holman, Britannia Road.

D. Matheson, Everton Street.

G. Clench, Chantry Road.

G. Church, Chantry Road.

F. Tamlin, Southampton Street.

Robert Hopkins, Woodstock Road.

W. C. Peters, Ludlow Road.

J. Anderson, Couzens Court.

W. Smith, Bridge Road.

F. O. Evans, Bond Street.

J. McGough, St. George Street.

J. Scarrott, Albert Road.

P. Vigett, Windsor Terrace.

W. Brice, Lower Canal Walk.

J. Poingdestre, Elan Road.

### Storekeepers.

A. Kenzler, Bleckendon Terrace.

A. Foster, Norwich Front.

H. Rudd, Chapel Street.

C. Newman, Latimer Street.

Edward Parsons, Robert's Road, Southampton.

H. H. Thompson, Eastwood, Lumsden Avenue, Southampton.

J. W. Keran, Avenue Road.

F. W. Prentice, Denzil Avenue.

G. Ricks, Hanley Road.

Arthur J. Williams, Peter Road, Walton.

C. F. Morgan, Bessboro' Road, Birkenhead.

E. J. W. Rogers, Oxford Avenue.

S. A. Stap, Bidston Avenue.

### Firemen.

W. Small, Liverpool, Russell Street.

James Keegan, Liverpool, West Place.

T. Threlfall, Liverpool, St. Martins Court.

F. Walker, Hants, Avenue Road.

Thomas Ford, Liverpool, Russell Street.

C. Hendrickson, Northumberland Road.

W. Mayo, Castle Road.

T. Davies, Church Lane.

J. Norris, Spa Road.

T. Graham, Downpatrick Street.

E. Watridge, Millbrook Street.

J. Wyett, Millbank Street.

J. Thomas, Newman Street.

C. Otken, Northumberland Road.

John Jactopin, Dukes Road.

C. Altrams, Charles Street.

C. Painter, Mortimer Road.

H. Sparkman, Spring Road, Sholing.

F. Reeves, Cable Street.

W. Lindsay, Coleman Street.

W. Jarvis, Canal Walk.

R. Price, Houndwell Gardens.

W. Brugge, Sailors' Home, Southampton.

T. Knowles, Lymington.

W. Butt, Cawle Road.

G. Rickman, Derby Road.

H. Smither, Ash Tree Road.

E. McGaw, Broadlands Road.

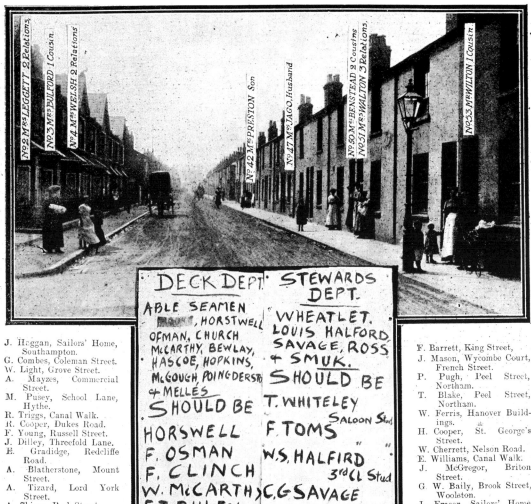

Labels on the image:
No 2 Mrs LEGGETT 2 Relations
No 3 Mrs PULFORD 1 Cousin
No 4 Mrs WELSH 2 Relations
No 42 Mrs PRESTON Son
No 47 Mrs JAGO, Husband
No 50 Mrs BENSTEAD 2 Cousins
No 51 Mrs WALTON 3 Relations
No 53 Mrs WILTON 1 Cousin

DECK DEPT. STEWARDS DEPT.

ABLE SEAMEN
, HORSTWELL
OFMAN, CHURCH
McCARTHY, BEWLAY,
HASCOE, HOPKINS,
McGOUGH POINGDERSTo
& MELLES
SHOULD BE
HORSWELL
F. OSMAN
F. CLINCH
W. McCARTH,
E.J. BULEY
C.H. PASCOE
R.J. HOPKINS
McGOFF
POINGESTER
S. WELLER
NOTE:
LYONS

WHEATLET.
LOUIS HALFORD,
SAVAGE, ROSS
& SMUK.
SHOULD BE
T. WHITELEY
F. TOMS Saloon Std.
W.S. HALFIRD " "
3rd Cl. Stud
C. G SAVAGE
H. ROSS " "
K. SMITH Cook
Stewardess

J. Haggan, Sailors' Home, Southampton.
G. Combes, Coleman Street.
W. Light, Grove Street.
A. Mayzes, Commercial Street.
M. Pusey, School Lane, Hythe.
R. Triggs, Canal Walk.
R. Cooper, Dukes Road.
F. Young, Russell Street.
J. Dilley, Threefold Lane.
E. Gradidge, Redcliffe Road.
A. Blatherstone, Mount Street.
A. Tizard, Lord York Street.
A. Shiers, Peel Street.
E. Hannan, Oxford Terrace.
E. Harris, Belgrave Road.
George Nettleton, Empress Road.
F. Mardle, Back of Walls.
H. Siniar, South Road, Clapham.
W. Watson, York Street.
F. M. McAndrews, New Capley Bridge.
S. Graves, North Front.
R. Hopgood, Ramsay Road.
D. Hanbrook, York Street.
J. Padesta, Chantry Road.
W. Neithear, High Street.
N. Toas, Bond Street, Southampton.
Thomas James, College Street.
J. Blaney, Sailors' Home, Southampton.
J. Taylor, Manor Road.
A. Head, Russell Street.
W. Sims, Charlotte Street.
J. J. Moore, Arthur Road.
J. Barnes, Woodley Road, Woolston.
J. Diaper, Derby Road.
T. Bradley, Green's Court.
E. Tegs, Kempley Road.
J. Ward, Hames Street.

F. Barrett, King Street,
J. Mason, Wycombe Court, French Street.
P. Pugh, Peel Street, Northam.
T. Blake, Peel Street, Northam.
W. Ferris, Hanover Buildings.
H. Cooper, St. George's Street.
W. Cherrett, Nelson Road.
E. Williams, Canal Walk.
J. McGregor, Briton Street.
G. W. Baily, Brook Street, Woolston.
J. Fraser, Sailors' Home, Southampton.
J. Chorley, Regent Street.
T. Hart, College Street.
T. Hunt, Queen Street.
F. W. Barrett, Bevors Street.
A. Slade, Chantry Road.
W. Ball, Brintons Road.
Thomas Slade, Chantry Road.
T. Laley, Spulling Road, East Dulwich.
G. Kemish, Shirley Road.
A. Streets, Lion Street, Shirley.
G. Roberts, Withers Street.
B. Moss, St. Peters Road.
G. Slade, Chantry Road.
George Milford, Graham Street.
E. Blien, Pound Street.
T. Instance, Guillaum Terrace.
W. Saunders, Edward Street.
C. Rice, Oriental Terrace.
R. Turley, Sailors' Home, Southampton.
W. McCastlan, French Street.
A. Black, Briton Street.
C. Biddlescomb, Kentish Road.

Southampton, where the majority of the crew lived, was a city of sorrow as soon as news of the disaster became known. The top photograph shows Milbank Street, one of Southampton's Streets of Mourning, with several of the bereaved homes marked. The other photograph is that of one of the notice boards outside the White Star Company's local office, where the names of rescued members of the crew were posted. Mistakes in cabling names were corrected from time to time, and each correction lifted a burden of sorrow from some home.

B. Hands, St. Michael's House.
M. W. Golder, Lansdowne Road.
William McQuillan, Sea View Street, Belfast.
John Noon, Sailors' Home.
B. Cunningham, Briton Street.
C. J. Hewert, Larndorf Road.
W. Burrows, Elm Street.
Thomas Shea, Briton Street.
J. Hall, Westgate Street.
C. Barlow, St. Mary's Road.
G. Beauchamp, Redbridge Road.
F. Saunders, Sussex Terrace.
Thomas McAndrill, Sailors' Home.
J. Cummins, King Street.
G. Marget, Elm Street.
S. Sullivan, Marsh Lane.
E. Biggs, College Street.
Archibald Scott, Lower Ditches.
J. Shaw, Northumberland Road.
Frank Holden, Albany Road.
W. McRae, Three-fold Lane.
R. Adams, Pound Terrace Road.
D. Cacceran, Sailors' Home.
F. Harris, Belle View Road, Gosport.
A. May, York Street.
F. Shafper, Brunswick Square.
W. Mintram, Chapel Road.
G. Hallett, Church Road.
H. Oliver, Nichols Road.
G. Snellgrove, Cecil Avenue.
C. Sangster, Bevon Street.
Charles Barnes, York Road.
Frank Painter, Bridge Road.
C. Judd, Derby Road.
J. Brown, Russell Street.
E. Flarty, Stamford Street.
F. Rendell, Woodley Road.
G. Thresher, Mount Pleasant Road.
J. Taylor, Russell Street.
W. Bessant, Henry Road.
W. Major, Oriental Terrace.
G. Burnett, Deal Street.
E. McGurney, College Street.
F. Wardner, Endle Street.
W. Hurst, Chapel Road.
Thos. Kerr, Hartley Street.
F. Mason, Waverley Road.
A. Burroughs, Adelaide Road.
A. Witcher, Nelson Place.
G. Godley, Mount Street.
T. Morgan, Sailors' Home, Southampton.
W. Vear, Spa Gardens.
H. Vear, Spa Gardens.
H. Allen, French Street.
W. Cross, Ludlow Road.
F. Drel, Richmond Street.
J. Pearse, Drummond Street.
John Coffy, Sperbourne Terrace.
E. Burton, Chapel Street.
W. H. Taylor, Broad Street.
H. Noss, Back Lane.
S. Doyle, Orchard Place.
E. Denville, Orchard Lane.
W. Clet, Paget Street.
W. Hodges, Britannia Road.
J. Priest, Lower Canal Walk.
H. Blackman, College Street.
L. Dymond, Farmers Court.
G. Pond, Sailors' Home, Southampton.
C. Light, Back of Walls.
Wm. Murdock, Sailors' Home, Southampton.
J. Thompson, Howe Street, Liverpool.
J. Canner, Shamrock Road, Woolston.
A. Curtis, Kingsley Road.
S. Collins, Sailors' Home, Southampton.
F. Taylor, Queen's Street.
H. Stubbs, Spa Gardens.
J. Richards, Summers Street.

**Trimmers.**

J. Dawson, Briton Street.
W. McIntyre, Floating Bridge Road.
W. Hinton, Cumberland Street.
James McCann, St. George's Place.
T. Casey, Sailors' Home, Southampton.
W. Evans, Manor Road, Hitchin.

J. Haslin, Sailors' Home, Southampton.
F. Carter, Cross Street.
W. Saunders, Suffolk Square.
A. Foyle, Charlotte Place.
F. White, Northbrook Road.
R. Proudfoot, Pear Tree Green.
S. Maskell, Albert Road.
B. Brewer, Foundry Lane.
B. Gosling, Lower York Street.
J. Read, Nelson's Place.
J. Brooks, Lion Street.
William Wilson, Queen's Street.
H. Lee, Bevors Street.
A. Farrang, St. Mary's Place.
G. Cavell, South East Road, Tholing.
R. Morrell, Malmesbury Road.
J. Bevis, Empress Road.
A. Morgan, Threefield Lane.
H. Brewer, Palmerston Road.
R. Reid, Wickham's Court.
H. Coe, Cross Court.
H. Perry, Rye Terrace.
Thomas P. Dillon, Sailors' Home.
A. Dore, Mount Street.
E. Smith, St. Mary's Buildings.
E. Tegs, Kempley Road.
A. Hunt, French Street.
F. Harris, Willow Street.
J. Bellows, Bell Street.
W. Morris, Marine Parade.
S. Webb, Sailors' Home, Southampton.
W. Snooks, Sailors' Home, Southampton.
A. Hebb, Bell's Court.
R. Moore, Manor Cottage, Headbourne Street.
B. Mitchell, Bevois Valley.
C. Shillaher, Nelson Road.
H. Stocker, Middle Road, Sholing.
A. J. Eagle, Lvm Street, Southampton.
F. Watts, St. Michael's Home, Southampton.
H. Ford, Royal Oak.
W. Skeater, King Street.
F. Sheath, Bell Street.
A. Penney, Chantry Road.
H. Calderwood, Sailors' Home, Southampton.
W. Birstead, Endle Street.
G. Kearl, Bay Road, Sholing.
H. Wood, St. Michael's Home, Southampton.
J. Hill, Kingsland Square.
C. Blake, Rumbridge Street, Totton.
F. Long, Sidford Street.
F. Perry, Ryde Terrace, Southampton.
P. Blake, Floating Bridge Road.
T. White, Colbert Street, Northam.
H. Crabb, Furgrove Road.
W. Long, Maine Terrace.
S. Gosling, French Street.
F. Snow, Lower Canal Walk.
T. Preston, Millbank Street.
G. Pelham, Sailors' Home, Southampton.
G. Green, Howards Grove.
F. Ingram, Lower York Street.
J. Avery, Hills Road.
J. Cooper, Pound Street.
G. Allen, Short Street.
W. Fredericks, Elm Road, Chapel.
R. Carr, Malvern Cottages, Winchester Road.
E. Elliott, Sailors' Home, Southampton.

**Greasers.**

A. White, Southampton Place.
J. Jukes, Moor Green, West End.
Fred Kanchensen, Latimer Street.
C. Keere, Chantry Road.
G. Phillips, Grove Street.
F. Beattie, Sailors' Home, Southampton.
A. Self, Romsey Road.
T. Polles, Upper Palmer Street.
O. Eastman, Cecil Avenue.
A. Veal, Imperial Avenue.
G. Pragnell, Brew House Court.
T. Rungem, Middle Road.
W. Pitfield, Albert Road.
C. Olive, College Street.

F. Godwin, Totton.
F. Woodford, Clovelly Road.
M. Stafford, Southhook Square.
A. Morris, Short Street.
W. Bott, Nichols Road.
J. Couch, Canton Street.
T. McInerney, Colston Street.
J. Kirkham, Chapel Street.
T. Fay, Stamford Street.
J. Jago, Millbank Street.
J. Tozer, Challis Street.
R. Baines, Union Place.
R. Moores, Northumberland Road.
D. Gregory, Floating Bridge Road.
E. Castleman, North Road, St. Deny's.
F. Scott, Clifford Street.
F. Goree, Belvedere Terrace.
J. Kelly, Woodleigh Road.
J. Dannon, St. George's Street.

**Stewards.**

A. Latimer, Glenwylin Row, Waterloo (chief).
George Dodd, Morris Road (second).
J. S. Wheat, Cobden Gardens (assistant second).
W. T. Hughes, Ivybank, Dyer Road (assistant second).
William Moss, Charlton Road (saloon).
W. Burke, Bridge Road (second saloon).
A. J. Goshawk, Coventry Road (third saloon).
W. Osborne, Hewitts Road.
John Strugness, The Poligon.
A. Dubb, Atherley Road.
W. Rovell, Liverpool, Malmesbury Road.
J. Smillin, Glasgow, Malmesbury Road.
James Johnston, Hants, Seamens' Home.
A. A. Howe, Cliff Road, Itchen.
C. D. Mackay, Hilton Road.
Henry Ketchley, Northcote Road.
W. Dyer, Stafford Road.
W. Brown, Ormskirk, Hillside Avenue.
C. Whalton, Liverpool, Bilmoor Road.
E. Brown, Holyhead, Suffolk Road.
A. Kutchling, Derby Road.
B. Oaket, Vaudrey Street.
A. Best, Malmesbury Road.
W. House, Derby Road.
H. Cove, London, Shirley Park Road.
W. Lucas, London, Cardigan Terrace.
Tom Weatherstone, Kenilworth Road.
E. Spinner, Oxford Street.
A. W. Barringer, Padswell Road.
A. McMickea, Suffolk Road.
F. D. Ray, Avenue Road, Palmer Park.
H. I. Lloyd, Oxford Street.
J. Shea, Portsmouth Road.
F. Allsop, Obelisk Road.
J. H. Boyes, Clovelly Road.
G. Knight, Ludlow Road.
A. J. Littlejohn, Weston Terrace, Chapel Road.
Ernest T. Barker, Grand Parade, Harringay.
R. Jones, Portland Terrace.
H. Bristow, Shortlands, Kent.
B. Boughton, Richmond Street.
P. Keen, Rugby Road.
F. Crafter, Albert Road.
J. McMullin, St. Mary's Road.
H. Fairall, Surrey Street, Ryde.
William Lake, Florence Hotel.
S. Nicholls, Brunswick Square.
F. Toms, Hillside Square.
E. Thomas, Avenue Road.
J. E. Cartwright, Western Terrace.
R. G. Smith, Stafford Road.
M. Rowe, Bridge Road.
George Evans, Richmond Road.
T. Turner, Terminus Terrace.
G. Cook, Bridge Road.
A. Coleman, Oaktree Road.
J. Symons, Church Street.
J. Ranson, Knowle, Bristol.
W. Cherubin, Mile Street, Newport, I.W.
H. Crisp, Macnaughten Road.

Wm. Burrows, Hanover Street, London.
J. H. Stagg, Commercial Road.
J. L. Pury, Manor Road, Itchen.
L. White, Romsey Road.
S. Rummer, Cranbury Road.
A. Stroud, Shirley Road.
L. Hoare, High Street.
A. Lawrence, Oxford Street.
E. Hendy, Paynes Road.
A. Derrett, Hillside Avenue.
A. M. Bagot, Park Road, Freemantle, Southampton.
C. Casswill, Oxford Avenue.
W. Pryce, Heatherdene, Newlands Road.
W. Ward, Millbrook Road.
B. Fish, Blackbury Terrace.
L. Whiteley, St. John's Park, Highgate.
E. Burr, Above Barr.
T. Veal, Forster Road.
F. Wormald, Pestwood Road.
P. Deslands, Portswood Road.

J. Boyd, Cranbury Avenue.
J. Butterworth, Priory Road.
J. W. Robinson, Vine Cottage, Carlisle Road.
J. R. Diverage, Cowle Road.
F. C. Simmons, Middlebrook Road.
Joseph Dolley, Devonshire Road.
Thomas Holland, Walton Village.
T. W. H. Cowles, Camden Place.
Ernest E. T. Freeman, Hanley Road.
W. Boston, Hanley Road.
W. Hawksworth, Lemon Road.
P. W. Fletcher, Liscombe Avenue.
E. Abbott, North Road.
R. E. Burke, Southampton Road, Chandlerford.
C. Back, Weymouth Terrace.
Brooke Webb, Hanley Road.
E. Hamilton, Shirley Road.
J. Stewart, Earles Road.
A. T. Broome, White Lodge.

W. Gwann, Shirley Road.
A. Hayter, Mayflower Road.
T. Clark, Hillside Avenue.
R. Wareham, Park Road.
R. Allen, Kenilworth Road.
F. McCarthy, Charlton Road.
W. Anderson, Queen's Terrace.
G. R. Davis, Hillside Avenue.
R. Ide, Lyon Street.
R. C. Geare, Grove Road.
H. Wittman, Richmond Road.
S. Gill, Suffolk Avenue.
J. Hill, Cromwell Road.
E. Harris, Greenhill Road, Winchester.
C. Edwards, Brunswick Square.
J. W. Marriott, Chilworth Road.
J. Akerman, Rochester Road.
S. Stebbings, Richfield Road.
H. Fellowes, Bridge Road.
C. Jackson, Graham Road.
W. Henry, Romsey Road.

## THE TERRORS OF THE NORTH ATLANTIC.

Our photograph shows a typical iceberg in the North Atlantic. A drawing on an earlier page gives a striking idea of the vast bulk of ice concealed beneath the water.

James Toshuch, Malmesbury Road.
W. Taylor, Morris Road.
W. F. Kingscote, Elgin Road, Freemantle, Southampton.
T. Warwick, Totton.
A. E. Lane, Victoria Road.
A. C. Thomas, Brunswick Place.
R. Butt, Carole Road.
J. McGrady, Platform Tavern.
P. Ahler, Northumberland Road.
P. Kilford, New Road.
H. Bruton, St. Andrew's Road.
F. Hartnell, Harcourt Road.
W. W. Dawes, Nelson Road.
C. Lydiatt, Brunswick Square.
A. Mellor, Carlton Place.
E. Bagley, Woodside Road.
George Lefevre, Orchard Place.
D. E. Saunders, Albert Road.

A. D. Harrison, Oakley Road.
H. Yearsley, Gloucester Passage.
G. F. Crowe, Milton Road.

T. Wright. Stern Street, Shepherd's Bush.
E. Bessant, Shirley Park Road.
J. Painton, Shakespeare Avenue.
Ernest R. Olive, Hanley Road.
S. Holloway, Hartington Road.
W. Carney, Caird Street, West Derby Road, Liverpool.
Alfred King, Dyer Road.
T. Allen, Short Street.
L. Perkins, Emsworth Road.
W. A. Watson, Oakley Road.
C. H. Harries, Short Street.
A. Barrett, North Road.
A. Mishelany, Criterion Restaurant.
E. T. Corben, Floating Bridge Road.
Samuel Ryler, Athenlay Road.
F. Morris, Shirley Road.
H. Broome, Thetis Road.
E. Major, Criterion Restaurant.
F. Pennol, Imperial Avenue.
Thomas Baxter, Atherley Road.
John P. Penrose, Southern Road.

E. J. Guy, College Terrace.
J. Scott, Upper Canal Walk.
S. Hiscock, Chantry Road.
F. Hopkins, Fanshaw Street.
W. Bunnell, Kingsfold Road.
E. Hogue, Alison Grove, Dulwich Common.
C. Light, Thorney Hill, near Christchurch.
J. A. Bradshaw, Portland Street.
P. Ball, Windsor Terrace.
Donald Campbell (clerk).
W. F. Janaway, St. George Road.
A. Cunningham, Charlton Road.
T. Hewitt, Devonfield Road, Aintree.
A. Cranford, Cranbury Avenue.
P. P. Ward, Ridgefield Road, Shirley.
W. Bishop, High Street.
E. Ward, Richmond Terrace.
T. Donoghue, Ludlow Road.
Charles Culling, Warburton Road.
William Faulkener, Romsey Road.

Thomas O'Connor, Linaker Lane.
W. McMurray, Empress Road.
C. Stagg, Pulver Street, Liverpool.
H. Roberts, Mildmay Road, Bootle.
Charles Crumplin, Shakespeare Avenue.
S. C. Siebert, Harold Road, Shirley.
A. Thussinger, French Street.
W. Bond, Handley Road.
E. Stone, St. Andrew's Road.
H. Etches, Gordon Avenue.
G. Brewster, Carlton Place.
J. Walpole, Stafford Road.
B. Tucker,. Suffolk Avenue.
G. Levett, Chilworth Road.
F. Smith, Ordnance Road.
F. B. Wrayson, Southampton Street.
J. Monks, Livingstone Road.
John Hardy, Oakleigh, Highfield (chief second class).
H. Jenner, Bellevue Road.
R. Sconnell, Foundry Lane, Freemantle.
P. W. Conway, Bentham Road, S. Hackney.
M. Rogers, Greenhill Avenue, Winchester.
R. J. Davies, The Polygon.
H. Philleine, Priory Road.
G. Bailey, Brooklands, Shepperton.
Alan Franklin, Egrement, Newton Road.
R. Parsons, Polygon Road.
R. Russell, Anchor Hotel, Redbridge.
G. E. Moor, St. Mary's Road.
W. Ridout, Queen Anne Buildings.
F. H. Randall, Empress Road.
A. Whitford, Richmond Street.
A. Jones, Woodfield Charlton Road.
W. G. Dashwood, Sailors' Home.
M. V. Meddleton, Felsham Road, Putney.
T. Seaton, Middle Road, Sholing.
N. Daughty, Bridge Road.
C. Harris, Short Street.
F. Benham, Bridge Road.
E. Stroud, Malmesbury Road.
C. Jensem, Morris Road.
W. E. Ryerson, Salop Road, Walthamstow.
R. Pfraffen, Washington Terrace.
John Charman, Latimer Street.
Joseph Heinen, Malden Hill House, Lewisham.
C. W. Samuel, Osborne Road.
Peter Alinger, Marsh Lane.
J. Hawkesworth, Milton Road.
Jacob V. Gibbons, Harbour View, Studland Bay.
F. Terrell, Grove Street.
W. Williams, Northumberland Road.
H. Christmas, Bruntons Road.
B. Lacey, Southampton Road, Salisbury.
W. Penny, Lodge Road, Southampton.
J. T. Wood, Merford Road, Upper Clapton.
C. Andrews, Millbrook Road.
G. Robertson, Mount Street.
H. Humphreys, Rockstone Lane.
G. H. Dean, King Edward Avenue, Shirley.
R. Owen, Earls Road.
H. Gunn, Bridge Road.
W. T. Kerley, Woodminton Cottages, Salisbury.
W. H. Nichols, Kent Road.
R. J. Pacey, Cambridge Villa, Millbrook Road.
F. Kelland, Commercial Street, Bitterne (library steward).
F. W. Edge Clovelly Road.
J. Witter, Dorchester Road, Woolston.
H. Bulley, Carrabrooke, Britannia Road.
J. Chapman, Belherne Road.
W. Perren, Bellemore Road.
G. Hinckley, Oxford Street.
J. G. Widgery, Oxford Street.
G. Barrow, Carminster, Foundry Lane.
F. Ford, Oxford Street.
C. Smith, Hollydean, Portsmouth Road.
W. Boothby, Ivey Road, St. Denys.
G. Mackie, Winchester Road.

J. Byrne, Balfour Road, Ilford.
C. Reed, Derby Road.
G. Beeden, Shrewsbury Road, Harlesden.
E. W. Hamblyn, Norman Villas, Dyer Road.
H. Bogi, Crescent, Eastleigh.
E. H. Petty, Orchard Place.
E. F. Stone, Shirley Road.
W. Suvary, Shirley Road.
C. Cook, Chantry Road.
A. Harding, Station Cottages, Swaythling.
J. Longmuir, The Crescent, Eastleigh.
Arthur E. Jones, Ludlow Road.
R. Fisher, Duncan Street, Portsmouth.
F. Hambley, Clarendon Road.
A. Burray, Emsworth Road.
Mrs. Snape, Well Lane, Sandown.
Mrs. Wallis, St. Mary's Place.
James Kiernan, Inglewood, Billemoor Road.
S. F. Geddunary, Emsworth Road.
L. Mullar, Oxford Street (inspector and steward).
A. Pearcey, Kent Road.
W. Dunford, Bridge Street.
J. Brookman, Richmond Street.
H. P. Hill, Oxford Street.
F. Ford, Burtons Road.
C. Taylor, Oxford Street.
R. Bristow, Western Road.
F. Edbroke, Lake Road, Portsmouth.
J. Mabey, Grove Road.
A. D. Nichols, Dulford Avenue.
G. Chitty, Bevons Valley Road.
V. Rice, Thackeray Road.
S. G. Barton, College Street.
W. D. Cox, Thirley Road.
A. Ackerman, Rochester Street.
J. A. Prideaux, Cotlands Road.
H. J. Flight, Bellevue Street.
S. Daniels, Albert Road.
R. Mankle, Brintons Road.
E. B. Ede, Manor Farm Road.
W. Sivier, Westbourne Grove Mews, Paddington.
L. Knight, Spring Lane, Bishopsgate.
A. Mantz, Grove Street.
H. Ingrouville, Hoxbury Bridge Road.
J. Hart, Foundry Lane.
G. Talbot, Lemon Road.
W. E. Foley, Monsons Road, Chapel.
F. Port, Rockthorne, Foundry Lane.
H. Finch, French Street.
M. Thaler, Station Road, W. Croydon.
W. H. Egg, Brixton Trent Road.
E. Hilemot, Orchard Place.
M. Leonard, Chatwell Street, Belfast.
Richard Halford, Latimer Street.
H. R. Baxter, Shirley Road.
A. E. Peasel, Richmond Street.
T. Mullin, Onslow Road.
C. J. Savage, Harold Road.
G. Evans, Nightingale Grove.
H. Prior, Padwell Road.
A. Pugh, Orchard Lane.
C. Cecil, Millbrook Road.
H. Ashe, Wiresdale Road.
C. Crispin, Station Hill, Eastleigh.
J. White, Thackeray Road.
W. Wright, Easworth Road.
W. Willis, Derby Road.
A. Lewis, Ratcliffe Road.
T. Ryard, Albert Road.
W. T. Fox, Totton.

**Stewardesses.**

M. Slocombe, Leopold Terrace, Tottenham.
A. Caton, Highbury Hill, London.
K. Gold, Glenthorne, Bassett.
Annie Martin, Posbrock Road, Portsmouth.
E. L. Leather, Park Road, Port Sunlight.
M. Bennett, Cranbury Avenue.
M. Gregson, Lawland Road.
B. C. Jessop, Shirley Road, Bedford Park.
M. Sloan, Kersland Crescent, Belfast.

E. Marsden, West Marland Street.
T. E. Smith, Balmoral, Cobbett Road.
M. K. Roberts, Chestnut Grove, Nottingham.
H. McLaren, Shirley Road.
A. Pritchard, Rosslyn Road, East Ham.
A. Robinson, Shirley Road.
B. Lavington, Manor Farm, Headbourne Road, Winchester.
E. Bliss, Upper Park Road, New South gate.
K. Walsh, Church Road.

**Cooks.**

W. Summons, Thackeray Road.
F. Gallop, Briton Street.
C. Ruskimmel, Park View.
M. J. Mew, Hillside, Bitleme Park.
W. Slight, Hillside, Bitleme Park.
J. Lovell, Highlands Road.
W. Caunt, Sidney Road.
J. Hutchinson, Oxford Street.
J. R. Ellis, Dukes Road.
G. Ayling, Wilton Street.
J. Orr, Coleman Street.
H. E. Beverley, Brunswick Square.
H. Welch, Northaven, Bond Road, Swatling.
P. Dawkins, Fleming Road.
F. J. Beauman, Londesborough Road Southsea.
C. Coombs, Dykes Road.
Wm. Thorley, John Street.
H. Jones, Regent Street.
W. Bedford, Manor Road, Itchen.

**Scullions.**

F. A. J. Hall, Sidney Road.
W. Bull, Chandos Street.
J. Collins, Ballicar Road, Belfast.
H. Ross, Inkerman Road, Woolwich.
F. Martin, High Street, Fareham.
Joseph Colgan, West Street.
W. Platt, Belgrave Road.
G. Allen, Grove Street.
G. King, Thrafield Street.
W. Inge, Stratton Road.
Reginald Hardwicke, Heysham Road.
Wm. Beere, Avenue Cottages, Shirley.
C. Smith, Grove Street.
Harry Shaw, Towcester Street, Liverpool.
A. Simmons, Bevon Valley Road.

**Bakers.**

C. Joujhi, Elmhurst, Leighton Road, (chief).
J. Giles, Lime Street.
J. J. Davies, Earlfield Road.
W. Hine, Lyndhurst.
C. Burgess, Bridge Road.
H. Neal, Cliff Road.
J. Smith, Torpio Road.
L. Wake, Gloucester Passage.
G. Ching, Bevons Valley.
F. Barnes, Parsonage Road.
A. Barker, Kingsworthy, Winchester.
E. Farenden, South Street, Emsworth.
A. Lauder, Fanshaw Street.
G. Feltham, St. Denis Road.

**Butchers.**

A. Mayhew, Stafford Road (chief).
T. Top, Millbrook Road, Farnborough.
F. Robe.. s, Derby Road.
C. Mills, Albert Road.
T. Parker, Upper Boyle Street.
W. Wilsher, Britannia Road.
H. G. Hensford, Malmesbury Road.

**Attendants, Barbers, Waiters, Ship's Cooks, etc.**

J. B. Crosbie, St. Dunstan's Road.
W. Ennis, Bedford Road, Southport.
Leonard Taylor, Sherbourne Road, Blackpool.
A. H. Whiteman, Ivy Bank, Dyer Road.
A. White, Parnell Road, Portsmouth.
H. Keene, Oakley Road.
P. Gill, Waverley Road.

H. Johnston, Albert Road.
H. Hatch, Portswood Road.
Ernest Brice, Apsley Villa, Acton.
Charles Furvey, Apsley Villa, Acton.
J. Phillips, Jessie Terrace, Southampton.
E. Yorrish, care of Gatti.
C. Scavino, Gatti.
Angelo Knotto, Gatti.
P. Pourpe, Gatti.
R. Urbini, Gatti.

David Beux, Gatti.
B. Bernardo, Gatti.
Louis Biatti, Gatti.
J. Monrós, Gatti.
Alfonso Meratti, Gatti.
G. Lavaggi, Gatti.
Lornetti Mario, Gatti.
Rinaldo Ricadone, Gatti.
Abele Rigozzia, Gatti.
Giovanni de Martiro, Gatti.

Jean Vicat, Gatti
**Other Men Engaged by Messrs. Gatti Were:**
Henry Jaillet.
Georges Jouanwault.
Pierre Vilvarlarge.
Morel Conraire.
Louis Dornier.
Jean Pachera.
Giovanni Monteverdi.
Louis Desornini.

## REQUIEM MASS FOR THE "TITANIC" DEAD.

A remarkable photograph of the impressive service at Westminster Cathedral, at which
many distinguished Roman Catholics were present.

Ettera Vahassori. Gatti.
Narsisso Bazzi, Gatti.
Enrics Ratti, Gatti.
Guitio Casali, Gatti.
Geno Jesia, Gatti.
Giovanni Batihoe, Gatti.
Robert Nieni, Gatti.
V. Gilandino, Gatti.
Benj. Theyn, Aubert Park, Finsbury.
E. Poggi, Bowling Green House.
E. Dinapoly, Gatti.
Orovello Louis, Gatti
Alonzia B. Aptix Di Antonio, Gatti.

Maurice de Treacq, Gatti.
Albert Provatin, Gatti.
Sebastino Serantino, Gatti.
Itilo Donnati, Whitefield Street, Tottenham Court Road.
Aber Pedrini, Bowling Green House, Southampton.
P. Rousseau, Gatti
G. Biatrix, Gatti.
Henri Bollin, Gatti.
Auguste Contin, Gatti.
Claude Janin, Gatti.
Adrian Charboisson, Gatti.

Adolph Maltman.
H. Voegelin.
Gerald Groxlaude.
Jean Blumet.
George Aspilagt.
C. Tietz.
Carlo Leiz.
F. Bertoldo.
Paul Mange.
G. Salussolia.
E. Testoni.
Tazez Sartori.

## MORE LIFEBOATS ORDERED.

Many shipowners whose vessels at present carry an inadequate number of lifeboats have placed orders with boat-building firms for new boats.

Inquiries made by The Daily Mirror show that already there is a shortage of lifeboats owing to the big demand, and that the rush for them will continue for several months hence.

The manager of a large Thames-side firm said that the large shipping companies had already begun to place orders for lifeboats.

"The strong public feeling which has been aroused by the *Titanic* disaster seems to have thoroughly stirred the shipping companies to action," he said.

"I doubt if, at the present time, there are a dozen available lifeboats in the country. They have to be built to order, and to make a single lifeboat takes from three weeks to a month."

*(Mirror, 22 April 1912)*

## MORE WIRELESS OPERATORS.

Before public business is reached in the House of Commons today seventy-seven questions, many of them relating to the *Titanic* disaster, will be addressed to Ministers.

Mr. Bottomley will question the President of the Board of Trade as to lifeboat accommodation for passenger ships, the performance of lifeboat drill, and the condition of lifeboat gear.

Sir Clement Kinloch-Cooke will ask Mr. Sydney Buxton whether he will consider the advisability of making such regulations as will ensure that on all vessels equipped with wireless a sufficient number of operators are on board to secure constant attendance at the instrument by night and by day.

*(Mirror, 22 April 1912)*

## ARRIVAL OF THE 'VIRGINIAN'.

The Allan liner *Virginian*, which was at first erroneously reported to have been towing the ill-fated

*Titanic* to Halifax, arrived at Liverpool yesterday morning.

Captain Gambell, the commander of the vessel, reports having received a wireless message from Cape Race at 12.40 last Monday morning stating that the *Titanic* had struck an iceberg and wanted immediate assistance. He altered his course to go to her help.

At 3.45 the same morning he was in touch by wireless with the Russian steamer *Berma*, which was then fifty-five miles from the *Titanic*. Later he was in communication with the Leyland liner *Californian*, the *Carpathia*, the *Frankfurt* and the *Baltic*. The *Californian* replied: —

Can see *Carpathia* taking passengers on board from small boats. *Titanic* foundered about 2 a.m.

At ten o'clock the same morning he received the following message from the *Carpathia*: —

Turn back. Everything O.K. Have 800 on board. Return to your northern track.

He then proceeded eastward, and coasted round a large field of heavy and close-packed ice, with numerous bergs, steering east finally to clear it.

Captain Gambell states that he can throw no light on the messages that the *Virginian* had the *Titanic* in tow and that other standing by.

He passed the place where the *Titanic* went down at a distance of about six or seven miles. There were no boats or wreckage to be seen. His passage was delayed about 160 miles in trying to reach the *Titanic*.

*(Mirror, 22 April 1912)*

## POPULAR CHIEF STEWARD.

Mr. A. Latimer, chief steward of the *Titanic,* was also chief steward on the first voyage of the *Olympic,* and had acted in that capacity for most of the later boats of the White Star Line.

Mr. Latimer was described by one who knew him as one of the most popular men crossing the Atlantic, both with passengers and crew.

*(Daily Mail, 22 April)*

# MEN IN CROW'S NEST.

**FIRST SIGHT OF THE ICEBERG.**

**UNKNOWN BABIES AS SURVIVORS.**

**RESCUED GIRLS WEDDING.**

*FROM OUR OWN CORRESPONDENT.*
*NEW YORK, Sunday.*

The Senate Committee departed today for Washington, where tomorrow it will continue its investigation of the *Titanic* disaster. Some fifteen members of the *Titanic's* crew are proceeding simultaneously to Washington under the custody of the sargeant-at-arms in order that they may be at hand when evidence is required.

The chairman of the Committee, Senator Smith, announces that every survivor whose testimony can possibly be of value in elucidating the facts will be summoned in due course to Washington. He adds that he is "by no means through with Mr. Ismay," and intends to "question him at much greater length in Washington that I have been able to do here."

The course of the investigation so far has led to a general de-mand not only for the equipment of every liner with an adequate supply of lifeboats but for the standardisation of wireless apparatus and for Governmental supervision of marine operators, such as exists in England and other countries. Amateur wireless operators must be rigidly controlled, and any violations by them of the regulations to be made must be treated as a criminal offence. This is the conclusion universally expressed.

Other points to which the legislators of the United States are directing attention are the training of sailors employed in great ocean steamships and the manner in which the ships are officered. It is argued that there are far too few officers on board big ships. In this respect the steamship companies, it is held, make it felt that they have not moved with the times. They employ for vessels of 20,000 or 40,000 tons no more officers than they did in the old days in small steamships.

In the Foreign Relations Committee of the Senate yesterday a resolution was passed calling upon the President to negotiate treaties with Great Britain, France, Germany, and other maritime Governments having for their object the standardisation of safety appliances and equipment. While the resolution was being debated energetic protests were lodged by Senators McCullum and Lodge against the virulent denunciations of Mr. Bruce Ismay which marked the proceedings of the Senate.

Yesterday, Mr. McCullum said, one of the survivors of the lost ship, on flimsy reports, had been tried, condemned, and executed in the Senate of the United States. "I wish to register a protest against this action and against the condemnation and denunciation of any survivors or surviving officers and seamen without the fullest consideration. When the feeling of the civilized world is that it desires a victim on which to vent its wrath, then of all times should we be deliberate."

**CHIEF STEWARD'S STORY.**

Among the statements made public today is one from Mr. Thomas Whiteley, first saloon steward, and now in St. Vincent's Hospital. Whiteley says he was saved by a boat that contained the two men who were in the crow's nest at the time of the collision. One of them, according to Whiteley, said, "No wonder Murdoch (the first officer) shot himself." They were both very indignant, saying that their warnings had been ignored.

"I heard one of them say," Whiteley states, "that at 11.15 p.m. he reported to the first officer, Mr. Murdoch, on the bridge, that he fancied he saw an iceberg. Twice after that, he said, he warned Mr. Murdoch that an iceberg was ahead."

After the collision, according to the testimony of Mr. A.A. Dick, a survivor, Mr. Thomas Andrews, one of the designers of the *Titanic*, announced his intention of going below to investigate. "We begged him not to go, but he insisted, saying that he knew the ship as no one else did and might be able to allay the fears of the passengers."

"When he came back we hung on his words. They were these: 'There is no cause for any excitement. All of you get what you can in the way of clothes and come on deck as soon as you can. She is torn to bits below but will not sink if the after bulkheads hold. She has been ripped by an underlying peak of ice, and it has torn many of the forward plates from the bolts.'"

"It seemed impossible to us that this could be true, and many in the crowd smiled, thinking that this was merely a little extra knowledge which Mr. Andrews thought fit to impart."

While detailed accounts are given of the last moments of Colonel Astor, Mr. Guggenheim, and others, few people seem to have observed Mr. Stead. He was seen walking the deck after the catastrophe, and discussed with one of the passengers the size of the iceberg that caused the damage. He said that it must have been over a hundred feet above the deck.

Two days before, the famous journalist sat until midnight telling ghost stories.

Mr. Stead was last seen by Mr. R.L. Brekwith, just before the *Titanic* sank, pacing the decks unmoved. He was in evening dress. Another passenger believes, but cannot say positively, that Mr. Stead found refuge with Colonel Astor on a piece of wreckage, and that both men were forced to loosen their hold by the intense cold.

**WRECKED GIRL'S WEDDING.**

Of the survivors few excited more interest than a pretty English girl, Miss Marion Wright, of Yeovil, and two little French boys, who are ignorant of their name and identity. Miss Wright came here to be married to Mr. Arthur Woolcott, an Englishman engaged in fruit-ranching. Her lover arrived here in great agony of mind and discovered his fiancee at the home of Mrs. Watt, who was saved in the same boat as she was.

She lost her trousseau and wedding gifts, but the Women's Relief Committee, hearing of the romance, quickly provided her with a fresh trousseau, and yesterday the couple were married at St. Christopher's Chapel in New York.

The unknown French boys have been temporarily adopted by Miss Margaret Hayes, a survivor. "I intend to keep these lost babies of the sea," Miss Hayes told her parents, "until someone appears with a better claim to them." Dressed in new clothes the little boys, aged 3 and 2, play delightedly in their new home oblivious of the tragedy. The French Consul-General yesterday visited them and questioned them adroitly, but beyond "Oui" and "Non" and something that was interpreted as "a big place," he could extract no information. They appear to answer to the names of Louis and Lola.

The Consul-General will scatter photographs of the boys, who appear to be of good family, throughout France and England. They are believed to have joined the *Titanic* at Cherbourg.

The White Star officials at Liverpool point out that the following appears in their list of second-class survivors: —

"Mr. Lolo Hoffman and Mr. Louis Hoffman, children of Mr. Hoffman."

The company do not know where the children joined the ship or where they came from, and have no other information.

*(Daily Mail, 22 April)*

# BRAVE WOMEN.

## LIGHTS SEEN BY PEOPLE IN THE BOATS.

*From Our Own Correspondent.*
*NEW YORK, Saturday.*

Those rescued of the crew who were not subpoened left today by the *Lapland*, returning as destitute British seamen who have the right to be taken home after shipwreck. They were very unwilling to talk. "We have our orders," some of them said.

Four of them, however, stated that they never had a boat-muster after the *Titanic* left Southampton. Such a muster was expected on Sunday, but the orders never came, and when in the middle of the night the need came for all men to make for their places in lowering and manning the boats they had to rely on their memories of the number assigned when they shipped.

They all told of lights they saw, little lights full of hope for them, when they knew the *Titanic* was foundering. These lights seemed five miles off, and were thought to be those of one or more fishing smacks. They signalled frantically, but got no response.

Alfred White, one of two oilers from the engine-room who were saved, said: "I was on the whale deck in the bow calling the watch that was to relieve me when the ice first came aboard. It was a black berg we struck — that is, it was composed of black ice and could not be seen at all by night. The collision opened the seams below the water-line but did not even scratch the paint above the line. I know that because I was one of those who helped to make an examination over the side with a lantern."

"I went down into the engine-room, where my station was, at 12.40 a.m. We even made coffee, so there was not much thought of danger. An hour later I was still working at the light engines. I heard the chief engineer tell one of his subordinates that No.6 bulkhead had given way. At that time things began to look bad, for the *Titanic* was far down by the bow. I was told to go up and see how things were, and made my way up through a dummy funnel to the bridge deck."

"By that time all the boats had left the ship, yet everyone in the engine-room was at his post. I was near the captain and heard him say, "Well, boys, it's every man for himself now.""

## A WOMAN'S SACRIFICE.

Much has been said of the heroism of the men who died in the *Titanic*, but the survivors say there were conspicuous instances of bravery among the women. Miss Evans, of New York, gave up her place in a lifeboat in order that her aunt might be saved. She declared that as she was unmarried while her aunt was married and had children, her aunt's life was more important. Miss Evans died.

"There was one woman in my boat as was a woman," said a seaman from Southampton. "She was the Countess of Rothes. There were thirty-five of us in the boat, mostly women. I saw the way she was carrying herself and the quiet, determined manner in which she spoke, and I knew she was more of a man than most aboard, so I put her in command at the tiller. There was another woman in the boat who helped, and was every minute rowing. It was she who suggested we should sing, and we sang as we rowed, starting with 'Pull for the shore.' We were still singing when we saw the lights of the *Carpathia*, and then we stopped singing and prayed."

195

Mrs. J.J. Brown, wife of a Denver mine-owner, said: "It was all so formal that it was difficult for anyone to realize it was a tragedy. Men and women stood in little groups and talked and laughed. I was looking down at the boats being filled when two men seized me, threw me into a boat, with the words, 'You're going too.' I owe my life to them. I can still see the men up on deck tucking in the women and bowing and smiling. It was a strange sight. It all seemed like a drama being enacted for our entertainment. It did not seem real."

**"AFTER YOU."**

"Men would say, 'After you,' as they made some woman comfortable and stepped back. I afterwards heard someone say that men went downstairs into the restaurant, and many of them smoked for a while. After we reached the water we watched the ship. We could hear the band, and every light was shining."

"It did not seem long before there was a great sweep of the water. A great wave rose once and then fell, and we knew the *Titanic* had gone. I saw no dead people. To me there was hardly one tragic or harrowing element near me. We were in a boat, we were safe, we were at work. I was simply hypnotised."

A certificate that he is honourably alive is exhibited by an officer of the Queen's Own Rifles of Toronto. The certificate runs:

"Major Arthur Peuchen was ordered into the boat by me owing to the fact that I required a seaman, which he proved to be, as well as a brave man. — C.W. LIGHTOLLER, second officer, late steamship *Titanic*."

To the same category belongs a message brought to the Guggenheim family by a rescued steward. It runs:

From Benjamin Guggenheim. Tell my wife I drowned. I've tried to do my duty.

The steward narrated that Mr. Guggenheim assisted the officers in getting the women into the boats. "I woke him and his secretary," said the steward, whose name is Etches, "and I dressed them in heavy sweaters. An hour after I found them working in dress suits. 'What's this for?' I asked."

"'We've dressed up in our best,'
replied Mr. Guggenheim, 'and
are prepared to go down like
gentlemen.'

Then he gave me the message
to his wife."

*(Daily Mail, 23 April)*

## A CLUE FROM NICE.

*From Our Own Correspondent.*
*NICE, Monday.*

The two children rescued from
the *Titanic* are believed to be
those of Mme. Narvatel, of Nice,
who is separated from her husband. About a month ago the
children, whose names are Louis
and Lolo, aged respectively 3
and 2 years, disappeared from
the mother's custody.

The husband, who is a tailor,
was heard to say that he intended to leave Nice for America,
and it is surmised that, having
obtained possession of the children, he may have sailed in the
*Titanic* under the name of
Hoffman or placed them in the
care of a friend bearing that
name. Mme. Narvatel has telegraphed to New York request-
ing that photographs of the two
children be sent her.

*(Daily Mail, 23 April)*

## 50 BODIES PICKED UP.

**BURIALS AT SEA OF THOSE NOT
EMBALMED.**

*NEW YORK, Monday.*

The White Star Company has
received the following wireless
message from the cable ship
*Mackay-Bennett:* —

"Heavy south-west squall interfered with operations. Fifty
bodies from *Titanic* recovered."

"All unembalmed will be buried
at sea at eight in the evening with
divine services. Can only bring
embalmed bodies to port."

Another message says that the
*Mackay-Bennett* reports having
recovered sixty-four bodies floating near the scene of the disaster.

These, it is thought, may still be
identified. Several others, which
were beyond recognition, have
already been buried at sea. — *Reuter.*

*(Daily Mail, 23 April)*

## IGNORANCE OF THE

## COMMITTEE.

Attention is called by The Times New York correspondent to an extraordinary question asked by Senator Smith, Chairman of the Senate Committee. Questioning Mr. Lightoller, the second officer, Senator Smith said:

Were there any watertight compartments in that ship? — Certainly, forty or fifty.

Do you know whether any of the crew or passengers took to these watertight compartments as a last resort? — It is quite impossible for me to say, sir. I should think it very unlikely.

Are the watertight compartments intended as a refuge for passengers? — Oh, dear no, sir, not at any time.

*(MAIL, APRIL 25)*

## CAPT. SMITH'S £1,250.

### EXCEPTIONAL SALARY.

The salaries paid to the captains and other officers employed by the great Atlantic shipping lines are furnished by our Liverpool correspondent. Captain Smith, the commander of the *Titanic*, received £1,250 a year, but his salary was exceptionally large.

### CAPTAIN SMITH'S INSURANCE.

The White Star Line's insurance and pension scheme applies to the senior members of the different departments on board ship. According to a table furnished by the company the payment due to the widow of Captain Smith is £1,168.

Any man on the ship's articles, whether officer or ordinary member of the crew, whose total earnings do not reach £250 will come under the scope of the Workmen's Compensation Act.

*(MAIL, APRIL 27)*

## THE OLYMPIC STRIKE.

### CAPTAIN'S SIGNAL TO A CRUISER.

### EXCITING SCENES ON BOARD.

### "THIS IS MUTINY."

### ARREST OF 53 SAILORS.

### VOYAGE ABANDONED.

The White Star liner *Olympic*, sister ship of the *Titanic*, yesterday abandoned her voyage to New York owing to the desertion of the crew. The great liner, which had been delayed since Wednesday in the Solent, returned to port last evening, when her passengers disembarked.

The trouble began on Wednesday, when some of the firemen alleged that the collapsible boats were unseaworthy, refused to sail, and left the ship. The company hastily recruited 100 men in Portsmouth and brought about 150 more by special train from Liverpool and Sheffield.

These men reached the *Olympic* by tug late on Thursday night. The loyal men on board took objection to the newcomers on the ground that they were non-unionists and not fit for their work. The seamen began to climb from the *Olympic* into the tug which had brought the strike breakers.

Captain Haddock, of the *Olympic*, ordered them to return without effect. He signalled by lamp to the cruiser Cochrane, whose captain came aboard and warned the men that they were guilty of mutinous behaviour and liable to heavy punishment. The men refused to return.

Yesterday morning the tug returned to Southampton with the deserters. Fifty-three seamen were arrested as they stepped ashore. They were brought before the magistrates and remanded till Tuesday.

The *Olympic* berthed again at eight o'clock last night. Seventy-two of the passengers had volunteered to work in the stokehold, but the offer was refused. The Duke of Sutherland tried to raise a crew of volunteer yachtsmen, but the deserters could not have been all replaced. The *Olympic* is laid up until May 15.

The passage money is being refunded. Some of the passengers are making efforts to catch the *Lusitania* at Liverpool today and others are taking German liners at Havre or Southampton.

*(MAIL, APRIL 27)*

## "NOT THE TITANIC."

**MYSTERY OF A SHIP WHICH SENT UP ROCKETS.**

*WASHINGTON, Friday.*
Ernest Gill, of Liverpool, aged twenty-nine, a donkey-engine man of the *Californian*, the ship nearest the *Titanic* when she

# THE GRAPHIC

## AN ILLUSTRATED WEEKLY NEWSPAPER

The entire contents of this paper, both Illustrations and Letterpress, are copyright.

No. 2213.— VOL. LXXXV.
Registered as a Newspaper

SATURDAY, APRIL 27, 1912

WITH EIGHT-PAGE SUPPLEMENT

PRICE SIXPENCE
By Post, 6½d.

## THE LAST CALL : CAPTAIN SMITH'S FINAL ORDER TO THE CREW OF THE DOOMED TITANIC

From the moment of the collision until the Titanic disappeared below the waves, Captain Smith did his utmost to save every soul, and when the end came he refused to be saved, and went down with his ship. Before he was washed from his post he is said to have shouted through his megaphone, "Be British!" to the crew on the deck below.

DRAWN BY DOUGLAS MACPHERSON

# DAILY SKETCH.

No. 978—SATURDAY, APRIL 27, 1912.    THE PREMIER PICTURE PAPER.    [Registered as a Newspaper.]    ONE HALFPENNY.

## OLYMPIC VOYAGE ABANDONED OWING TO MUTINY.

As a protest against the introduction of non-unionist firemen the Olympic's fifty seamen and quartermasters deserted and jumped into the tug which had brought the new firemen to the liner. Captain Haddock signalled to the cruiser Cochrane and the commander failed to persuade the deck hands to return to the Olympic. The shore police were sent for, and early yesterday morning the deserters were placed in custody and conveyed to Portsmouth to be charged at the police court. The first photograph shows the loyal firemen looking through the portholes of the great liner during the testing of one of the collapsible boats by the deputation. Below is a picture showing the position of the Olympic at Spithead, with the cruiser Cochrane to the right.—Photographs by *Daily Sketch* and Cribb.

DAILY SKETCH,

# CREW DESERT THE OLYMPIC AND ARE ARRESTED

The sailors of the Olympic on board the tug Albert Edward as she made fast at Portsmouth on bringing the deserters from the Olympic. The seamen are seen leaving with their kits.

As each of the Olympic crew left the tug at Portsmouth with non-union

## TESTING THE COLLAPSIBLE BOATS.

The testing of the collapsible boats by the firemen's deputation. Captain Haddock says the alleged insecurity is pure nonsense. Forty collapsible boats from troopships are on board, and they have been tested and passed by the Board of Trade.

One of the firemen pointing out a rent in a collapsible during the launching and trials of the boats. It was such discoveries that led the men to refuse to sail.

## Hoping Against Hope: Painful Vigil of Anx

The scene outside the offices of the White Star Company in New York before the Carpathia broug and stood for hours, filling the small Bowling Green Park, etc

# HEY COME ASHORE FOR DISOBEYING THE CAPTAIN.

...narge by a policeman. The sailors who refused to work ...ing off under arrest.

The seamen marching to the Portsmouth Town Hall under police escort from the Harbour Railway Station. The onlookers raised cries of encouragement, and the deserters seemed to be in excellent spirits. They sang sea songs in the cells and were remanded on bail.

## ...ives Before Survivors Arrived in New York.

## THE SAILORS AND THE FIREMEN—A CONTRAST.

The long file of Olympic deserters, accompanied by the police, walking along the road after coming ashore at Portsmouth.

...re last week. The offices were besieged by relatives and friends of the passengers, who sat ...ble news after the lists of the survivors had been given out.

The Olympic firemen who are on strike sitting about on their kits on the quayside yesterday awaiting developments. Some of the men, as will be seen, are enjoying a nap in the sunshine.

sank, was called before the Committee.

Senator Smith first read an affidavit made by Gill on Wednesday. He said that he saw the *Titanic* most plainly. Ten minutes after midnight he saw a white rocket ten miles away. A second rocket went up seven or eight minutes later. He said to himself, "That must be a vessel in distress." He did not notify the bridge, because it was not his business. They could not have helped seeing the rockets.

At 6.40 a.m. he was awakened by orders to turn out to render assistance as the *Titanic* had gone down. The *Californian* was then proceeding at full speed. He heard the second officer, Evans, telling the fourth officer, Wooten, that the third officer had reported rockets during his watch. Gill said that he knew then that it must be the *Titanic* he had seen. Mr. Gibson reported rockets to the captain, who told him to continue Morse to the distressed vessel until he got a reply. No reply was received. Gill said that the next remark he heard Evans make was, "Why the devil don't they wake the wireless man?" The entire crew, according to Gill, talked among themselves about the disregard of the rockets.

**CAPTAIN'S DENIAL.**

Captain Stanley Lord, of the *Californian*, who was prepared to give a sweeping denial to Gill's statements, then took the stand.

How far were the *Californian* and *Titanic* apart when you sent the message to the *Titanic* telling him that you were blocked in the ice? — We were about nineteen and a half miles apart.

Did the *Californian* receive the *Titanic's* distress call? — No. We got it from the *Virginian* about six o'clock in the morning. We made 13 knots when we were going to the *Titanic*. We were driving her all we could.

Did you see any of the *Titanic's* signals or anything of the ship herself? — No.

Was the *Titanic* beyond your range of vision? — Yes; nineteen and a half or twenty miles away.

On Sunday night, he continued, the watch was doubled. We had reports two or three days before of the presence of ice ahead, and I took precautions.

From whom did you receive those reports? — Captain Barr, of the *Caronia*, gave us the report on April 13. The day before he told us that west-bound steamers had reported a field of ice.

What was your next warning? — The *Parisian* was ahead of us. I asked the *Parisian* on April 14 in the daytime. She said that she had passed three large icebergs. The *New Amsterdam* also warned us.

If you had received the distress call on Sunday evening how long would it have taken you to reach her? — At the very least two hours.

Do you know whether your wireless operator was on duty on Sunday night after he sent the warning message? — I think not. I went by his room about 11.45. There was no light, and that would indicate that he had gone to bed.

I did not see any distress signals. When I came on to the bridge at 10.30 on Sunday night the officer said he thought he saw a light. It was a peculiar night. We had been having trouble with the stars, mistaking them for lights. Then a ship came up.

I asked the operator if he had heard anything. He replied that he had, from the *Titanic,* to which he had given the ice message.

**ANOTHER SHIP'S ROCKETS.**

Then this ship came up and lay within four or five miles of us. She lay there all night, but we couldn't hear from her. It was not the *Titanic*, I am sure of that.

About one o'clock I told the operator to call this ship again. She sent up several rockets, but would not answer. I told him to ask her who she was. I heard him calling her when I went to bed, but she did not answer. I have a faint recollection of hearing the cabin boy about four o'clock saying something about the ship still standing by. Soon after she steamed away.

This boat sent up several white rockets, but they were not distress signals. In the position in which the *Californian* lay, eighteen miles away from the *Titanic,* it would have been impossible to see either Morse or distress signals. The ice conditions that night were very deceiving.

Cyril Evans, the wireless operator in the *Californian* said:

I called the *Titanic* and said, "Say, old man, we surrounded ice." He replied, "Shut up, I'm working with Cape Race." and said I had jammed him. I did not hear him again direct, but I knew he was sending messages to Cape Race. I didn't take them down.

I went to bed at 11.30. I was awakened at 3.40 by the chief officer, who said he had seen rockets and wanted to get some information.

I called, and the *Frankfurt* answered with the news of the sinking of the *Titanic*. The *Virginian* called before I left the key and furnished more information. I have none of the messages which passed because they were merely conversational.

Did anyone tell you about Captain Lord being informed three times that night about a ship sending up rockets? — I think Gibson, the apprentice, told me that the captain was called and told about the rockets. The rockets were talked about in the ship generally by the crew. While the *Californian* was on the way to the scene he heard the men say that five rockets had been sent up and that the captain had been roused. The apprentice got out Morse signals and tried to get into communication with the distressed vessel. No effort was made to use rockets in the *Californian*.

Gill expected to get £100 for his rocket story from some newspapers when he got ashore. — *Reuter's* Special.

*(MAIL, APRIL 27)*

## ANOTHER MYSTERY.

**SHIP THAT WAS SEEN FROM THE SINKING LINER.**

*WASHINGTON, Friday.*

Edward J. Baley, able seaman, of Southampton, of the *Titanic*, testified that another steamer with two lights at her masthead was visible when the *Titanic* struck.

She passed right by us, he said, and we thought that she was coming to us. If she had everyone could have boarded her. The lifeboats started for those very lights, and it was these

206

lights which kept the boats together. For about three hours the steamer was stationary, and then she made tracks. Mr. Fletcher: Why could she not see your sky-rockets? – She could not help seeing them. She was close enough to see our lights, and we could see the ship itself. I saw this steamer before I left the *Titanic* and told the passengers that it was coming to our assistance. That was what kept the passengers quiet. The steamer gave no signal whatever, but they must have known the *Titanic* was in distress for they must have seen our rockets. – *Reuter's* Special.

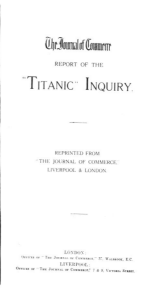

*The British enquiry found that the Titanic was travelling too fast, a proper look-out was not kept and the lifeboats were not manned properly. It also stated that in their opinion, the Californian might have made more effort to reach the Titanic, although Captain Lord said he was too far away. Since the recent discovery of the Titanic, it has been proved that the Californian was actually too far away to help. The enquiry's recommendation was that more watertight compartments were to be installed in ocean liners, better look-outs, and lifeboats for all.*

The accident to the *Titanic* calls attention to another great ship for the White Star Line, the keel of which was laid during the past week in Messrs. Harland & Wolff's Belfast yards  The vessel which will be named the *Gigantic,* and at 924ft will be considerably larger than any other vessel. (**Author's note**: This ship was re-named *Brittanic*. Launched in 1914, she was requisitioned by the Government, and after fitting out as a hospital ship, was mined in the Aegean Sea in 1915, with the loss of 28 lives. Over 1000 passengers and crew were saved.)

# DAILY SKETCH.

No. 979.—MONDAY, APRIL 29, 1912.　　　THE PREMIER PICTURE PAPER.　[Registered as a Newspaper.]　ONE HALFPENNY.

## FIRST SURVIVORS OF TITANIC TO REACH ENGLAND.

The Lapland, the Red Star liner, arriving in Cawsand Bay, off Plymouth, yesterday morning with the Titanic survivors on board. The crew of the lost liner were not brought ashore immediately, but waited on the tender (Sir Richard Grenville) until the mails and passengers were got away from Plymouth. In the lower photograph the Titanic men are seen leaning against the taffrail of the tender.—*Daily Sketch* Photographs.

# The GREATEST WRECK in HISTORY
## THE LOSS OF THE WHITE STAR TITANIC
### THE LARGEST SHIP IN THE WORLD, WHICH SANK ON ITS MAIDEN VOYAGE WITH A LOSS OF 1635 LIVES

### LEAVING THE SINKING LINER: A PERILOUS MOMENT FOR THE LIFEBOATS

"'Stop lowering 14,' our crew shouted, and the crew of No. 14, now only 20 feet above, cried out the same. The distance to the top, however, was some seventy feet, and the creaking of the pulleys must have deadened all sound to those above, for down she came fifteen feet, ten feet, five feet and a stoker and I reached up and touched the bottom of the swinging boat above our heads. The next drop would have brought her on our heads. Just before she dropped, another stoker sprang to the ropes with his knife open in his hand. 'One,' I heard him say, and then 'Two,' as the knife cut through the pulley-ropes. The next moment the exhaust-stream carried us clear."—Mr. Beeston's narrative.

## The First Photograph of Titanic Passengers on the Carpathia Arrives on

Beds on the floor and tables laid for a meal.  The men strenuously opposed being detained, and when they saw the arrangements that had been made to keep them " prisoners " became quite unmanageable.

Mr. and Mrs. George A. Harder, a h the Carpathia to Mrs. C. M. H

An undertaker about to leave for the scene of the disaster with coffins.

Some of the survivors of the Titanic who arrived on the Lapland ye

Not even yet has the extraordinary interest in the Titanic disaster and its sequels dropped.  Every day brings a new incident; in fact, drama is piled on drama.  Yesterday, when the men w

## apland, Which Brings also Rescued Sailors Who Refused To Be "Housed."

saved from the Titanic, talking on
onaire husband was drowned.

A boat in which were trade union officials alongside the tender. One of them (holding the sail) is addressing the survivors. Later the president and secretary of the Seafarers' Union were allowed on board. Then the men refused to be kept "prisoners."

ken ashore in a tender. They said they would not be "prisoners."

The Lady Mayoress and Sir William Soulsby with relief fund cheques.

om the Titanic crew arrived at Plymouth, they jeered at the arrangements made to house them while their depositions were taken, and went home instead.—(*Daily Mirror* photographs.)

# THE RULE OF THE SEA — "WOMEN AND CHILDREN FIRST"

FINAL FAREWELLS BETWEEN WIVES AND HUSBANDS IN THE SINKING TITANIC

# WHAT HAPPENED — THE UNDOING OF THE TITANIC
## THE PRECISE NATURE OF THE DAMAGE WROUGHT BY THE ICEBERG

Note. The above Section is taken between the Foremast and the First Funnel. For explanation of Bulkheads see page 592.

# IF ONLY WE COULD FLY THE ATLANTIC!

## ONE WAY BY WHICH THE ICEBERG DANGER WOULD BE AVOIDED

This diagram tells its own story of how we have conquered time and space. In prehistoric days, America was a week's journey from Europe. V. Martin, in an aeroplane fitted with floats, proposes to attempt a flight across from New-foundland to Ireland in fort hours, so that he can cover the two thousand miles in forty hours. Once accomplished, it will not be long before the journey is made in a single day.

DRAWN BY SID TREEBY

214

# FAMILY OF EIGHT, WHO WERE ON THE TITANIC BY CHANCE, ALL DROWNED IN THE DISASTER BECAUSE THERE WERE NOT ENOUGH LIFEBOATS.

the many sad cases of the Titanic disaster, few are more tragic than that of Goodwins, of Kensington, all of whom were drowned. The family consisted ather, mother and six children, and it was only by chance that they were on the nic. They originally intended to sail during Easter week, but waited for the York on account of the coal strike. At the last minute, however, they were sferred to the ill-starred liner. They were on their way to join Mr. Good-

win's brother at Niagara, where they intended to settle. (1) Mr. and Mrs. Goodwin and five of their children. (2) Sidney, the baby, aged eighteen months. (3) Mme. Navratil, of Nice, with her two children, who are believed to be Louis and Lolo, the French boys who were rescued. Mme. Navratil is certain they are hers, because of a number of coincidences she has noted. She is divorced from her husband, who took the children away.

# DISASTER TO TITANIC

**THE SCENE AT THE WHITE STAR OFFICES AND SOME OF THE TITANIC'S PASSENGERS.**

The White Star Line offices at Charing Cross were without first-hand information during the earlier part of the day, and anxious inquirers could gain no more information as to the Titanic's fate than appeared in the afternoon editions of the evening papers. Paper-boys in good numbers gathered outside the offices, and did a brisk business. The portraits here given are of some of the Titanic's distinguished passengers. Top (left to right): The Countess of Rothes, Mr. Norman Craig, and Mr. W. T. Stead, editor of the "Review of Reviews." Below (left): Mrs. Levison, a well-known New York hostess; (right) Colonel J. J. Astor.

("Daily Graphic" photograph; top portraits by Lafayette, Bond Street.)

May 1, 1912

# FUNERAL BOAT ARRIVES AT HALIFAX

### Mackay Bennett Brings 190 Bodies Into Port.

The funeral ship, the Mackay-Bennett, which has recovered a large number of bodies, including Colonel Astor's.

The Mackay-Bennett, which is steaming towards the scene of the disaster in search of bodies. Coffins are being taken, and several undertakers and embalmers are on board. She also carries a Church of England clergyman.

An undertaker about to leave for the scene of the disaster with coffins.

The sole relic of the Titanic disaster. It is an oak dining-room chair, and was picked up by the steamer Mackay Bennett, the vessel which was sent to search for bodies.

## LOUIS AND LOLO.

### Two Titanic Babies Sail for Their Home with Their Mother.

**(From Our Own Correspondent.)**

NEW YORK, May 19.—The Titanic babies, Louis and Lolo, are on their way home after their terrible mid-ocean adventure.

Mme. Navratil, happy at the recovery of her two little boys, Louis and Edmond, sailed yesterday on the Oceanic for Cherbourg and Nice.

As the little chaps were carried aboard the big liner they seemed nervous at the sight of the water, and evidently still remembered the dark night voyage in the open boat when they left the sinking Titanic.

There are only sixty-one first class passengers on the Oceanic for this trip.

## HALIFAX AWAITS TITANIC'S DEAD.

### Sad Preparations for Arrival To-day of Funeral Ship.

## ANGUISHED RELATIVES.

**(From Our Own Correspondent.)**

NEW YORK, April 28.—Preparations are now practically completed at Halifax for the reception of the bodies of the Titanic victims which arrive by the Mackay Bennett to-morrow.

Undertakers are arriving with quantities of embalming fluid, and rows of coffins are piled high on the pier of the navy yard. Undertakers' wagons are to be seen driving through the streets in all directions.

The most recent message received at Halifax from the Mackay Bennett is:

"Confirm report that the bodies of Colonel Astor and Mr. I. Straus are on board. Due Monday with bodies."

It is known that the ship has picked up 219 bodies, and now great anxiety prevails among relatives as to which have been buried at sea owing to the lack of embalming fluid on the funeral ship.

Private cars, which will be waiting at the station, will carry away the bodies of Colonel Astor, Mr. Widener and Mr. C. M. Hays, president of the Grand Trunk Railway.

Only officials will be permitted to board the funeral ship.

The identified dead will be placed in the mortuary parlour, but those as yet unidentified will be conveyed to the Mayflower Curling Rink on the outskirts of Halifax. The public will be excluded, only relatives being allowed admission.

### 190 IDENTIFIED.

The White Star Company, says a Reuter's message from New York, has received a wireless message from the Mackay Bennett stating that eighty-two additional bodies of those who perished in the Titanic disaster have been recovered and identified.

Up to Saturday the number of dead identified was stated to be 171. Yesterday the total reached 190.

Among the bodies identified is that of Mr. Wallace H. Hartley, the gallant leader of the ship's band, who went heroically playing to their doom.

Another victim identified is Mr. Frank D. Millet, the American painter and journalist. Mr. Millet had resided in London for a considerable time, and was in his sixty-seventh year.

## WAS THIS THE ICEBERG THAT SANK THE TITANIC?

The liner Amerika, which passed close to the spot where the Titanic sank eight hours after the catastrophe, reported having seen numerous icebergs, one of which was estimated to have been 100 feet high and 1,000 feet broad. Photographs of this berg, which is believed to have sunk the giant liner, were taken by the passengers, and above is a reproduction of one of them.—(From the "New York Herald.")

ⱃAILY SKEⱃ

# THE SURVIVORS ALLOWED TO RETURN: MEN WHO ESCAPE

The survivors of the crew of the Titanic who were not required for the American Senatorial inquiry and allowed to return by the Lapland saw the  tender, Sir Richard Crenville, for some shores of the Old Country again when day broke on Sunday morning and they sailed quietly into Cawsand Bay, Plymouth.  They were kept on the / accommodated on the dock premises.

The Titanic firemen and seamen listening to the remarks of Mr. Phillips, president of the Seamen's Union, who instructed them to ask to see him on landing.

The steerage passengers of the Lapland deeply interested in the bustle of the t class passengers, who travelle

DAY, APRIL 29, 1912.

EATH WITH THE TITANIC THANKFUL TO SEE ENGLAND AGAIN.

photograph shows the men gazing eagerly over the rails. Afterwards the men were
or the forthcoming official inquiry, by the Board of Trade and the White Star Company.
—*Daily Sketch* Photograph.

Preparing the dockyard buildings at Plymouth to accommodate the men of the Titanic whose evidence
is required, and whom the White Star Company and Board of Trade desire to seclude from intruders.

The union firemen booing the "blacklegs" (with whom the seamen refused to work on the Olympic) when
the non-union firemen left Southampton by special train to return to the North on Saturday.

the return of the survivors of the Titanic. The Lapland also brought the mails, and first and **second**
special train. *Daily Sketch* Photographs.

**As a** precaution against eventualities the police guard on the docks at Southampton was maintained
throughout the week-end. It is feared the revolt may spread.

THURSDAY, MAY 2, 1912

# THE BOARD OF TRADE INQUIRY INTO THE LOSS OF THE TITANIC

## TO BE OPENED IN LONDON TO-DAY.

Lord Mersey, who will preside over the inquiry.

Captain A. W. Clarke.

Rear-Admiral S. Gough-Calthorpe.

## TITANIC'S BOATS.

Model of the Titanic, made for the inquiry. Portrait, Mr. E. C. Chaston.

Titanic lifeboats at New York. They are all that remain of the vessel.

DAILY SKETCH, TUESDAY, MAY 7, 1912.

## CLOTHING THE TITANIC SURVIVORS.

The officials of the Seamen's Home, New York, fitting out the surviving members of the ill-fated Titanic's crew with new clothing

## THE TITANIC

### THE UPPER DECK OF THE TITANIC.

A view showing some of the lifeboats by which many of the survivors left the ship. Most of the boats were filled with women and children, and all these boats have been accounted for.

("Daily Graphic" photograph.)

## AT FULL SPEED.

### Head-On Collision Might Have Saved the Ship.

### UNFILLED BOATS.

Men Turned Away from Families When There Was Room.

NEW YORK, Friday.

The *New York World* contains a complete story of the disaster written by their staff correspondent, Carlos F. Hurd, who chanced to be a passenger on board the Carpathia. Mr. Hurd writes:

The facts which I have established, as positively as they could be established in view of the silence of the few surviving officers, are that the Titanic's officers knew several hours before the crash of the possible nearness of icebergs; that the Titanic's speed was nearly twenty-three knots; and that this speed was not slackened.

That women went first was the rule. In some cases it was applied to the extent of turning men back who were with their families, even though there were not enough women to fill the boats available at that particular part of the deck. Some few of the boats were thus lowered without being completely filled, but most of these soon filled with sailors and stewards, who were picked up out of the water, and helped to man them.

The bulkhead system, though it was probably working in the manner intended, availed only to delay the ship's sinking. Had the ship struck the iceberg head on, at whatever speed and with whatever resultant shock, the bulkhead system and the water-tight compartments would probably have saved the vessel.

**THE CLICK OF THE LEVERS.**

The night was starry. The sea was glassy. The lights in most of the state rooms were out. Only two or three congenial groups remained in the public rooms. In the crow's nest the look-out on the bridge, the officers and members of the crew were at their places awaiting relief at midnight from their two hours' watch. At 11.45 p.m. came the sudden sound of two gongs warning against immediate danger.

The crash against the iceberg, which had been sighted when it was only a quarter of a mile away, came almost simultaneously with the click of the levers, operated by those on the bridge, which stopped the engines and closed the watertight doors.

Captain Smith remained on the bridge until just before the ship sank, leaping from her only after those on the decks had been washed away.

When one of the cooks sought to pull him aboard a lifeboat Captain Smith exclaimed, "Let me go!" and, jerking himself away, went down.

**A NUMBING BATH.**

As the end of the Titanic became manifestly but a matter of moments the oarsmen pulled their boats away. The chilling water began to echo with splash after splash as the passengers and sailors with life preservers leaped overboard and started swimming away to escape the expected suction.

Only the hardiest constitution could endure more than a few minutes of such a numbing bath, and then their first vigorous strokes gave way to heartbreaking cries of "Help! Help!" Then their stiffened forms were seen floating with their features relaxed in death.

**BOATS SET ADRIFT.**

After the boats were picked up by the Carpathia they were unloaded and set adrift for lack of room in which to put them.

Few of the men of the Carpathia's passenger list slept in bed on any of the nights that followed. They lay on chairs on the deck, on the dining table, or floor. The captain was the first to vacate his room, which was used as a hospital.

In the first cabin library women of wealth and refinement mingled their tears and asked eagerly for news of the possible arrival of a belated boat or a message telling of the safety of their husbands.

Those who talked with Mrs. Astor said that she spoke often of her husband's ability as an oarsman, and said that he could save himself if he had a chance.—Reuter's Special Service.

*Left: Some of the Titanic stewardesses on arrival at Plymouth. They were the first of the crew to be released from their temporary detention at Plymouth. (Southampton Museums)*

*Right: Some of the imprisoned stewards enjoying their lunch at Plymouth. This virtual imprisonment of the survivors was a disgrace, and thanks to union officials who told the crew not to discuss the sinking with the authorities, most of the crew were freed the following day, April 29th (Southampton Museums)*

*Left: Mr Pascoe of 68 High Street, Itchen, Southampton, re-united with his family on April 29th 1912. (Southampton Museums)*

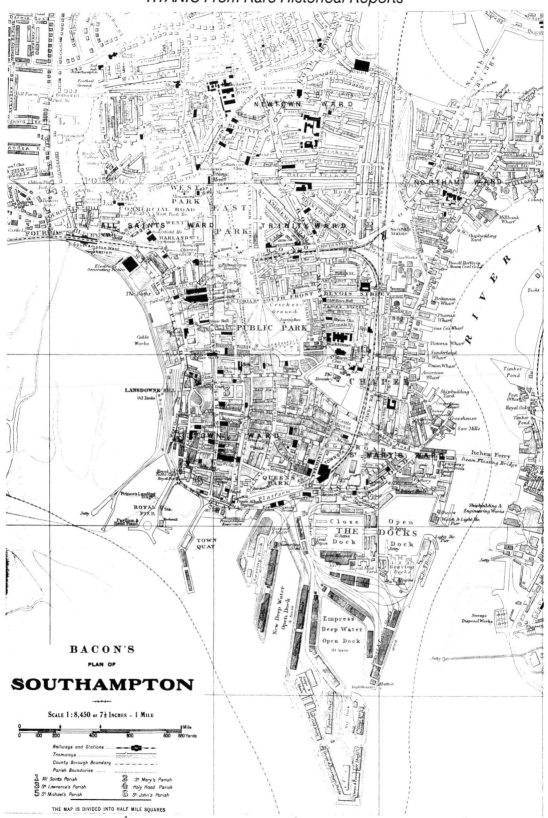

BACON'S

PLAN OF

# SOUTHAMPTON

SCALE 1 : 8,450 or 7½ INCHES = 1 MILE

Railways and Stations ......
Tramways ......
County Borough Boundary ......
Parish Boundaries ......

1 All Saints Parish      2 St Mary's Parish
3 St Lawrence's Parish   4 Holy Rood Parish
5 St Michael's Parish    6 St John's Parish

THE MAP IS DIVIDED INTO HALF MILE SQUARES

*Previous Page: Street map of Southampton, showing the main areas where the crew lived. Titanic sailed from the new deepwater dock, shown on this map, then along the river towards Dock Head where the New York was berthed.*
*The following streets all had crew-members living in them. most went down with the ship:*
*Albert Rd, Argyle Rd, Bellevue Rd, Belvedere Terrace, Bevois St, Bevois Valley Rd, Black Lane, Briton St, Brinton's Rd, Cable St, Canute Rd, Cedar Rd, Chantry Rd, Chapel Rd, College St, Coleman St, Cranbury Ave, Crosshouse Rd, Derby Rd, Denzil Ave, Elm Rd, Empress Rd, Earls Rd, Floating Bridge Rd, Field Lane, Fanshawe St, Golden Grove, Jessie Terrace, Kingsland Square, Latimer St, Lower Ditches, Lower Canal Walk, Marine Terrace, Millbank St, Northumberland Rd, Orchard Lane, Ordnance Rd, Paget St, Palmerston Rd, Park View, Queen's Park Terrace, Rochester St, Ryde Terrace, Russel St, St. Mary's St, St. Mary's Rd, St. Peter's Rd, St. Andrew's Rd, Sailor's Home, Short St, South Front, Terminus Terrace, Union Place, Windsor Terrace, York St.*

*Left and below: These two photographs, believed to be unpublished show a brother and sister who were crew members on the Titanic. The man died, the lady was saved. Frank Richard Allsop of 73 Obelisk Rd, Woolston, Southampton was a saloon steward aged 43. Mrs McClaren (nee Allsop) of 9 Shirley Rd, Southampton was the saved sister.*

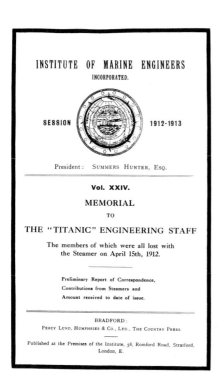

INSTITUTE OF MARINE ENGINEERS
INCORPORATED.

SESSION 1912-1913

President : SUMMERS HUNTER, ESQ.

**Vol. XXIV.**

MEMORIAL

TO

THE "TITANIC" ENGINEERING STAFF

The members of which were all lost with
the Steamer on April 15th, 1912.

Preliminary Report of Correspondence,
Contributions from Steamers and
Amount received to date of issue.

BRADFORD :
PERCY LUND, HUMPHRIES & CO., LTD., THE COUNTRY PRESS.

Published at the Premises of the Institute, 58, Romford Road, Stratford,
London, E.

*Left: The Institute of Marine Engineers started a fund to raise money for a memorial to the engineers who stayed at their posts and kept the dynamos working as long as possible. Non survived, and this small book contains photo's and biographies of those engineers.*

*On April 29th 1914, the Titanic Engineers Memorial was unveiled in Southampton's East Park. The unveiling was watched by a crowd of many thousands including the author's grandparents. Today, this is the best known and most visited Titanic memorial in the world.*

*Above: Spectators at the unveiling.*

**Since 1912, many items have been made commemorating the disaster. The following few pages show a small selection of some of those items...**

*A rivet, supposedly from her hull, left over during construction and engraved with the ship and date of sinking. This one was purchased by a survivor in 1912.*

*Above: Two items of commemorative chinaware produced in 1912.
In later years, similar items would be produced for the Lusitania.*

*Right: A tin 'in memoriam' badge.
These were also made in a form of
crude plastic.*

*Left: These paintings on glass were
inlaid with mother of pearl so that the
portholes, on reflecting the light,
appeared to glow.*

*Left: A tobacco tin with Olympic on the front. The message inside the lid reads: 'Olympic and Titanic, the two largest steamers in the world.'. The bottom of the tin has a serrated section for striking matches.*

*Below: This embroidery was made by a lady whose brother perished on the Titanic. When it was completed, she could not bear to look at it, and folded it in tissue paper. When the author purchased it in 1979, he was the first person to see it since 1912.*

*Some of the many books written about the Titanic since 1912.*

# The Titanic Disaster!

**A NIGHT TO REMEMBER** tells in terrifying detail the tragic events which led to the loss of over 1,500 men, women and children in *the greatest sea disaster in living memory*—the sinking of the Titanic.

THE RANK ORGANISATION
PRESENTS WITH PRIDE

## Kenneth More

# A NIGHT TO REMEMBER

FROM THE BOOK BY WALTER LORD
SCREENPLAY BY ERIC AMBLER
PRODUCED BY WILLIAM MacQUITTY
DIRECTED BY ROY BAKER

*Previous two pages: The Titanic disaster was a good story for the film companies, and in 1953, a Titanic feature was made featuring Clifton Webb and Barbara Stanwyck.*
*In 1958, the most famous Titanic film ever made: "A Night To Remember" starring Kenneth More, was released. The author still remembers going to see this film with his parents. Now, many years later, it is his own son's favourite film.*

*A jigsaw spin-off from the film.*

# BRITISH LINER.

# SUNK:

### THE CARPATHIA SUNK.

## FAMOUS LINER SUNK ON WAR SERVICE.

The Carpathia, formerly a famous Cunard liner, which has been sunk while on war service. She will be remembered as having picked up the only survivors from the ill-fated Titanic.

# CARPATHIA

The Cunard liner Carpathia was sunk in the Atlantic [west of Ireland] last Wednesday, when outward bound. Five men were killed through the torpedo entering the engine-room.

The survivors number 215, including thirty-six saloon and twenty-one steerage passengers.

Members of the crew state that just after the passengers had breakfasted a torpedo struck the vessel slightly forward of the engine-room, and a minute or two later a second torpedo crashed into the engine-room.

#### CARPATHIA'S FATE.

There was no panic of any description on board.

The passengers and the surviving members of the crew got away in small boats

The Carpathia looked like remaining afloat for a long time, but then the U-boat came to the surface and fired a third torpedo.

The liner filled rapidly and sank about two hours after the firing of the first torpedo.

After her disappearance the submarine approached the Carpathia's boats, but did not fire on them.

It is stated that the U-boat was a large two-masted vessel of the latest type.

The survivors were in the boats two hours when picked up by the steamer

The Carpathia was a steel twin-screw steamer, 13,603 gross tonnage, built by Messrs. Swan and Hunter, Newcastle, in 1903. It was the Carpathia which rescued survivors from the Titanic.

## CHILD WHO MISSED DEATH

### SEVEN WEEKS OLD BABY SAVED FROM THE TITANIC:

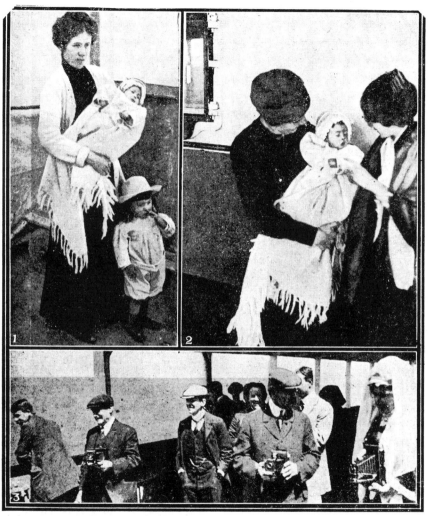

The youngest survivor of the Titanic disaster arrived at Liverpool on Saturday on board the Adriatic. Baby Dean, who is only seven weeks old, was the pet of the liner during the voyage, and so keen was the rivalry among the women to nurse this lovable mite of humanity that one of the officers decreed that first and second class passengers might hold her in turn for not more than ten minutes. Mr. Dean was among those drowned, but Mrs. Dean and her two children were saved. (1) The two little Deans. (2) Women passengers petting the baby while (3) others wait with their cameras to snapshot her.

*Bertram Dean at three years of age with his younger sister on the Carpathia after being rescued.*

*Right:* **Bert** *Dean in 1990 at the re-dedication of the plaque to the Titanic's musicians in Southampton. Bert is seen here with fellow survivor Eva Hart.*

*Right: A crew badge from the 1987 French dive on the wreck, during which several hundred artifacts were raised.*

*Above: In 1983, marine artist Chris Mayger painted The Maiden Voyage of the Titanic. It was turned into a large print and then a jigsaw puzzle, as shown here.*

*Above: 1982 70th Anniversary painting by Lawrence Bagley. One of 350 made and signed by survivor Bert Dean*

**Actual items from the Titanic are, understandably, very rare, and apart from letters and postcards posted at Southampton and Queenstown, seldom appear.**

**However, visitors and crew-members took items from the ship whilst she was fitting-out in Belfast, and later in dock at Southampton, so occasionally items do appear.**

**Items like these...**

*Above: A spoon with the ship's portrait in the bowl and name on the handle. This item was made to be sold on the ship in the hairdressing salon, and is the only one known to exist. The lady who originally owned this spoon told the author that her father had the concession to sell them in the salon where he was employed, and that her mother designed the spoon. This one was kept as a souvenir and is now on display in Southampton Maritime Museum.*

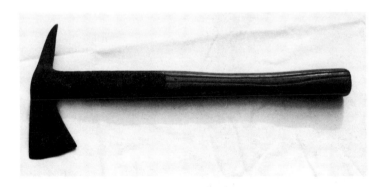

*Above: A ship's fire-axe stamped Titanic and found in a lifeboat by one of her quartermasters.*

*Above: A demitasse coffee cup and saucer taken in Southampton and bearing the batch mark for Titanic.*

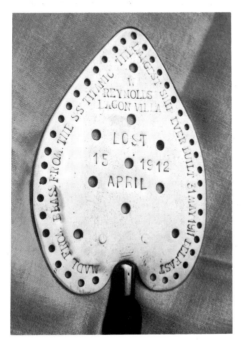

*Left: Brass trivet (or iron-stand) made in 1911 from brass used in the construction of the ship. The owner later had it stamped with the loss of the ship .*

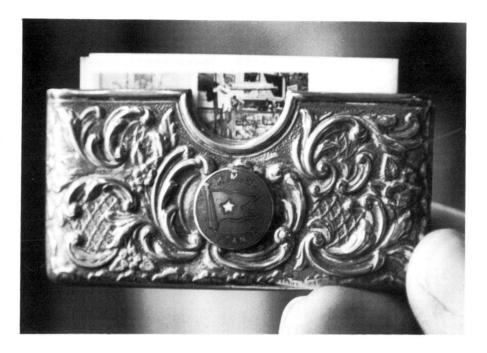

*Above: This silverplated visiting card case was taken from the ship by a disgruntled crew-member who was transferred to Olympic after bringing Titanic from Belfast. He also took ashtrays and glassware, but the card case is all that has survived.*

*Above: This brass crumb-tray was taken from the ship in Belfast, and after the sinking was engraved by the owner. It was purchased from an English auction house in the early 1970's.*

*Bringing us more up to date now are these two commemorative items (a trend that looks set to continue for the foreseeable future). Here we see a limited edition china plate and a thimble, both produced in 1989.*

FAREWELL TO BELFAST.
DEPARTURE OF THE LARGEST VESSEL IN THE WORLD,
THE WHITE STAR LINER "TITANIC," 46,328 TONS, APRIL 3rd, 1912.

WHITE STAR LINER TITANIC
LEAVING SOUTHAMPTON DOCKS
APRIL 10TH 1912

Titanic. triple Screw. 45,000. tons.
Largest Steamer in the World.

## AUTHOR'S POSTSCRIPT

The story of the *Titanic* will continue to fascinate generations as yet unborn, and provide material for books and films for a long time to come.

I hope that eventually the diving on her will stop, and that she will once again be allowed to rest in peace.

You can contact me at:

**Cobwebs Ocean Liner Memorabilia**
78 Northam Road
Southampton
Hampshire
England
SO14 0PB
Southampton 227458

## SOCIETIES.

**British Titanic Society.**
P.O. Box 401,
Hope Carr Way,
Leigh, Lancs. WN7 3WW,
England

**Titanic Historical Society**.
P.O.Box 53,
Indian Orchard,
M.A. O1151 OO53.
U.S.A.

**Titanic International**,
Regency Building,
Suite D,
31 Schank Road,
Freehold,
N.J. O7728.
U.S.A.

**Nordic Titanic Society**.
Den Nordiske Titanic
Foreningen,
Formervegen 24,
Klevfos, 2345
Aalsbruk,
Norway.